The American Walk Book

The American WALK BOOK

AN ILLUSTRATED GUIDE
TO THE COUNTRY'S MAJOR
HISTORIC AND NATURAL
WALKING TRAILS FROM
NEW ENGLAND TO THE
PACIFIC COAST

Jean Craighead George

A Sunrise Book

E . P . DUTTON

New York

For information contact:
E. P. Dutton, 2 Park Avenue, New York, N.Y. 10016

Library of Congress Cataloging in Publication Data:
George, Jean Craighead, 1919–
The American walk book.
Includes bibliographies.
1. Hiking–United States. 2. Walking–United States. 3. Trails–United
States–Description and travel. 4. United States–Description and travel–
1960– I. Title.
GV199.4.G46 1978   917.3′04′92   78–8567

ISBN: 0-87690-315-4

Published simultaneously in Canada by
Clarke, Irwin & Company Limited, Toronto and Vancouver

10 9 8 7 6 5 4 3 2

To Bob

CONTENTS

PART THREE
Short Trails Near Cities

PART FOUR
Biotic Communities

A C K N O W L E D G M E N T S

Walkers:
Twig C. George, John Craighead George, Thomas Luke George, Charlie Hall, William and Alice Craighead, Dorothy Laker, James A. Kern, Woody Marmore, Vincent Schaefer

Maps:
Meredith Melvin, John Craighead George, Thomas K. Melvin

Calligrapher:
Kim Webster

Artists:
John Craighead George, Jean Craighead George

Natural History Adviser:
Dr. F. C. Craighead, Sr.

Research:
Meredith Melvin, Twig C. George, Jana Craighead

Introduction:
The American Walk

On Sunday afternoons for many generations, an American family would leave the mid-day dinner table and walk the streets of their town, peering into store windows, strolling past civic buildings or lingering at railroad stations to observe the new technology.

For some, however, the streets were a reminder of sweatshop jobs, and the regimentation of a confining world, and these set out to seek nature in all her wild freshness.

The numbers of these nature walkers increased, and in 1876 the Appalachian Mountain Club was formed to "explore the mountains of New England and adjacent regions for both scientific and artistic purposes and, in general, to cultivate interest in geographic studies."

The footpaths blazed by the Club led not from village to village but from mountain top to mountain top, from steep cliff to thundering waterfalls where one might pause and contemplate nature. For the Sunday walker, AMC's "scientific" trails soon became trails of esthetic purpose: the scent of pine, the texture of tree trunks, the color of wildflowers, the songs of birds. The national movement to walk in the woods had begun.

In 1910 the Green Mountain Club of Vermont blazed the first extensive nature path, from the Massachusetts to the Canadian borders. A few years later the Appalachian Trail concept was conceived by Benton MacKaye, of Massachusetts. He envisioned a path down the entire spine of the Appalachian Mountains that would be met by trails leading out from cities, along which workers, confined to urban areas by industrial jobs, would find beauty.

Enthusiasts of the concept volunteered to blaze trail, and within eleven years the 2023-mile footpath had been completed, and hammered to the mountain crests by the boots of walkers. On the West Coast, the Pacific Crest Trail was initiated by the U. S. Forest Service, and a new trail came into being for the first time—"the long path into nature."

After World War II, the proliferation of automobiles and the manufacturing of lightweight camping gear made it possible for millions to walk in the woods. As they poured into remote areas, The National Park Service extended footpaths and camping facilities; state and municipal outdoor recreation departments were formed; and by the 1960s the nation had nine million walkers and 28,000 miles of trail.

During that decade, walkers realized the footpaths were losing ground to developments, industrial complexes, and highways and, as a result of urging, in March 1968 the U. S. Congress passed the National Scenic Trail Act, placing two footpaths—the Appalachian and Pacific Crest, under the stewardship of the U. S. Department of Interior's National Park Service and the Bureau of Outdoor Recreation. Funds were also provided to acquire private land along these trails and to consider others for possible inclusion in the National Trails System. Nature trails studied were the Long Trail of Vermont, the Long Path of New York, the Florida, North Country, Continental Divide, and Potomac Heritage trails. Historic trails are the Santa Fe, Lewis and Clark, Natchez Trace, Chisholm and Oregon trails. President Lyndon B. Johnson signed the bill into law and officially launched the American walking era.

Seven years later the Bureau of Outdoor Recreation estimated that forty million people walked nature trails, and more were laid out, some in sections of the country where it had not been fashionable, the South and the desert. Now on the drawing board are the Bartram Trail, a 750-mile route tracing the travels of the eighteenth-century naturalist William Bartram through North Carolina, South Carolina, Georgia, Alabama, Mississippi, Louisiana, and Tennessee; the Daniel Boone Trail, following the 300-mile course of the famed woodsman from Statesville, North Carolina to Frankfort, Kentucky; the Nee-Me-Poo Trail, a 1350-mile route tracing the epic retreat of the Nez Percé Chief Joseph through Oregon, Idaho,

Wyoming, and Montana; the Desert Trail, a 2000-mile walkway from Canada to Mexico through the deserts of Idaho, Oregon, Nevada, and California. These trails are designated to be blazed in the 1980s.

Also provided for under the National Trail System Act were funds for shorter trails out of cities, to be known as the National Recreation Trails. Sometimes no more than a mile in length, these can be reached by public transportation. At this writing they number more than ninety.

Perhaps the greatest boon to walking and one that changed the character of the American walk was the advent of field guides, the little hip-pocket books for identifying the birds, mammals, wildflowers, mushrooms, insects, trees, and minerals. Together with the long pathways these handy books gave rise to a new type of excursion—for identifying natural wonders along the trails. Since the country is so enormous it is easier to learn these plants and animals by biotic areas. Naturalists have zoned the United States into areas, or biotic communities each supporting a unique combination of trees or other plant life, and named for the stable plants rather than the mobile animal life. By learning the biotic areas a walker eliminates the confusion of thousands of species and can concentrate on the plants and animals that dwell in the life zones through which he passes.

These biotic areas stretch out, fit in and patch the continent with landscapes that give each trail its own mood and tone. The Southeastern Riverbottom Forest, with its cypress swamps and screaming pileated woodpeckers, creates a primitive atmosphere along the Natchez Trace. The sparse Desert Community makes the Grand Canyon Trail a silent and lonely path, while the birds and sunshine of the Subtropic Zone lend an air of bright activity to the southern section of the Florida Trail.

Together the biotic areas are known as the Scheme of Things, a nation-wide jig-saw of creatures and plants that have adjusted to the soils, weather, light, and other living things. Awareness of these life zones on the trail enriches the walking experience and makes time pass swiftly and without boredom.

Finally, the American Walk has become a health trip. With walking at the top of the list of healthy activities, more and more people are seeking the national trails for exercise. Not only is it a good workout but nature is so infinitely varied that a walk stimulates the mind, the spirit, and the five senses.

There is something about the walk in the woods that does call strongly, for at the last estimate (no one is really sure) from fifteen to twenty million people had hiked our national trails last year, and another forty million took to the short nature trails.

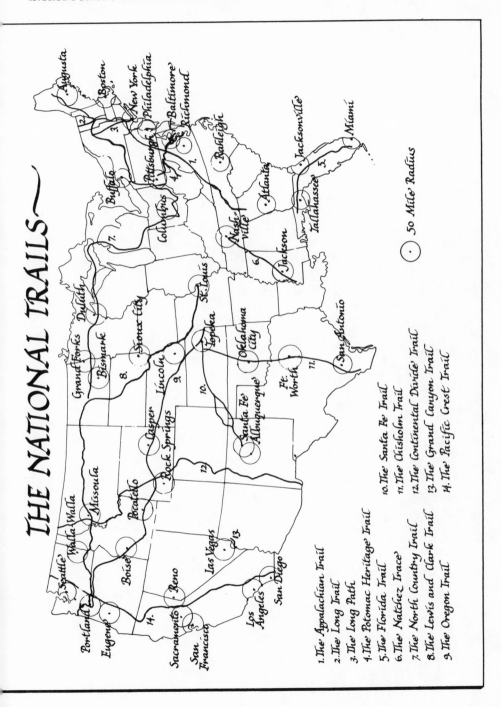

THE NATIONAL TRAILS —

50 Mile Radius

1. The Appalachian Trail
2. The Long Trail
3. The Long Path
4. The Potomac Heritage Trail
5. The Florida Trail
6. The Natchez Trace
7. The North Country Trail
8. The Lewis and Clark Trail
9. The Oregon Trail
10. The Santa Fe Trail
11. The Chisholm Trail
12. The Continental Divide Trail
13. The Grand Canyon Trail
14. The Pacific Crest Trail

PART ONE

Nature Trails

1

THE LONG TRAIL *

The Long Trail traverses the entire state of Vermont from border to border as it follows the ridges and valleys of the Green Mountains. This wild footpath is rugged and much of it is strenuous, for it seeks out gorges and windy tors as it winds through gardens of ferns, and beneath spruce and fir trees. The oldest of our national long trails, it is the grandfather of the concept "a trail into nature for nature's sake."

The genesis of the concept goes back to a snowy night, March 10, 1910. That night in the town of Burlington, Vt., James P. Taylor, the assistant principal of the Vermont Academy for Boys, called together twenty-three enthusiastic walkers and enlisted their help in building a 29-mile trail through the Green Mountains, from Camel's Hump to Smuggler's Notch, so that the students might have healthy exercise. By the time the meeting closed near dawn the Green Mountain Club had been organized, and had a plan to build shelters, fireplaces, and lookouts along the twenty-five dark wilderness miles.

Like most originators, however, the men at that wintry meeting around a log fire had no idea they were initiating a new movement, one that would put footpaths down the Appalachian, Rocky, Sierra Nevada, and Cascade mountains or that in sixty years the concept of the Long Trail would have spawned more than 300,000 miles of footpaths.

The Long Trail was begun the following summer. Green Mountain Club members gathered at Camel's Hump and scouted the

* For information about biotic communities along this trail, see pages 260–261, 272, 273.

area for the best possible route to the Notch. As they bushwhacked over the rough mountains they agreed that the trail should not be easy, but should seek out the most beautiful hills and ridges. that it should twist, turn, and climb in such a manner as to stun the eyes and lift the spirits of the walker as he rounded bends or struggled out onto rocky peaks.

A year later, twenty-nine "long" miles of footpath threaded up and down the Green Mountains in the halflight of the ancient forest.

Rain during the following summer hampered the lengthening of the Trail, and only the short distance from Smuggler's Notch to Sterling Pond was added. William Adams of Summit House, a local resident, paid woodsmen to cut the route from his home to the Trail.

As word of the trail spread, more Vermonters joined the club, and by the winter of 1912 about 500 members had formed subgroups all along the Green Mountains. That year the Killington and Bread Loaf Club raised sixty dollars in private donations to hire help in extending the Trail. With this financial support, the state Forest Service, which had been cutting a short trail for their own use, linked it to the new project. The idea of a long trail was now a fact.

In the summer of 1913 the watchword was "Mansfield to Killington."

News of the trail-blazing reached Boston's Appalachian Mountain Club, founded in 1876 "to explore the mountains of New England and adjacent regions both for scientific and artistic purposes," and several of its members journeyed to Vermont to walk the new footpath. They arrived at Camel's Hump on September 5, 1913. While seated around the campfire that evening, Robert M. Ross of the Vermont Forestry Service strode into camp and joined them. He described the untouched middle of the Green Mountains between Lincoln and Brandon Gaps. There, he said, the forests were dark with great firs and lit with the white birches; they were haunted by bears, huge cats, and wild rivers that tore through deep gaps. Ross so enthralled his audience that they gave him a hundred dollars to bring the Trail through that wildness.

The next week in a thunderstorm and high wind, the trail crew slashed into the mountains, completing the footpath ten days ahead of schedule. Inspired by this achievement, the Green Mountain Club at Johnson went into the forest the following spring and cut trail up over Sterling Mountain to meet the path at Sterling Pond.

By the summer of 1914, the slogan had become "Killington to the Massachusetts Line," and suddenly everyone saw a vision— a footpath from Massachusetts to Canada. In 1916 the Long Trail reached the Massachusetts border to complete almost 200 miles of trail, and the Vermont forests with their variety of wildflowers, trees, mammals, and birds were accessible to all who could walk.

In the next ten years the Trail inched toward Canada, finally stopping twenty miles short of the goal. In 1931 two faculty members of the University of Vermont, Charles G. Doll and Phillips D. Carlton, agreeing that "almost to Canada" was not good enough, packed off into the mountains with axes, saws, and tents. On the club's twenty-first birthday the professors completed the wilderness path, slogging through snow and wind. News of America's longest nature trail soon spread from coast to coast.

The Long Trail lies in the Vermont section of the Green Mountains which are part of the Appalachian Mountain Chain, the oldest mountain range in the United States. Stretching from Canada to Mississippi, the Appalachians have arisen and been worn down three times. Rocks of the Green Mountains are granite, schist, shale and gneiss, banded and chunks of white quartz.

They came to be more than 420 million years ago when a Cambrian sea flowed over the area that is now Champlain Valley, and formed a limy seabottom. Two hundred thirty million years ago, a violent earth disturbance, called the Appalachian Revolution, buckled the submerged igneous rocks to the surface and created the first Appalachian chain.

During this upheaval the stress and heat transformed the rocks lying under what is now Vermont into huge blocks of marble that bent and surfaced, were eroded and arose twice more.

The present features of the Green Mountains were carved 10,000 years ago by the glaciers which filed them down by 500 to 600 feet into domes and canyons. The ice chipped off ledges, polished surfaces, and shoved tons of boulders in unsorted piles of sand, clay, and gravel, then retreated. Today they are rubble on the mountains and make the walking tough.

It is the forest, however, that makes the Trail memorable. The entire footpath is in the Northeastern Hardwood and Coniferous forests. In the valleys and low on mountainsides grow the trees of the stunning beech–birch–maple–hemlock complex for which Vermont is famed. The tops of the Green Mountains are crowned with the white, red, and black spruces and balsam fir, all trees of the boreal forest. Dark patches of partridgeberry and moss quilt the floor and treat the walker to visions of primeval America, for the Green Mountains of Vermont are much as they were when Columbus reached the New World. Warbling vireos and barred owls haunt the umbra and occasionally black bears take to the path. The birds and flowers are, however, the wonders that most walkers seek. Although more than 200 different birds can be found in woodlands, meadows, and along streams and lakes during the year, in summer the uncommon Louisiana waterthrush, a wood warbler, can be seen along the swift-moving streams as it bobs its tail and sings its three clear notes followed by a descending jumble. Under overhanging banks it builds its nest of moss and leaves. Another dweller along this trail is the saw-whet owl. Small, quiet, and tame, it stares out from the branches of coniferous trees where it perches during the day.

The wildflowers of the beech–birch–maple–hemlock forest are a remarkable group. Trillium, bloodroot, spring beauty, hepatica, columbine, jack-in-the-pulpit, lady's slipper, all flowers of the Northeastern Forest, are everywhere along the Trail.

The Long Trail takes its start northward in the small town of Blackinton, Massachusetts, four miles from the Vermont border. Just off *State Highway 2*, at the junction of Hoosic River and the Boston and Maine Railroad, where bouncing bets flower in the dry cinders, the Long Trail and the Appalachian Trail come together, and remain merged for almost half the Long Trail's extent in Vermont.

At the Vermont border the path descends through hemlocks to a brook, following an old woods road and climbing to the ridges for views of hills and farms.

On the sandy site in the low areas grows the handsome white pine, the unrivaled timber tree of colonial times. Once entire forests of these trees stood 150 feet tall and measured three or four feet in diameter. These giants were used to build ships, wharves, and buildings. Today white pines are primarily planted for land-

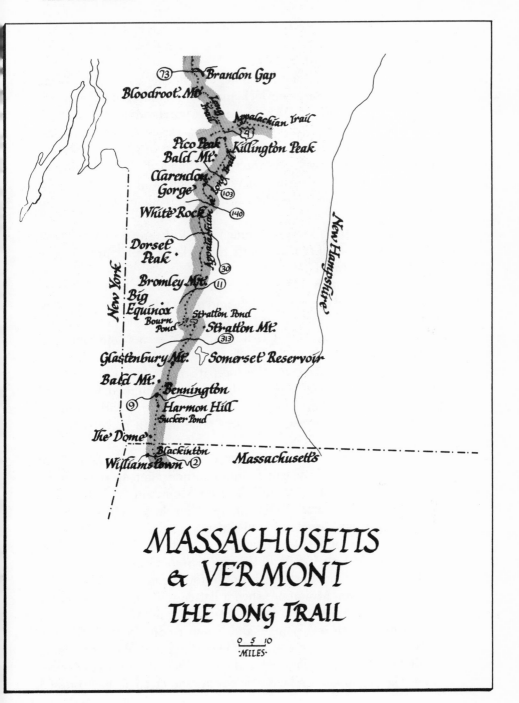

MASSACHUSETTS
& VERMONT
THE LONG TRAIL

0   5   10
·MILES·

scaping and soil control; some second-growth trees are cut for lumber. In profile the trees have a soft and oriental look with branches well separated in pagoda-like tiers.

From Warner Shelter, seven miles over the border, the Long Trail seeks out views of Mt. Greylock and the Taconic Range, then descends to Sucker Pond. Where it winds up Harmon Hill, catbirds call from field edges and towhees toss up leaves as they search for food in the forest litter. From the top, the little town of Bennington can be seen snuggled in the valley, the needle monument that commemorates the Revolutionary War heroes of Vermont piercing the sky. Rising behind the town and monument is the graceful Mt. Anthony.

The Trail drops steeply through hemlock groves, where great carpets of moss and ferns decorate the rocks of Walloomsac Brook, all the way to *State Highway 9.*

Winding through a field edged with sweet birch and red oak, the footpath makes use of bridges and old roads as it ascends Glastenbury Mountain and enters the northland's spruce and balsam fir forests. These spiked trees that crest the Green Mountains also cover northern Maine and Canada all the way to the Arctic Circle. Their needles are deep on the footpath and pine siskins whistle softly among their branches. A dip of a few hundred feet brings the walker into stands of old yellow birch, the tree with gleaming yellow-brown bark whose wood was once used to make yokes for oxen.

From the top of the Glastenbury Mountain fire tower, more wilderness can be seen than from any other point on the trail. In the distance ski trails identify Stratton Mountain, and the valley below cradles Somerset Reservoir, sparkling in its setting of conifers and hardwoods. The Trail ascends into dark timber where nuthatches, woodpeckers, chickadees, and titmice enliven the soundscape with their calls all the way to *State Highway 313.*

Beyond the road the path is boggy for the first four miles as it starts up Stratton Mountain: then it flattens out in a forest of sugar maples and beeches, the wonderful trees that fire the October hills of Vermont with red, orange, and lemon colors. Beyond, the way is rocky as the footpath climbs through a forest of old trees riddled with hollows in which tree swallows, bluebirds, and chickadees nest. Skirting mountain bogs where bears and raccoons have pressed their footprints, the Trail crosses acres of fallen logs and finally enters open woods, carpeted with ferns and tree-like club mosses, the crowfoot, and ground pine. An icy brook splashes off into the shadows, drowning the clicking note of the slate-colored junco. Roots mix with rocks as the Long Trail descends to crystal Stratton Pond, where elfin newts and spotted salamanders twist in the shallow water. Following the shoreline of this largest of the lakes on the Long Trail, the path arrives at Stratton Shelter, famous for views of the sunrise over the lake and misty mountains.

Keeping to the high ledges, the Trail strikes west toward beaver ponds, over slopes where the red spruce mingles with its constant companion, the balsam fir. These two trees live in such intimate association that early settlers called them He-balsam and She-balsam. The latter name was given to balsam fir because of the swollen blisters of resin under its bark, which look like breasts filled with milk. Foresters distinguish the two trees by crushing the needles. The spruce has an aroma of orange rind, and the fir smell is familiar from balsam pillows and Christmas trees.

Beyond *State Highway 30 and 11* the Long Trail slopes gently up Bromley Mountain, over earth damp with seeping spring water. Through the dense forest the muffled roar of Bromley Brook is heard.

Along this part of the Trail the rusty-hoof fungus, which lives on dead birch and beech trees, decorates the umbra with its shelves of shining platters. Enormous glacial boulders are scattered among the trees. Suddenly the Trail takes a bend and a white, quartz-filled ledge blazes above the dark forest. The Trail narrows; birches, maples, and beeches grow more densely overhead and the path is rocky as it threads upwards to the crest of the ridge. Along the way pure stands of smooth-barked beech give a silver sheen to the mountainside. Then the Trail breaks out onto glacier-polished rocks and connects with a Bromley ski trail. From here the ascent is straight up this rockpile to the top of the mountain, where Equinox Mountain can be seen to the west and, beyond it, the hazy Taconic Range.

The Trail plunges over rocks and through dark forests into Mad Tom Notch, then kinks, twists, and turns onward to Peru Peak and Griffith Lake. Weaving through pristine stands of canoe birch, whose blazing white bark typifies the northern forest, the Long

Trail crosses acres of loose rock to a ledge and a view of seemingly endless greenery.

A rocky route leads to the summit of Baker Peak (2850 feet). Below *U. S. 7* twists up the valley, and beyond it is Dorset Peak, with its white marble quarries that shine like snow patches, marking the veins from which a fine grade of marble was quarried in the early 1800s. On the horizon loom the jagged points of the Adirondack Mountains.

The Trail plunges down into beech, birch, and maple forests, crosses hemlock-bordered streams, and eventually loops up Green Mountain to gem-like Little Rock Pond. North of the pond the Long Trail keeps to the high country, reaches a clearing, and then begins a steep ascent to White Rock Mountain. Passing beneath the summit, the Trail circles White Rock Cliffs and takes to fields and open country before arriving at *State Highway 140*.

North of the highway, the Long Trail follows an old farm road beside a brook with cold and excellent drinking water. Raspberries edge the path on its steep ascent to Mill River, which is followed by an even steeper descent into picturesque Clarendon Gorge. This dark canyon is crossed on a suspension bridge built in 1957 by Emil and Cecile Boselli of the Green Mountain Club.

After a short climb the path crosses *State Highway 103*, and ascends steeply to the bare summit of Beacon Hill, a mammoth boulder of gneiss. Next the Trail drops into a sugar-maple forest where in February the landowner makes maple syrup, Vermont's most famous product.

Trekking through private campgrounds, open fields, and hardwood forests, the Trail climbs steadily up the south slope of Little Killington and Consultation Point before arriving at Tamarack Shelter, named for the graceful deciduous evergreen that grows farther north than any other tree in North America.

Canoe birch and white ash give way to spruce and fir as the Long Trail climbs into the wilds of Killington Peak (4281 feet) and then at the top finds itself back in civilization. The summit buzzes with activity around the radio tower, gondola terminal, and restaurant. On this mountain top, so the story goes, Reverend Sam Peters of Connecticut, who in 1763 was traveling through the region to preach and baptize, looked down upon the forests and lakes of the Green Mountains, and gave the state the name "Verd-Mont."

Plunging past groves of osier dogwood, a shrub with red branches and deeply veined leaves, the Long Trail crosses through fields of meadow parsnip, nightshade, primrose, and aster which grow along the summer ski trails, and enters the forest of Pico Peak (3947 feet). The shamrock-like oxalis, a plant with large yellow flowers, covers the damp forest floor. Juncos call from the mossy rocks and bats swing out from ledges as the Long Trail slices under a jutting ledge and creeps between giant slabs where the walker can barely squeeze through. With suddenness the rocks come to an end and the woods open onto a flat meadow. Song sparrows trill here, and flycatchers wing overhead, catching insects in the sunlight of this famous clearing where the Appalachian Trail leaves the Long Trail and heads east to the White Mountains.

Continuing straight northward, the Long Trail passes old birches whose enormous roots twist like a wall of serpents for miles along the Trail. Roots become the hallmark of the Trail from this point north.

Circling Deer Leap Mountain the footpath climbs Blood Root Mountain, named for its acres of this white spring flower. Then, twisting through beeches and maples, the Trail comes into Blood Root Gap and the smell of bracken fern permeates the air.

Beyond *State Highway 73* the path wends through Brandon Gap where staghorn sumac and roadside grasses abound, then ascends Mt. Horrid. On a steep slope halfway up it passes through a memorable stand of yellow birch. The leaves measure from four to five inches long, the largest in the birch family, and are dull dark green above and pale below. After twisting through balsam firs the Trail bursts out upon an enormous patio of rock that juts 600 feet above a small lake speckled with dead stumps and surrounded by wispy tamarack trees. The downy young of wood ducks and mallards swim among waterlilies and spatterdock. In every direction the forest appears unbroken by civilization, and the greenness of Vermont is all-encompassing.

A gradual slope brings the Trail down *State Highway 125*, then abruptly up Silent Cliff to Silent Cave. With twists and turns the path snakes up and down Mt. Boise and Mt. Battell to Skylight Pond. Then it descends to Steam Hill Meadows, the site of an old logging camp, and takes a steep climb to the top of Bread Loaf Mountain. Following old logging roads, crossing brooks, the Long

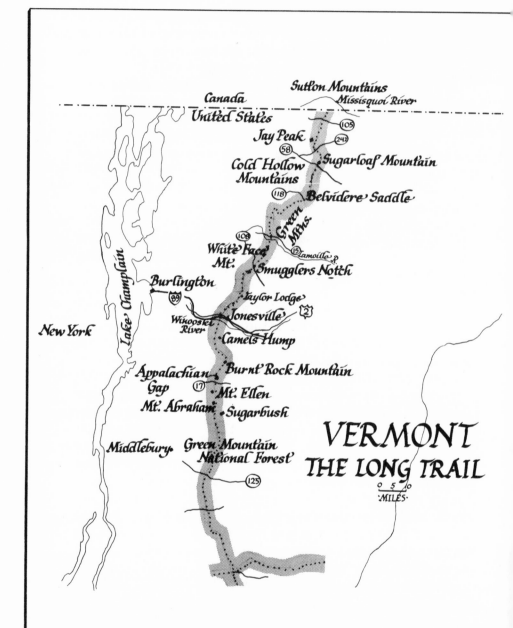

Canada
United States
Sutton Mountains
Missisquoi River

105

Jay Peak 242

58

Cold Hollow
Mountains

Sugarloaf Mountain

118 Belvidere Saddle

Green Mtns.

108

White Face
Mt.

15 Lamoille R.

Smugglers Notch

Lake Champlain

Burlington

89

Taylor Lodge

2

Winooski
River

Jonesville

New York

Camels Hump

Burnt Rock Mountain

Appalachian
Gap

17 Mt. Ellen

Mt. Abraham Sugarbush

Middlebury

Green Mountain
National Forest

VERMONT
THE LONG TRAIL

125

0   5   10
·MILES·

Trail ascends Mt. Roosevelt and curves northward to the wooded summit of Mt. Cleveland. With a sharp thrust it descends along several galloping streams, tributaries of the New Haven River, and out onto *State Highway 17* in Lincoln Gap.

After climbing the steep road the footpath begins a rocky ascent of Mt. Abraham. Halfway up it passes between two enormous glacial rocks, the "Carpenters," named for brothers who worked on the Long Trail. Just beyond is a glimpse of the mountain that explains why it was originally named Potato Hill. The hump does indeed strongly resemble a mound of mashed potatoes. In the late 1800s the mountain was purchased by Colonel Joseph Battell, who renamed it Mt. Abraham after his favorite American president, Abraham Lincoln.

In a forest of slender birches, tree roots again dominate the Trail, mosses and ferns abound, and rocks leak silver streams of spring water. Then the Trail threads between stands of red spruce and balsam fir, creeps up dry rocks to the summit of Mt. Abraham, where a circular wall of stone has been built over the years by walkers to protect themselves from the gusty winds that scream and howl up there. In the distance lie Lake Champlain and the Adirondack Mountains. To the south stands Killington, and to the east is the Presidential Range of New Hampshire.

Mossy ravines and almost impenetrable forests mark the way to Little Abe and Mt. Sugarbush, another Vermont ski mountain. Taking to the ski trails, the footpath dips and then ascends to Mt. Ellen, the third highest mountain in Vermont (4135 feet), then passes lodges and parking areas on the way to the Mad River ski area. The trail is wet and slippery as it goes down precipitous Stark's Wall to cross *State Highway 17*, in Appalachian Gap.

From here on the Long Trail becomes even more rugged winding upward through swatches of sharp-leaved wood asters and over boulders and rocks to a small glacial pothole that forms a natural cup. Not far beyond, the path leaves the wood and ascends to the top of Burnt Rock Mountain (3168 feet). In the distance, Camel's Hump looms above Wind Gap. Farther on, a short, steep ascent to the peak of Mt. Ethan Allen is followed by another climb to the top of North Peak, with expansive views to the east.

In Wind Gap the original twenty-nine miles of the Long Trail begin. Winding west of the Hump, the Trail traverses a ridge, passing beaver ponds and scrub pines to arrive at the northern side of Camel's Hump. It ascends to the summit of Camel's Hump from the southwest. A more descriptive name could hardly have been given to this mountain, for it is indeed a camel's hump.

Continuing north, the Long Trail drops into a clearing, enters woods, and descends to Gorham Lodge, a log cabin with bunks for twelve. Crossing knobs and brooks, the Trail begins a steep climb up Robbins Mountain to *U. S. Highway* 2 and into the picturesque town of Jonesville. Here the Trail crosses a span of farmland and open pastures where every bend opens upon a Christmas-card scene of cattle, gates, and weathered barns.

The Trail switches up through the Bolton ski area and makes a steep climb to Taylor Lodge, named for James P. Taylor, the father of the Long Trail. The view is down on Lake Mansfield, tucked like a silver coin between wooded ridges. To the north, rugged cliffs tower above green valleys as the Trail leaves the shelter and slabs along the west slope of Mt. Dewey (3371 feet) to Butler Lodge, the most picturesquely located of all the lodges. Passing through the Needle's Eye, a pile of glacial debris, most walkers are forced to take off their packs. A steep and rough climb over rocks and ledges, and even up ladders brings the walker to the top of Mt. Mansfield.

An Indian legend gives a poetic account of the geological history of this mountain, whose bald top forms a man's profile against the sky. One day the crippled son of an Indian chief, ashamed of his distorted body, crawled up the great mountain called Mishawaka, to uphold the honor of his family by a show of courage. High in the crags he died from the cold. At his death the screaming winds blew and storms raged. When the sun finally came out again, the crest of the mountain had been cut and chiseled into the profile of the young Indian brave. From the valley the walker can see the Indian face looking up to heaven. Each feature has been named: Adam's Apple, Chin, Upper Lip, Nose, and Forehead. The mountain's present name has a less charming origin: it simply commemorates an English Chief Justice, Lord Mansfield. But for walkers the Indian brave is still there to see.

At the windy summit of The Chin, the highest peak, only an occasional walker sees the sun, for clouds and rain envelop it most of the year. The Trail winds tortuously over boulders, into canyons and across lichen-draped ledges to scale the Adam's Apple. Eventually it descends to Smuggler's Notch, where it crosses *State Highway 108*, completing the last of the original twenty-nine miles.

Beyond *State Highway 118* the footpath heads for Belvidere Head and Madonna Peak. A gentle ascent through spruce and balsam fir brings the walker into a serene valley before a rugged trek to the top of White Face Mountain (3715 feet), to *State Highway 15* and the Lamoille River Bridge. Going up Bowen Mountain, then down to Devil's Gulch, the Long Trail crosses acres of glacial rocks where the wind screams endlessly through the firs and birches in winter and summer.

Beyond *State Highway 18* the footpath heads for Belvidere and a breathtaking view of the Northeastern Coniferous Forest. Numerous switchbacks bring the Trail to the top of Belvidere, where the Sutton Mountains of Canada shine to the north. Descending through slopes covered with grasses and wildflowers, the Trail dips into Hazen's Notch and takes briefly to *State Highway 58*.

A granite marker on this road commemorates General Moses Hazen, a hero of the Revolutionary War, who built a military road through the remote pass in 1778.

Passing through a mix of civilization and wilderness, where cable cars are neighbors to beds of fairy moss, the Long Trail goes up and over Mt. Sugar Loaf to *State Highway 242*. Beyond this, it penetrates a dense forest of spruce and fir, then makes its steep ascent up the southeast spur of Jay Peak (3800 feet). Yellow-green lichens splotch the limbs and trunks of the tangled trees, red squirrels scream, and blue jays yell. Mercifully, the Trail breaks out onto the mountain top with spectacular views in all directions.

A bumpy rollercoaster now, the pathway goes up and down two mountains, over rocks and ledges, finally crossing a glacier flat to arrive at Shooting Star Shelter, so named, the story goes, after the trail crew watched a brilliant meteorite burn across the black night sky.

Below the shelter are massive rocks and boulders, piled up by the ancient glacier. Winding among these the Trail descends to *State Highway 105*. Here may be seen the stumps cut by the two professors in their race to the border in 1932, as well as Line Post 592, erected in 1842 when the United States–Canadian boundary was finally agreed upon. This section of the Long Trail is called Journey's End Trail and terminates in a dark forest at Journey's End Camp.

A logging road leads to *Canada Highway 105*, the route to North Troy, Vermont, and buses that will carry the walker back to civilization.

Highways Crossed by the Long Trail

Massachusetts:
  State Highway 2

Vermont:
  State Highway 9
  State Highway 313
  State Highway 30 and 11
  State Highway 140
  State Highway 103
  State Highway 73
  State Highway 125
  State Highway 17

U. S. Highway 2
State Highway 108
State Highway 15
State Highway 18
State Highway 58
State Highway 242
State Highway 105

Canada:
  Canada Highway 105
  (Glen Sutton Highway)

Bibliography and Maps

GREEN MOUNTAIN CLUB. *Guide Book of the Long Trail: A Footpath in the Wilderness.* Burlington, Vermont: Green Mountain Club, 20th ed. 1974. Contains excellent maps and shelter-by-shelter descriptions of the Trail. May be obtained for $3.00 from the Green Mountain Club, Inc., P. O. Box 94, Rutland, Vermont 05701.

PETERSON, ROGER T., and MARGARET McKENNY. *A Field Guide to Wildflowers of Northeastern and Northcentral North America.* Boston: Houghton Mifflin Company, 1968.

SADLIER, RUTH and PAUL. *Fifty Hikes in Vermont: Walks, Day Hikes, and Backpacking Trips in the Green Mountains.* Somersworth, N.H.: New Hampshire Publishing Company, 1974. Provides maps that are less detailed than those in the Green Mountain Club Guide. Twenty of the fifty hikes coincide with the Long Trail.

SARGENT, CHARLES S. *Manual of Trees of North America* (2 v.). New York: Dover Publications, Inc., 2nd ed. 1965.

U. S. FOREST SERVICE. A folder containing a map and lists of picnic and camping areas maintained by the Forest Service. Can be obtained by writing U. S. Forest Service, Rutland, Vermont 05701.

VERMONT DEPARTMENT OF FORESTS AND PARKS. *Vermont State Parks and Forests.* A folder giving information on picnic and camping areas maintained by the State. Available from the Vermont Department of Forests and Parks, Montpelier, Vermont 05602.

2

THE APPALACHIAN TRAIL *

The 2023-mile-long Appalachian Trail stretches from Springer Mountain in Georgia to Mt. Katahdin in Maine. It is the people's trail, boot-worn and well-loved. Although to walk its entire length is a tough, three-to-five-month trek, much of the path near roads and highways is relatively easy. Deep into the forests, the route becomes more difficult for the Trail was blazed along high ridges that afforded the most beautiful views of rivers, mountains, fields, and towns. Every inch of the Appalachian Trail is a refreshment.

The Trail was conceived in 1921 by Benton MacKaye of Shirley, Massachusetts, a philosopher, author, and forester who had often met and talked with the members of the Green Mountain Club of Vermont as they were building the Long Trail to the north of him. He took the concept one great step forward and conceived the first continental outdoor recreational project. "The Appalachian Trail," he wrote in the *Journal of the American Institute of Architects*, 1921, "should be a seemingly endless trail that would link the wilderness areas along the eastern seaboard." The author envisioned the Trail in the shape of a fish skeleton, the spine being the main footpath, with connecting paths leading out from cities and towns into the primeval environment.

Almost immediately his idea became a reality. The Appalachian Mountain Club of Boston had a system of footpaths in New Hampshire, members of the Dartmouth Outing Club were blazing trails between the White and Green Mountains, and New Yorkers

* For information about biotic communities along this trail see pages 259–261, 272–274.

18

were cutting paths through the Bear Mountain and Harriman sections of the Palisades Interstate Park. After the publication of MacKaye's article, these trailblazers met and began the Appalachian Trail to unite the separate trails into one long chain.

In 1925 the Appalachian Trail Conference was formed to co-ordinate the effort. A year later, however, work had degenerated into fireside talk and the project came to a standstill.

At the end of that year Arthur Perkins, a retired Connecticut lawyer, asked Myron H. Avery of Lubec, Maine to take on the assignment of inspiring volunteers to work on the Trail once more. Before the next snows flew, Avery had talked more than a hundred people into joining him in the hills with axe and paint bucket. Under his impetus the Trail moved rapidly northward and south-ward, and by 1937 the last two miles completed a herculean effort that has not been matched since: in less than sixteen years two thousand miles had been cut and blazed, entirely by volunteers.

In the summer of 1975 the Appalachian Trail Conference cele-brated its fiftieth anniversary in Boonetown, North Carolina. Gone were Avery and Perkins, but Benton MacKaye, then 98, was still very much alive and alert.

"Little did I dream more than fifty years ago," he wrote in a message to the Conference from his home in Massachusetts, "when I sat down with two men in the New Jersey Highlands and out-lined to them my idea of a footway through the Appalachians, that such plans would be translated into the institution that has now come to pass. I did little more than suggest the notion: I set the match to the fuse and set the chain reaction that has come about." MacKaye died quietly at home in January 1976, having lived to see his dream become the first National Trail by an act of Congress in 1968.

Contrary to a widespread assumption, the Appalachian Trail does not follow the old Indian warpath which lies in the Appalachian Valley, but parallels it on the mountain crests.

The AT covers fourteen eastern states, the longest stretch being the 465 miles in Virginia, and the shortest, five miles in West Vir-ginia. Every seven or eight miles there are shelters with three walls, bunks, and dirt floors, providing 230 resting places.

The Appalachian Trail is not, and never has been in the true sense "a footpath in the wilderness." More than half of its length passes through farmland and small towns, lingering in fields and woodlots, following dirt roads, and winding off to crests and ledges with views of rivers and cattle in valleys.

At this writing four million hikers tread at least part of the AT each year and about 300 men and women spend four months or longer walking the entire 2023 miles. The first to do so was Myron H. Avery, the energetic first president of the AT Conference, who inspired the volunteers to complete the great effort. The first woman to walk the Trail alone, and the oldest person to do so twice, was Grandma Emma Gatewood of Ohio. She plodded up the path in 1955 at the age of 65 and again when she was 68. At the end of a long hard day, well-booted and supplied with tents and food, today's Trail walkers still tell tales of this five-foot-two mother of eleven, who trekked the entire length in sneakers, using six pairs to a trip. She never carried a sleeping bag, only a blanket, a rain cape, and a plastic curtain; never cooked a meal (she opened cans) and carried no more than 20 pounds. This amazing lady of the Appalachian Trail began her day at 5:30, ended it at 3 or 4 in the afternoon, and created dramas as she went. One unfolded on the side of Mohawk Mountain, Connecticut. Under the pines near the summit is the log where a bobcat threatened Grandma Gatewood for her can of sardines. "If you come any nearer," she shouted to the snarling beast, "I'll crack you." The cat backed off.

Also along the Trail are spots immortalized by Dorothy Laker, now a resident of Florida and a trailblazer on the Florida Trail, who three times hiked the Appalachian Trail alone in 1957, 1962, and 1964. Terrified of bears and snakes, she braved encounters with both and courageously fought rain and snow; but primarily her walks are remembered for her berry-gathering. Miss Laker harvested more fresh wild strawberries, blueberries, and raspberries than any of the other 2000-milers. The hillsides where she found luscious crops are now called The Laker Fields.

A controversial Appalachian Trail personality is the fastest man on the Trail, Warren C. Doyle, who completed the 2023 miles in sixty-six and one-half days by sleeping many nights in the back of his father's station wagon, carrying only a light daypack, and often walking by night with a flashlight on his head. He averaged 30.6 miles a day, with an average walking time of 15 hours and 20 minutes. Critics of Warren's trek call it a marathon not befitting the spirit of the Trail. He disagrees.

"I learned," he said, "just who I thought I was, how much I felt I could take, and more importantly, how much I reasoned I could give. It turned out to be a successful character-confirming experiment."

As hikers stride the lonely, rugged back stretches of the Trail, a lexicon of new words and phrases has evolved. To "truck" is to hike the Appalachian Trail; the "through-hiker" or "2000-miler" is one who is going the whole way; "bush-leaguers" are day-and-weekend hikers. "The Big K in the Sky" is Mt. Katahdin, the destination of those going north.

Since much of the Trail is far from newspapers and radio, as April arrives and the walkers again take to its pathway, the Appalachian Trail becomes a crackling grapevine of news. Names of through-hikers, their deeds and cunning are sped along the Trail as walkers meet, pass, drop back, and move on. John Silva of Rhode Island, a Connecticut College student at the time he hiked, became a back-country journalist, writing down and passing on Trail news.

Although Silva walked to see the views, he soon found the AT community more exciting. "It's a small town on the move," he wrote. "We kept track of each other through a truly incredible grapevine which was possible since we would repeatedly leapfrog each other as we passed through the 14 states on our way to Katahdin." As Silva listened he discovered that the woods were full of Dickensian characters. Damascus-to-Dalton Bob got his name by walking from Damascus, Virginia to Dalton, Massachusetts without washing his clothes. The Mad Englishman got his when he was almost arrested in Virginia for taking off all his clothes in a laundromat, to wash them. Gabby Dan talked constantly on subjects ranging from the theory of relativity to gossip about the youngest general in the Civil War.

The reputations of some of the characters were hair-raising. There was Crazy Frank, who smashed his flashlight on the back of a mouse he had stayed awake all night to kill. Crazy Frank raided the refrigerator in a rooming house just off the Trail and walked out without paying; in rain and fog he could be heard to swear and rave. Silva kept hearing about him, but did not meet him until he reached Virginia. There he wrote:

Vegetarian Charlie and I were trucking along in the rain in late May on the fifth day of what was to become the Six Day Rain. The Trail was a river of water pouring down the mountainsides and eroding the ancient Appalachians, but not fast enough to make our hike easier. When we reached the Cornelius Creek Lean-to in Jefferson National Forest, Virginia, we whooped and shouted to find that it was ours alone. We ate a feast of lentils and brown rice, watched the rain, and then Vegetarian Charlie put his sleeping bag in the left-hand corner of the shelter.

Suddenly through the magnified sound of rain pounding on the corrugated steel roof, we heard voices coming our way. We cursed simultaneously at the prospect of company, then two wet hikers appeared. One was Hi Carl, a through-hiker who had the knack of suddenly appearing behind you on the Trail and of evoking the exclamation "Hi Carl." The other was a stocky man wearing plastic-rimmed glasses who was swearing his head off.

Hi Carl took off his pack and addressed his companion as Frank. It struck me instantly who he was: Crazy Frank. I stared in silent awe.

Suddenly Crazy Frank strode over to Charlie's sleeping bag. "Is anyone sleeping in this corner?" he roared. "I like corners." Fearing murderous violence I quickly said "No," and grabbed Charlie's bag. "We're sleeping way over here." We lay down our bags and crawled in, a watchful eye on Frank all night.

At dawn Charlie and I hurried off into the rain, glad we had escaped the fate of the mouse.

The Appalachian Mountains were named by the Spaniards for the Appalaches, a southeastern Indian tribe. Their geology is complex, as might be expected of a range that has been uplifted and eroded away three times. Sedimentary, metamorphic, and igneous rocks are found along the Appalachian Trail. Although the range is one system that stretches from Newfoundland to Alabama, from region to region it has been given a whole series of names: the Green, the White, Sutton, Allegheny, Blue Ridge, Cumberland, Smoky, and Black mountains.

The opulent forests, however, not the geology, is the outstanding feature of the Appalachian Trail. A mix of four out of the eight biotic areas found in the temperate deciduous forests shade the Trail: the birch–beech–maple–hemlock; chestnut oak–tulip-tree; oak–pine; and at its northern reaches and on high mountain tops, the black, red, white spruce–balsam fir. More than 190 tree species and 1300 native flowering plants live along it, as well as 50 native mammals, 300 birds, 2000 species of fungi, 300 species of moss, 250 of lichens, 70 toads and frogs, and 45 fishes, snails, and salamanders.

The forests are laced with cascading streams and the shapes, textures, and colors are almost endless. The sounds vary from thin song to thunder roll. When MacKaye conceived the Appalachian Trail he had a clear objective: to fulfill people's need for variety by cutting a path into the multiformity of this biotic area, known world-wide as the Great Forest. Other such forests exist in parts of Europe, in the hills above the Yangtze River in Middle China, in the Manchurian Highlands, and in central Korea. The genesis of the Great Forests has been traced back some ninety million years to a period when all the continents were one (known as Gowandaland). It supported a vast and luxuriant forest reaching up to the, then, warm top of the world. Over the millions of years the land split into continents, and the original Great Forest was fractured into widely separated fragments, one of which is the Eastern deciduous forest of the United States. In time, the waters around the Pole turned to ice, glaciers crept southward, and the American trees, flowers, birds, and beasts were shoved along its leading edge. When the ice retreated, the forests spread northward again to southern New Hampshire and Maine.

The leaf-dropping habit of the deciduous trees of the Great Forests makes for a dramatic change and defines the four seasons: the leaflessness of winter, the flowering and budding of spring, the green canopy of summer, and the riotous colors of autumn. The four seasons, perhaps more than any other factor, make even a mile on the Appalachian Trail an adventure for the spirit.

Off *State Highway 52*, near the northern border of Georgia, a slender footpath climbs seven miles up Springer Mountain, through oak and sassafras trees with rare glimpses of the loblolly pine, the once dominant tree of the Southeastern Pine Forest. High up among hemlocks and maple, amid trillium and columbine, the Appalachian Trail begins. A bronze plaque on a rock reads: "A footpath for those who seek fellowship with the wilderness— Georgia to Maine." Near by stands a register where several hundred through-hikers and thousands of bush-leaguers have signed their

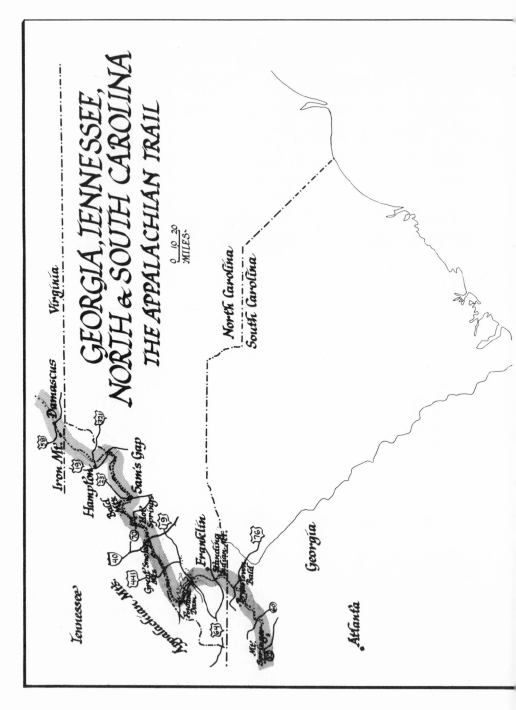

GEORGIA, TENNESSEE,
NORTH & SOUTH CAROLINA
THE APPALACHIAN TRAIL

names. Most have registered on April 1, the traditional day to begin the long walk. Less than ten feet beyond is the first of several thousand blazes: a white rectangle two by six inches (two such rectangles indicate a turn is coming up) that will guide the walker through forest and field for one or for 2023 miles.

The path plunges down into a valley of cedar and oak, in view of hillsides covered with shining laurel. It crosses swamps and rivers and comes to *State Highway 60*.

North of the road the Trail dips to Dick's Great Gap, where whippoorwills cry in the twilight and the screech owl hunts through the night. At dawn the Carolina wren sings from moist brushland.

North of *Interstate 76* the Trail is festooned with the famous Southern chinquapin of shiny serrated leaf and spiny fruit that is sweet and chestnut-like. The tree rarely grows taller than fifty feet and seeks out sandy ridges and the borders of swamps. On the Appalachian Mountains it occurs at altitudes up to 4500 feet, but no farther north than southern New Jersey. The chinquapin's fame goes back to Captain John Smith, who mentioned it in his first account of Virginia.

At Bly Gap, fifteen miles beyond the highway, the Trail crosses the North Carolina border and plunges into gardens of bluets, hobblebush, and the pale gold azalea unique to this state. Carving through this wet area where the annual rainfall is 80-plus inches, and the footpath is drenched two out of three days, the Trail passes evidence of the deluge in that mosses and ferns grow all the way up Standing Indian Mountain (5498 feet), an ascent that many consider one of the hardest on the route. The rain flowers—oxalis and columbine—grow in profusion at 4500 feet. Here, too, are hidden the nests of the slate-colored junco, the summer bird of the high country. For loud sounds along this section of the Trail the drumming of the ruffed grouse is surpassed only by the hammering of the pileated woodpecker.

The fifty-four miles from Bly Gap to Nantahala River, North Carolina, is flowered with Dutchman's breeches and jack-in-the-pulpit, violets, and huckleberry blossoms. Strawberries bloom and ripen on the sandy open hillsides.

For the next twenty-five miles, past *U. S. Highway 19* to Fontana Dam, the Trail is rocky and occasionally venomous. That snake-hater Dorothy Laker wrote of seeing "a three-foot blacksnake that vibrated his tail in the grass and produced a sound just like a rattle-snake. I camped a mile off the trail and spent a very cold, wet night."

Gardens of azalea and rhododendron dominate this region, where bluebirds sing and the yellow-billed cuckoo hatches its odd tree-climbing young. The pink lady's slipper abounds in the red oak forests and the scent of sassafras permeates the air. As seen from the lookouts, the deep valleys are threaded with roads leading to small villages.

Rocks assail the walker at *State Highway* 28 through the Stekoah region to Fontana Dam, the highest dam in the eastern United States, 480 feet above sea level. A few miles on is the border of Great Smoky Mountain National Park. Now for seventy-miles, the Appalachian Trail penetrates the core of the Great Forest. A greater variety of trees, animals, and flowers grow in this park than in any other comparable spot in the world, and together they fuse into a green that is a living diadem, supported by an annual rainfall of 100 inches.

A steep climb brings the walker up through the Northern hard-woods and into the spruce and balsam fir on Clingman's Dome for a brief taste of the northland ahead. The juncos are so tame here that Howard Bassett of Connecticut wrote home in perplexity, "One little bird, a junco, kept coming within a few feet of me." The ovenbird sings its piercing "teacher, teacher, teacher" as the Trail goes downward through the blazing azalea and laurel, where the alarm notes of chipping sparrow and hooded warbler warn of snakes and owls.

Past *U. S. Highway* 441 the Trail winds to Newfound Gap and joins the Charles Bunion Trail on a narrow shelf that leads to Mount Cammerer. Waterfalls plunge over ledges in feathery plumes, and black bears often block the path.

Interstate 40 ends the walk through Great Smoky Mountain National Park, and the Trail weaves on, crossing the line between North Carolina and Tennessee for almost 192 miles, and taking the walker into the Pisgah and Cherokee National forests. This is the country of the big "Balds," a succession of domed mountains that rise from 4500 to 6000 feet high. With soils so thin they cannot support trees but only grasses and wildflowers, their treeless summits shine like bald heads above the forest. From their tops the view is of clouds resting on mountains and mist fingering valleys across this Cherokee Indian country.

Isolated near the bottom of the last bald are a cluster of gravestones from the Civil War, which haunt almost every walker with thoughts of that melancholy conflict. From the graves the Trail descends to Sam's Gap and *State Highway 23*.

Chickens crow, ducks quack, and dogs bark along the next stretch of farmland, which brings the Trail to *State Highway 321* and the town of Hampton, Tennessee. The green fields and bright orchards are a pleasant patchwork in the unvarying greenness of the surrounding forests.

Beyond Hampton, abandoned farmlands culture wild strawberries, and the Trail is exposed to blazing sunshine and crashing storms. Then it climbs Iron Mountain and arrives in the abandoned apple orchard where Dorothy Laker found "raspberries and green-horned caterpillars." The green-horns are the larvae of the monarch butterfly, and are found only on the milkweed plants from which the handsome caterpillars acquire a shot of a heart stimulant causing whatever birds that swallow them to suffer an uncomfortable heart flutter. Most soon learn not to eat green-horns. The adult monarch, an orange and black butterfly, is the only butterfly that migrates. These fragile creatures fly not only from Canada to the Gulf and California in October, but back again in spring.

Iron Mountain is noted for its rattlesnakes, its carpets of rue anemone, and its trailside bellworts. Walkers also speak of the olive-backed thrush and yellow orchids in this moist woodland.

And then comes Damascus, Virginia, the midway rendezvous of the Appalachian Trail, where many walkers get on or off. Beyond *U. S. Highway 58* the Trail begins its 240-mile penetration of Jefferson National Forest, which ends at the James River and meets *State Highway 130*. In the month of May, hundreds of box turtles meet in the forest, tap one another's shells in turtle courtship, and eventually mate. At almost precisely 6 o'clock in the evening female turtles dig into soft soil with a sunny exposure and lay their eggs. Virginia deer crop the grasses along the Trail and vanish into the understory of twinleaf and dogwood to watch the walker pass. Strawberries abound in abandoned fields, and in June the local people join trail-walkers in harvesting the crop. Near the end of the forest the Trail takes to country roads, passes open fields and

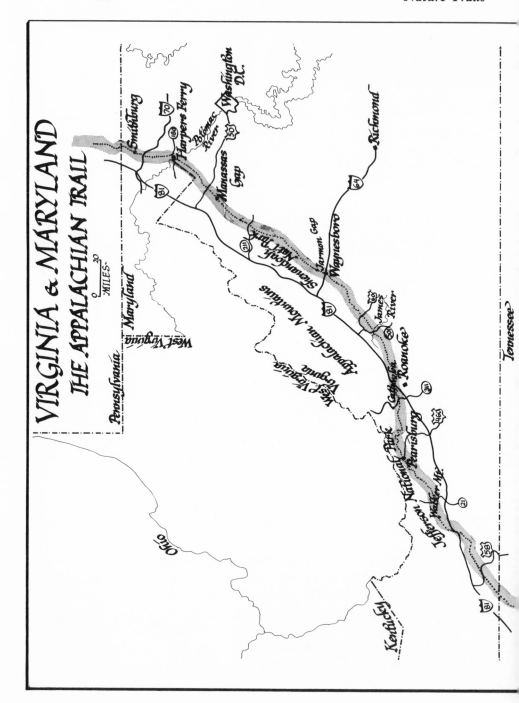

VIRGINIA & MARYLAND
THE APPALACHIAN TRAIL

farms, then crosses *Interstate 81* and ascends Walker Mountain (3406 feet), and is once again engulfed in wilderness. Walker Mountain is black bear country, and wise hikers hang their packs high.

Clouds and mist hang over Walker Mountain for much of the year and almost everyone who makes the trip is drenched at least once on the way to Pearisburg and *U. S. Highway 460*. To the north of this road stretches farmland, and miles of June- and July-ripening blackberries. Orchards are red with cherries and mulberries at this season, the deer are hiding their fawns in the meadows, and red-winged blackbirds are defending their nests along the streamsides. Passing fencelines of beggarweed, the Trail climbs Sinking Creek Mountain, tilts up through cow pastures bright with daisies, and arrives at *State Highway 311*. Apple orchards line the Trail to Catawba Mountain, and around them grow blueberries that ripen in late June and July. At Bear Wallow Gap skunks and black bear take to the path, leaving their footprints all the way to *Interstate 81*.

The Trail winds through farmland to Snowden Campground, the home of a profusion of red-and-yellow columbines and the rare trailing arbutus. Frogs sing from the pond's edges and from the floating lily pads where waterlilies are in bloom. Just before *State Highway 130* the walker can glimpse the graceful James River between the sycamores and red maples. A steep and brambly way goes up Bluff and Punchbowl mountains to George Washington National Forest at the tip of the Blue Ridge Range. For seventy-eight miles the Trail rollercoasts up and down rugged mountains deeply sliced by river gorges.

The summit of Bald Mountain is a black rock with views in every direction. Then the way is down through cattle meadows and miles of stinging nettles. Poison ivy, blackberries, huckleberries, and thistles grab at pants and shirts and hummingbirds whirl from flowering bramble to honeysuckle. The long descent to *Interstate 64* in Waynesboro takes the walker through bobolink and meadow-lark country, where songs announce the invisible fence that surrounds each caroler's territory.

To the north, the Trail over Calf Mountain, farmed almost to its summit, becomes a pastoral scene all the way to Jarmans Gap. Next the Shenandoah National Park offers ninety-four miles of forest and estate-like footway. The famed Skyline Drive parallels this part of the Trail, and about every four miles there are hot showers, snack bars, and dining rooms available to the walker. Yellow-throated vireos sing, mourning doves coo, and huckleberries hang ripening. Streams are blocked by beaver dams, and deer with fawns leap from clearing to forest shadow. Climaxing the wild beauty is a taste of camping luxury, the Black Rock Gap Shelter, an attractive structure with fireplace and commodious bunks. Appalachian Trail walkers gather here to sing and philosophize. From the shelter the Trail winds through brushy goldfinch country to the ledge at Bear Fence Meadow and a superlative view of the Conway River Valley.

North of *U. S. Highway 211* is Elk Wallow Gap, a name to remind the walker that the now extinct Eastern wapiti once cropped the grasses and wallowed in the mud here. The Trail winds down to Chester Gap, past barnyards and cattle fields to *U. S. Highway 50*.

Some of the most spectacular views of the entire Appalachian Trail are found at several points on Loudoun Heights. Below the bluffs, carved into the landscape in the shape of a Y, is the shimmering confluence of the Shenandoah and Potomac rivers.

The footpath comes down to *State Highway 180* for five short miles in West Virginia, to enter the attractive Revolutionary and Civil War town of Harpers Ferry.

On a quiet street in this comely village is the home office of the Appalachian Trail Conference. Here walkers can obtain maps of the latest Trail changes, guidebooks, and free information. Without exception every through-walker stops by the office, for at this point each feels proprietary about the great pathway and wants to talk with other trail experts. Although this is an historic town, the Appalachian Trail goes straight through it seeking nature. (*See Chapter 6, "The Potomac Heritage Trail," for the history of the town.*)

The red maple and sycamore forest along the Potomac bottomland shades acres of blue and pink-violet Virginia bluebells, fairy flowers of the river country. The tiny nests of the wood pewee and hooded warbler are fastened to branches high above the blue gardens. Their songs are wistful and sad.

Crossing *Interstate 70* the Trail enters Smithburg; then, angling past fields and farm woodlots, it crosses the Maryland–Pennsylvania

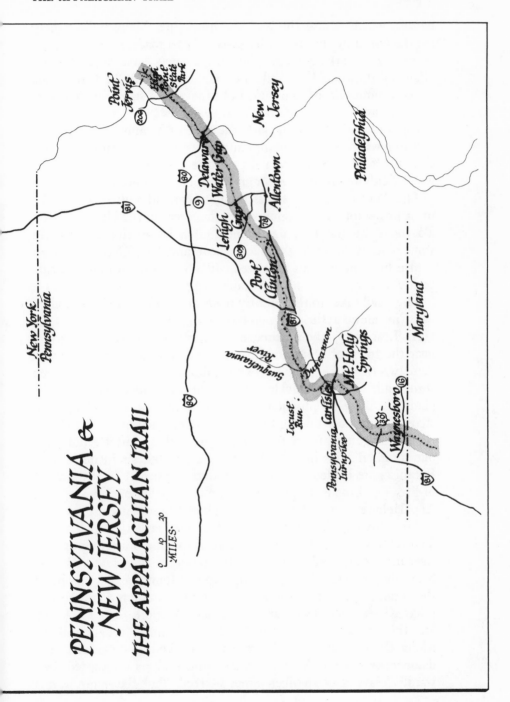

PENNSYLVANIA &
NEW JERSEY
THE APPALACHIAN TRAIL

border, which is also the Mason–Dixon line. Many walkers here are distressed by the footpath's proximity to roads, resorts, garbage dumps, and barking dogs. The unsightliness ends beyond *State Highway 16*, where the Trail enters Caledonia State Park, descends a steep mountain of hemlock and pine where hairy woodpeckers hammer, and crosses *State Highway 94.*

Past old mills, the path skirts the edge of Mount Holly Springs, and follows the foot of the mountain past wooden farmhouses and church steeples. Sparrowhawks on the tops of telephone poles watch fields and fencerows for grasshoppers and mice.

The Trail moves out across the Cumberland Valley, one of the most prosperous and unspoiled farming areas in the United States. To the right and left, handsome Dutch barns and 200-year-old stone houses stand in fields of wheat and hay. Occasionally an Amish husband and his bonneted wife on their way to Carlisle ride beside the Trail in their horse-drawn buggy.

The Trail takes to the country roads and walkers find themselves whistling along in this flat, rich farmland.

At Lost Run, about three miles northeast of Macks Corner, near the town of Duncannon on the Susquehanna River, grows a plant worth walking the six extra miles to see. It is an evergreen shrub called the bog huckleberry, *Gaylussacia brachycera.* A sterile plant incapable of producing seeds, it sends out an underground stem, as it has been doing for 12,000 years, which makes it the oldest and largest plant in the world—one and a quarter miles long, one hundred acres in area. The stem grows but six inches a year. Botanists are baffled as to its origin and its purpose in the scheme of life. The Lost Run specimen and a few smaller ones in southern Appalachia appear to be the only bog huckleberries in existence.

After crossing the Susquehanna at Clarks Ferry, the Appalachian Trail climbs Third Mountain, creeps through a scattering of wild tiger lilies, oaks, and sumacs and twice crosses *Interstate 81* before beginning a long, bleak pitch up Stony Mountain. At this point the Trail begins its famous trek over the eastern Pennsylvania ridges. These long flat plateaus are seldom more than 1500 feet, but their rocky, sparsely vegetated wastes make tough walking. Many through-hikers finish off old boots here and bush-leaguers damage new ones. "Water is scarce and shelters are spaced awkwardly," says through-hiker James Leitzell, "but the ridges were a

joy to traverse. Objectively, I do not understand why, the Trail surface alternated between gravel road, rocky patch and jumbled rock
pile. But I probably felt good because the halfway point in the Trail
had been passed."

The stony way continues between Lehigh Gap at *State Highway
9* and the Delaware Water Gap, one of the East Coast's geological
masterpieces. The river has cut through rock to form a three-mile-
long gorge whose walls rise 1400 feet on each side. Mt. Tammy
lies on the New Jersey side and Mt. Minsi on the Pennsylvania one.
They hug the river like bear paws and shade the walker across the
river to *Interstate 80*.

Ahead lie the dark forests of New Jersey's Kittatinny Mountains.
The Trail climbs through maple, ash, tulip, and hornbeam into one
of the loveliest sections of the Great Forest anywhere on the entire
route. Lakes shine green-blue, the black-billed cuckoo calls, and
the nature of the land changes; for the Trail has now entered a
land where the glaciers scoured the mountains smooth.

Following a rural road pinned down on each side with black-eyed
Susans and alive with female cowbirds eyeing the brush for nests of
other birds to lay their eggs in, the footpath weaves back and forth
between New Jersey and New York, then strikes out for the ridges
of New York's southern highlands.

The aptly named Agony Grind is a descent over boulders and
down cliffs to *Interstate 87*. The Trail enters Harriman and Bear
Mountain State Parks, and within a few miles the walker is on the
original section of the Appalachian Trail, a deeply worn, well-
traveled path that winds through oak and hickory, mountain laurel
and trillium, to the top of Bear Mountain. The Hudson River
moves serenely below.

Plunging down the steep mountainside, the Trail arrives at Bear
Mountain Inn, a log and stone hotel built around the turn of the
century and refurbished recently.

Taking to a sidewalk, the Appalachian Trail circles through the
Trailside Zoo, the first of a number of such zoos displaying not
exotic animals from Africa and Australia but those indigenous to
the area. Skunks, beavers, turtles, bears, great horned owls, and
rattlers are part of a collection so complete that the trail-walker who
has missed many of the shy wild mammals and reptiles can pause
to observe them here.

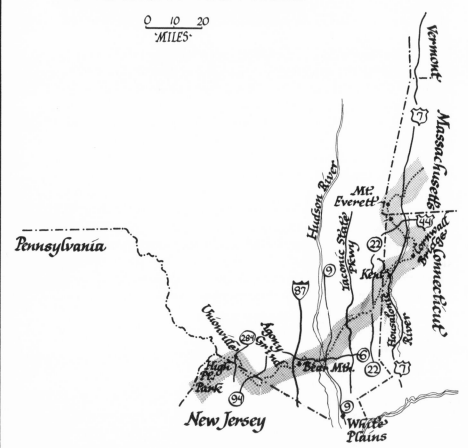

NEW YORK
THE APPALACHIAN TRAIL

0   10   20
·MILES·

The Trail leads over Bear Mountain Bridge, the lowest point
on the trek, 115.4 feet above sea level. In mid-bridge the view is
of mountains that come down to the water to form the Hudson
fjord. Boats of all descriptions move on the river and trains crackle
down both shores. The once blue-purple water is brown with
pollutants, but cleaner than it was in 1974 when the singer Pete
Seeger and his sailing ship *Clearwater* began a battle for a clean
and clear Hudson.

The climb up Anthony's Nose, off *State Highway* 9, leads around
swatches of laurel, twisting through chestnut oak to the summit.
Backtracking off the Nose, the Trail jogs off to Lake Alice, near
Graymoor Monastery. On summer nights the lightning bugs turn
this bog into a theater of lights, where shadowy flying squirrels
volplane to a chorus of frogs.

Plying through fields of Queen Anne's lace, the Trail crosses the
Taconic State Parkway and enters the twilight of the ancient hemlock forest at Fahnestock State Park. In the shadows deer snort
to warn each other of the approach of a walker. Crossing the *Taconic State Parkway* the footpath wends into Pawling, New York
on *State Highway* 22, skirts the home of the former governor,
Thomas E. Dewey, then strikes out for New England.

Old stone fences and second-growth forests edge the route to the
foot of Mt. Algo in Connecticut. The climb up and down this
giant staircase of boulders and rocks is tortuous and risky in rain or
snow. At the foot of Algo next to the Kent School for Boys,
the path crosses a road and climbs to the oak-covered bluff and a
view of the Housatonic River. The wood pewee calls in the stillness; the hermit thrush sings from leafy thickets. Northward over
rocks, through red oaks and scrub pine, the Trail keeps for a while
to the top of the ridge, then drops straight down into Macedonia
Brook State Park where a clear stream dashes through a forest of
hemlock and beech. Bluets decorate the mossy rocks and stargrass
grows in bright clumps on the bank. At twilight the nighthawk
gives its buzzing cry as it hunts insects overhead. In this park, a
2000-miler, Thomas McKone, met his parents for a one-day picnic
on his way north. When his family had departed, McKone wrote:

As I walked through the darkening woods I felt a little lonely. I
wanted to go home to Hartford. When I reached the next lean-to, be-

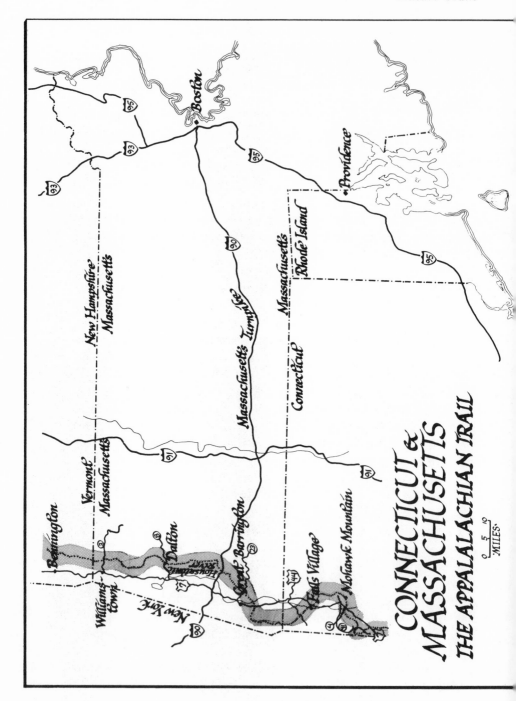

CONNECTICUT &
MASSACHUSETTS
THE APPALALACHIAN TRAIL

ing very conscious of the weight of my freshly loaded pack, I introduced myself as Colin Fletcher (famous for his heavy pack and author of the *Complete Walker*). One of the people went along with it. "Well, hello, Colin Fletcher, I'm Sam Prentiss," he said.

Soon I felt good again. I had my pack, I was at a lean-to with a white Appalachian Trail blaze on a tree beside it, and I was sitting by a campfire with good people. I wondered why I would want to go back to the city.

Across the Housatonic River in the town of Cornwall Bridge, the Trail meets *U. S. Highway* 7, then plunges into Dark Entry Ravine. Six miles farther along, it enters the Cathedral Pines—an awesome forest. Towering 150 feet above the Trail, this grove of virgin white pines dwarfs the footpath and shows what much of this country looked like before the forests were cut.

A few miles farther, the footpath climbs Mohawk Mountain and goes steeply past Grandma Gatewood's bobcat log. Beyond it, the trees have been felled for a ski trail and the view is of the rolling blue mountains of Connecticut.

White-throated sparrows softly call "old Sam Peabody" from the understory and marsh hawks hunt through the dell.

A long, rugged trek along streams, through yards, and over mammoth boulders brings the walker to the top of leg-breaking Barrack Mountain and to the end of one of the most exciting stretches on the Trail—Connecticut's fifty miles of ledges and vistas.

Past Falls Village and *U. S. Highway 44* the Trail climbs up Mt. Riga, the highest point in Connecticut (2316 feet) and crosses into the Berkshire Mountains of Massachusetts.

The walkers of the Appalachian Trail are legendary and so are many of the people who dwell along it. Of these there has been none more famous than Mrs. Fred Hutchinson of Washington Town Hall in the Berkshires. Mrs. Hutchinson, who died in 1975 at the age of 89, lived in a handsome Revolutionary house beside the Trail, and for 51 years involved herself with each 2000-miler many days before he or she turned up at her door. Word of such a hiker's arrival would come to her by way of newspaper articles and the back-country grapevine. When the hiker drew near she would send out scouts with an invitation to a shower and breakfast. No such through-hiker would fail to recall with pleasure the pungent taste of her coffee and home-cooked food. Before departing the guest was asked to sign her register. Mrs. Hutchinson would then read him or her a verse by her favorite poet, Robert Frost, and finally would draw a star beside the name. "Please send me a postcard when you reach Katahdin," she would say. "Then I will color your star."

As the pathway wends through Massachusetts, it penetrates the rural landscape where the plants of roadside life zone predominate. Queen Anne's lace, chicory, raspberries, and yarrow ribbon the Trail. Toads, catbirds, and towhees enliven it with song.

After crossing *State Highway* 8, the Trail leads into Greylock State Reservation, a deciduous forest of dark waterways overhung by the translucent leaves of birches. Here the rains collect in the clay soil, and long stretches of the Trail are crisscrossed and corded with logs to keep the walker from sinking into the mire.

Fields and greenways fill the landscape, white pines appear not just high on the mountain ridges—as on the southern part of the Trail—but in the valleys as well, announcing the beginning of the Eastern Pine Forest.

In the little town of Blackinton, Massachusetts, at the railroad bridge just across *State Highway 2*, the Appalachian Trail joins the grandfather of all American trails, the Long Trail.

Heading directly north at the Vermont border, the path climbs past white pines, cedars, and clumps of closed gentians—the flower of the cool, wet northern meadows—to the Seth Warner Shelter. On Prospect Ski Mountain, the Trail takes off through the hemlocks and canoe birch to *State Highway 9*. Plunging into some of the most valuable hardwoods of the National Forest system, the path is shadowed and cool all the way to *State Highway 30 and 11*. On the ascent to Emerald Lake, one of the most glittering and gemlike in a state of beautiful lakes, the Trail becomes wet and boggy and walkers are slowed to a toad's pace.

The footpath darkens beyond *State Highway 140* as it enters the Northeastern Coniferous Forest, the zone of spruce and balsam fir, and begins a battle with roots and stones that lasts all the way to the border of Maine. Porcupines rustle in the branches, and come at night to the shelters for salt left by the contact of human hands and bodies with boards and posts. Brian Winchester, a 2000-miler, wrote of porcupines on a sleepless night: "Each bite made a sound like the breaking of a pencil."

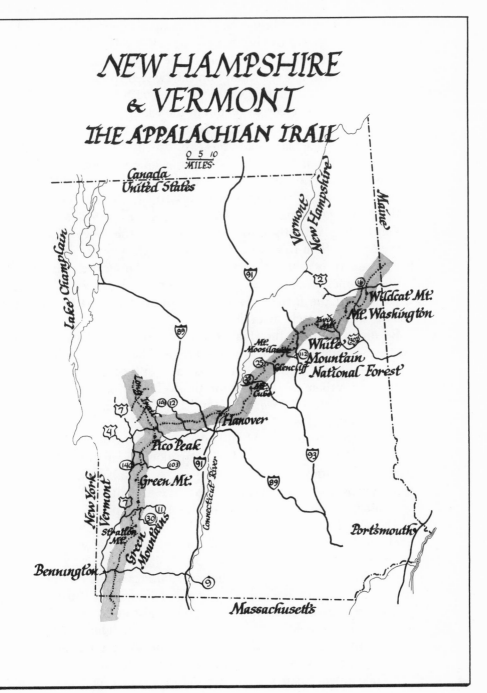

NEW HAMPSHIRE
& VERMONT
THE APPALACHIAN TRAIL

State Highway 103 brings the walker up Killington Peak (4241 feet). Reigning over the horizon to the east are the White Mountains of New Hampshire, monarchs of the Appalachian chain.

Icy blasts have left their mark on the twisted spruce and fir trees of Killington Peak, some of which, bearded with lichens and yellow moss, lie down and creep to get out of the wind.

In a meadow not far off *U. S. Highway 4*, as the Long Trail goes north, the Appalachian Trail veers east, driving steeply through the last rocky miles of the Green Mountains and Vermont. Thunderstorms often make these miles terrifying. Ed Kuni, a 2000-miler from Wilkes-Barre, Pennsylvania, was frightened by "close calls with lightning walking these ridges during electrical storms."

Descending abruptly into West Hartford, the footpath crosses *Interstate 89*, then *Interstate 91*, and finally the Connecticut River, the boundary between Vermont and New Hampshire. The Trail fittingly comes into Hanover, home town of the Dartmouth Outing Club, one of the first outdoor clubs and an active participant in blazing the Appalachian Trail.

Beyond the town the Trail leads northwest to Velvet Rocks, via paved roads hugged by cow pastures and hayfields. A stiff climb to Holts Ledge, through porcupine and spruce grouse country, brings the walker to the edge of the White Mountain National Forest and *State Highway 25*. Here the "far northland" in all its wild splendor begins.

The path tilts up Mt. Moosilauke to a view of both the Green and the White Mountains, then drops down a smooth rock face, angled precipitously at 30 to 40 degrees. A veritable sliding board, this is dangerous wet or dry. Below the mountain the Trail is soaked with runnels and the walker leaps and hops for a good part of the way to *State Highway 112*. In spring, wild Canada geese honk and guard young, and myrtle warblers sing as of wonders still to come.

Within a few miles one of the most famous sights of the Trail rises into view, the mountain sculpture of Franconia Ridge. Lofty projections, carved from the shale and mudstone by the glaciers, loom like monuments. One of these is known as The Great Stone Face. On the ridge the winds often gust up to 60 miles per hour. Clouds put caps on rocks and turn them into witches.

A 2000-miler, Brian Winchester, set down his experiences here:

When the misty cover broke on the Franconia Ridge my companion and I would glimpse the next wall of clouds hurtling up out of Franconia Notch with terrific velocity. Then we would be engulfed once again with visibility shrinking to twenty or thirty feet. It was necessary to lean well into the wind to maintain any semblance of balance, and any abrupt decrease in wind speed usually sent us reeling forward, a potentially dangerous situation if we were on a downward sloping incline. To make it a little more exciting some of the downward sloping inclines had thousand-foot precipices on either side.

The treacherous Trail crosses over *U. S. Highway 302* for a rocky climb up Webster Cliff. In this wildwood the Trail stays above 4000 feet, frequently climbing to 5000 and moving up beyond timberline at 5500 as it pitches across the summit of Mt. Washington (6288 feet), the windiest spot in the world. Here winds from the Atlantic, the Great Lakes, the far-distant Gulf of Mexico and the frigid Arctic meet. Their collision, unprecedented anywhere in the world, tears and pummels beast, bird, and man. A blast 231 miles per hour, the highest ever, has been recorded in the weather station on the summit.

Above timberline, across the jumble of rocks where the Northern raven hunts and storms boom, stand twenty-nine white crosses that mark the spots where walkers have died on this angry mountain. Three hundred and four days of the year are foggy or stormy and all walkers are urged to carry compasses when they ascend into the violent weather of Mt. Washington.

Down in the famous Tuckerman's Ravine, the Trail skirts the headwall where late-season skiers seek snow in May and June. Below in the cover of trees is the beautiful Lake of the Clouds Lodge, a shelter where many weekend hikers meet the 2000-milers and cheer them on to the finish.

The stony trail down the east slope of Mt. Washington crosses roaring streams, with occasional glimpses out upon dark Wildcat Mountain, and descends to *State Highway 16* and the Appalachian Mountain Club Lodge, the site of the club's first venture in wilderness living.

On wind-beaten Wildcat Mountain, the Trail passes through some of the richest stands of balsam fir in the United States, and consequently one of the darkest of the Northern forests. Canada jays scream from the shadows, porcupines stare solemnly down from the trees.

At *U. S. Highway* 2 the Trail leaves the White Mountain National Forest to plow through boggy land up and over Mt. Moriah to Gentian Pond. Here the spruces, collapsed by the force of the wind, huddle into dwarf krummholzes (German for "crooked timber"). The view is of the pointed trees of the north woods, spruce and fir.

In a few miles the Trail enters Maine. From the lakes and tarns comes the call of a loon, a sound so mournful that through-walkers move swiftly as they approach *State Highway* 26 and the Mahoosuc Range. The road is lonely on the way to Mahoosuc Notch, the most terrifying part of the Trail.

"This famous Notch," wrote Dorothy Laker,

which might have been named Nightmare Valley, was a channel between steep walls, jammed with giant boulders tossed one upon the other. There were spaces between and under the boulders. Moss and roots grew over everything. Trees were growing wherever they could find enough soil and their roots were of great help in getting over the boulders. The bare tree roots frequently formed part of the trail.

The water that flowed beneath the rocks was very cold, and frigid air welled up along the trail from the ice and icy water below. More often than not the trail went under and over the boulders. Pack and person must go through separately. It was a very strenuous trail, very time-consuming, very dangerous, and very hard on gear and the seat of the pants. At one point I lay down on the rocks and cried.

I had my pack off and on for what seemed like a million times going under boulders, through boulder tunnels and between boulders. I couldn't believe a trail could be so rugged. This was absolutely the most strenuous part of the trail for me. I took hours to go the one mile through Mahoosuc Notch.

State Highway 17 brings the Trail into the land of sphagnum moss, lakes, and moose. Rounding Rangeley Lake, it crosses Sandy River and climbs Saddleback and Spalding mountains.

State Highway 16 *and* 27 cuts brief lines across the wet Trail before the ascent of Moxie and Bald mountains. The way is enlivened by the acrobatics of the belted kingfisher right up to where it crosses *Interstate 201.*

State Highway 6 *and* 15 is the last road to cross. The end of the

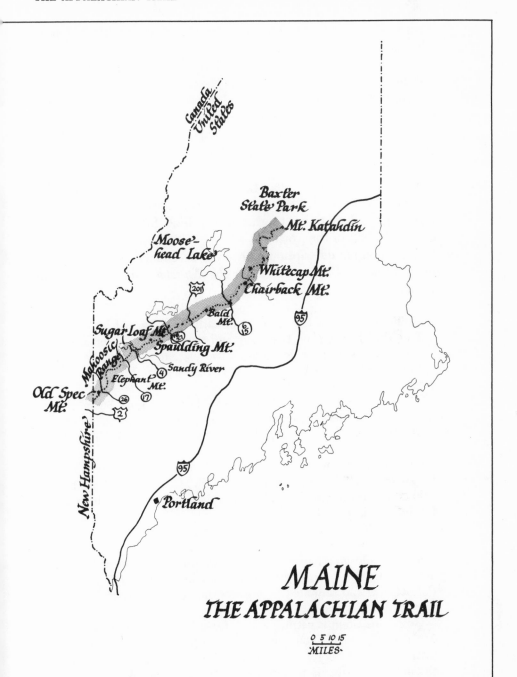

MAINE
THE APPALACHIAN TRAIL

0 5 10 15
MILES·

Trail is not far ahead. After rounding a sparkling succession of lakes, springs, and rivulets, the footpath winds up Chairback Mountain. To the north above the trees looms "the Big K in the Sky." Katahdin is lost from view on the descent to the west branch of Pleasant River, but a complex of beaver dams and other slides entertain the walker along the way to Nahmakanta Lake.

The last miles to Mt. Katahdin, in Baxter State Park, are different from all others. The trees have become shorter, the flowers are more brilliant, and the air is vibrant all the way to the Pitman Campgrounds. Here walkers camp and wait for the right weather to make the ascent of "Big K." On foggy and wet days park rangers urge anxious 2000-milers to wait for sunshine, for the last five miles can be the best or the worst.

A memorable description of the last ascent was written in 1969 by Andrew C. Giger, in *Hiking the Appalachian Trail* (Rodale Press):

Katahdin stands in the halflight of early morning as I look up at it.

The Trail breaks from trees here and there. There is a breeze, many very large rocks, and touchy going. A bad place to slip if you're alone.

Now what's this? Steel handholds in the rocks, and very necessary to get up over these big boulders.

This must be the ridge. I can't be sure in fog. It must be an exposed ridge. The wind had gotten very much stronger now. Geez, it's blowing hard. Don't be a weather casualty. Maybe the wind is just bad on this ridge.

Go on up the rocks. . . . The wind seems less, I'll go on. This freaky weather. It looked clear from below. Is Katahdin angry because I think it is just a formality rather than the tremendous northern anchor for the Appalachian Trail?

Now across the backside for more than a mile. This is some scrubby growth, but mostly rock and lichen. A Trail junction sign, turn right and climb. On up a half-mile, not too steep here. The wind at my back increases until it's pushing hard. It roars in my ears if I face into it. Foggier now and saturated with water droplets. The next blaze where? There, then that one.

Gosh, this cloud is getting thick. If you lose those blazes you'll be in one hell of a mess. You can just see to the next mark. My parka is plastered tight to my wool sweater by the wind and both are wet clear through. The wind is intense. There, what's that? A sign. That's it! That's it! The top! The top of Mt. Katahdin!

I made it! I made it! I made it!

No one hears the yelling. The wind blows the words out over the precipice. . . .

Highways Crossed by the Appalachian Trail

Georgia:
State Highway 52
State Highway 60
Interstate 76

Tennessee–North Carolina:
U. S. Highway 19
State Highway 28
U. S. Highway 441
Interstate 40
State Highway 23
U. S. Highway 19
State Highway 321

Virginia:
U. S. Highway 58
Interstate 81
U. S. Highway 21
U. S. Highway 460
State Highway 311
Interstate 81
State Highway 130
U. S. Highway 60
Interstate 64
U. S. Highway 211
U. S. Highway 50

West Virginia:
State Highway 180

Maryland:
Interstate 70

Pennsylvania:
State Highway 16
State Highway 94
Pennsylvania Turnpike 76
Interstate 81
State Highway 309
State Highway 9

New Jersey:
Interstate 80
U. S. Highway 206

New York:
Interstate 87
State Highway 6
State Highway 9
Taconic State Parkway
Interstate 84
State Highway 22

Connecticut:
State Highway 341
U. S. Highway 7
U. S. Highway 44

Massachusetts:
U. S. Highway 7
State Highway 23
Interstate 90
State Highway 8
State Highway 2

Vermont:
  State Highway 9
  State Highway 30 and 11
  State Highway 140
  State Highway 103
  U. S. Highway 4
  State Highway 12
  Interstate 89
  Interstate 91

New Hampshire:
  State Highway 25A
  State Highway 25

State Highway 112
Interstate 93
U. S. Highway 302
State Highway 16
U. S. Highway 2

Maine:
  State Highway 26
  State Highway 17
  State Highway 4
  State Highway 16 and 27
  Interstate 201
  State Highway 6 and 15

Bibliography and Maps

APPALACHIAN TRAIL CONFERENCE. Guidebooks and other literature are available from the Conference's headquarters at P. O. Box 236, Harpers Ferry, West Virginia 25425.

BURT, W. H., and R. P. GROSSENHEIDER. *A Field Guide to the Mammals.* Boston: Houghton Mifflin Company, 1952.

DANA, W. S. *How to Know the Wildflowers.* New York: Dover Publications, rev. ed. 1963.

GARVEY, EDWARD B. *Appalachian Hiker: Adventure of a Lifetime.* Oakton, Va.: Appalachian Books, 1971.

HARE, JAMES R., ed. *Hiking the Appalachian Trail* (2 v.). Emmaus, Pa.: Rodale Press, Inc., 1975.

PETERSON, ROGER T., and MARGARET McKENNY. *A Field Guide to Wildflowers of Northeastern and Northcentral North America.* Boston: Houghton Mifflin Company, 1968.

Rand McNally Road Atlas of the United States, Canada, and Mexico (51st ed.). The Appalachian Trail appears as a dotted line on maps of the region.

ROBBINS, CHANDLER S., BERTEL BRUUN, and HERBERT S. ZIM. *Birds of North America: A Guide to Field Identification.* New York: Golden Press, 1966.

SARGENT, CHARLES S. *Manual of Trees of North America* (2 v.). New York: Dover Publications, Inc., 2nd ed. 1965.

WHERRY, EDGAR T. *Wildflower Guide.* Garden City, N. Y.: Doubleday and Company, Inc., and the American Garden Guild, Inc., 1948.

3

THE PACIFIC
CREST TRAIL *

T he Pacific Crest Trail extends for 2610 miles from the
Mexico–California to the Washington–Canada border.
Passing through California, Oregon, and Washington, it
takes to the crests of the Laguna, San Jacinto, San Bernardino,
the Sierra Nevada, and Cascade mountains. Designated a National
Scenic Trail by Congress in 1968, the PCT is fed by highways and
trails that lead out of metropolitan areas to meet it, the same fish-
bone plan as Benton MacKaye's for the Appalachian Trail.

The Pacific Crest Trail is difficult, more so than the Appalachian;
the peaks are high, and snowstorms strike its northern section even
in summer. Only a handful of people have walked its entire gruel-
ing length, for there are long stretches where food must be carried
for as long as ten days or two weeks, and the entire trip requires
endurance and at least five months of time.

Valleys surrounded by jagged peaks, snowfields, flowers, and
waterfalls are the rewards of walking this trail, blazed high on ridges
and passes.

The PCT is a trail of biological diversity, for it crosses the desert,
winds among the tallest and oldest trees on earth, and climbs some
of the highest mountains on the North American continent.

The Trail's history dates back to 1920. That year the U. S. Forest
Service sent foresters on foot and horseback up canyons and across
ridges to find routes along the tops of the Cascade and Sierra
Nevada ranges that were esthetically most pleasing. Twelve years
later, when Clinton C. Clark of Pasadena, California, conceived

* For information about biotic communities along this trail see pages 258–259,
262–269, 279–283.

47

the idea of a blazed path down the mountainous crests between Canada and Mexico, most of the way was already mapped. In 1932 Clark organized the Pacific Crest Trail Conference, and within months volunteers were clearing the crest footpath, a job that took thirty-four years of work in a dangerous and storm-ridden terrain to complete. The Trail was finished in 1968.

The geology of the region dates back twenty-eight million years, to a period when the continent shifted and the earliest forerunners of the present Sierra Nevada and Rocky Mountain ranges arose where only seas and swamps had been. Through eons they were lifted twelve or thirteen thousand feet into the sky, forced upwards by the subterranean pressures moving from the east and the west. In time these movements released blasts of hot magma to the north, and the Cascade Range was spewed up. Between eleven and twelve million years ago, hot lava broke through the granite giving birth to ten now-dormant volcanoes, all of which can be seen from the PCT: Mt. McLoughlin, 9495 feet; Crater Lake, 12,000 feet; The Three Sisters, 10,358, 10,447, and 10,085 feet; Mt. Jefferson, 10,497 feet; Mt. Hood, 11, 235 feet; Mt. Adams, 12,267 feet; Mt. Rainier, 14,410 feet; and Glacier Peak, 10,568 feet.

Over the eons the lava blew out fissures and cracks in the Cascades and laid down deposits six miles deep over the original granite. Then at one stage of geological activity, a fault opened in the North Cascades, and intrusions of molten granite pressed up through the cracks. It is over these ribbons of granite, some tens of miles wide, the Trail passes today.

About ten thousand years ago the most recent glacial age slowed down the volcanic activity. The frequency of eruptions dwindled from one about every ten years to no more than one about every hundred years.

When the landscape was still puffing and hissing, the granite to the east of the Cascades broke open and spewed forth a sea of basalt that flooded what is now southern Washington and northern Oregon. Into the low spots came a trickle of water that eroded the basalt; growing in volume as the rains fell, it became the Columbia River.

Today the jagged Cascades are rain-makers. As the warm clouds off the Pacific Ocean strike the high barrier, they are slowed down, and the stalling precipitates more than a hundred inches of rain every year on the west side of the range. In these moist soils grow the great redwoods, Douglas fir, Western hemlock, and the giant cedars of the Northwestern Coniferous Forest. On the other side of the mountain range, for lack of water the plant life is quite different. Here grow the drought-tolerant white fir, lodgepole and yellow pines.

The biotic areas of the PCT comprise eight communities that have become variously adapted to the rocks, sunlight, storm, drought, and altitude along the West Coast. The Trail penetrates the Southwest Woodlands of chaparral and mesquite, plunges across the blistering Desert and Desert Shrublands, climbs into the Western Pine and Western Mixed forests to reach the Western Alpine Tundra that lies above the treeline from 7000 to 10,000 feet. On the northern section of the Trail the footpath enters Northwestern and Western Subalpine Coniferous forests.

The PCT begins in gravel and cacti at Monument 251 on the Mexico–California border. It strikes out over Hauser Mountain through a low cover of chaparral, a thorny, two-foot forest of holly-leaved cherry, quinine bush, and oaks. The most conspicuous shrub is the small chaparral oak, an evergreen with smooth yellowish-green leaves about two inches long and one inch across.

Beneath the chaparral the California quail, a black plume curving dandily forward from its crown, wistfully calls "Where are you?" Ground doves hunt seeds around bright clumps of California poppies, and the California thrasher, a handsome tannish-red ground feeder, tosses leaves as it hunts insects. Here also flits the scrub jay, a bird with blue head, wings and tail, and the source of the screaming "check-check-check" heard in the chaparral.

North of *State Highway* 94 and *Interstate* 8 the Trail ascends slabs of rock dating back sixty-five million years, when they were but the dust laid down by erosion of the granite mountains. Folded down into the hot furnace of the earth by a geological revolution the dust became gneiss.

Here the last of the endangered California Condor, no more than from 40 to 60 in number at the time of this writing, cruises the sky, and here lives the diminutive bush rabbit, which amazes walkers because it never drinks but metabolizes water from plant fats.

The Trail goes along the eastern rim of the Laguna Mountains, which look down on the enchanted Anza-Borrego Desert and off

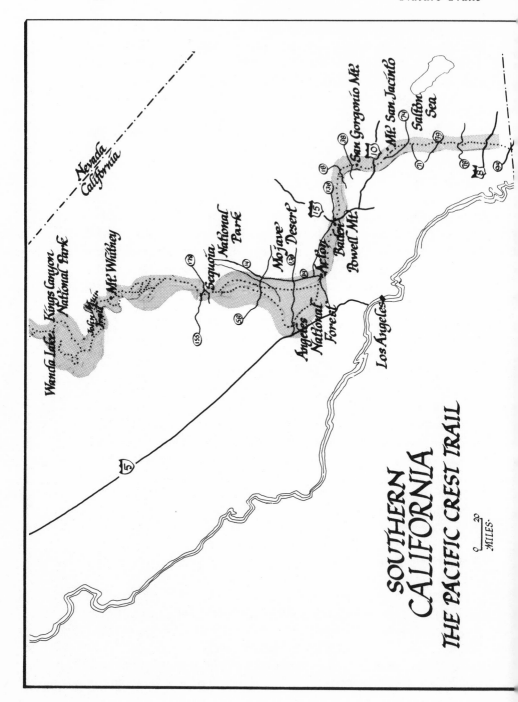

SOUTHERN
CALIFORNIA
THE PACIFIC CREST TRAIL

0   20
MILES·

toward the distant Salton Sea, a vast lake created by the Colorado River in 1905–7 when it burst through irrigation ditches and was trapped in the desert lowlands. Below the rim, green oases where Indians dwelled are tucked in canyon heads. In these bright green niches springs flow from rock walls, and Washington palms, birds, and wildflowers flourish.

As the Trail climbs, the chaparral gives way to Jeffrey pine and black oak. This largest and most abundant oak of southern California has thick leaves that are dark yellow-green, three to six inches long, and tipped with distinctive bristles. These trees obtain their maximum growth, 100 feet high and four feet in diameter, at altitudes of around 6000 feet.

Arid Chariot Canyon, beyond Cuyama Reservoir, is the home of the whiptail lizard, a reptile that gives birth to females which give birth to females, ad infinitum, by parthenogenesis. To date no scientist has found a male, although Professor Marsden of the University of Denver, Colorado, has kept many of these lizards isolated for over ten years.

To the north of *State Highway* 78 the PCT takes off through the hot cattle land of San Felipe Valley. An occasional oak gives welcome shade to the walker. The silver bubble to be seen on the skyline is the dome that covers the Mt. Palomar telescope.

The Trail meets *State Highway* 79 near Warner Springs, the last watering hole before a long dry hike through ribbonwood and acres of manzanita, a member of the heather family. In this semi-desert, gallons of water are needed by those who make the ascent to the top of San Jacinto Peak (10,831 feet) beyond *State Highways* 71 and 74. On the summit the view is eastward, a yellow and gold tapestry of sand, oases, and hills.

Near the top of San Jacinto, white streams leap down the sheer east face of the San Jacinto fault, making the earthquake line a wall of beauty. The PCT then plunges through ribbonwood and scrub oak forests to clumps of pinyon or nut pine, once the staff of life for the native Americans of the Southwest and Mexico. The pinyon needles are stout and appear in two-leaved clusters on small trees 40 to 50 feet tall. Their erect branches form a narrow head, and their thick irregular bark is tinged with red or orange. These trees abound in the region at altitudes of between 3000 and 7000 feet.

Beyond *Interstate 10* the PCT ascends the highest peak in southern California, San Gorgonio (11,500 feet). Since each hundred feet of elevation is equivalent to about 17 miles of latitude from the Equator to the North Pole, the ascent to the top of snow-crested San Gorgonio is like a climb up the globe. The biotic communities change from desert life to snowfield. At altitudes of from 1000 to 2000 feet the life community is chaparral. Then come the California live oak, digger pine, ponderosa, incense cedar, sugar pine, giant sequoia (Yosemite and Sequoia National Parks), red fir, Jeffrey and lodgepole pine. Still higher grow the Western white pine and the mountain hemlock. The whitebark pine of the timberline region grows prone at snowline to avoid the wind and ice. Beyond lies the treeless tundra.

After a long climb up San Gorgonio, the Trail comes into Fish Creek Meadows with their tall cool grasses. Winding higher, it enters a forest of pine, incense cedar and live oak trees, then zigzags down into Lone Pine Canyon to follow the San Andreas Fault, the earthquake line. The slippage of this fault set off the fire that nearly destroyed San Francisco in 1906. In 1940 it slipped again, rocking the Imperial Valley, and in 1971 a third movement set Los Angeles quaking. The PCT teeters on this gargantuan fracture. One side of the break is clean granite; on the other is metamorphic rock. The very sight of it hastens the walker along the fracture toward the slender pines that shade the route to Wrightwood.

Beyond *Interstate 15* the PCT climbs Mt. Baden-Powell (9399 feet), named in tribute to Lord Robert Stevenson Smyth Baden-Powell, founder of the Boy Scout movement. High on this mountain are a few gnarled patches of limber pine, a relative of the oldest tree on earth, the bristlecone pine. These pines have been filed by the winds and twisted by time into living gargoyles.

Descending into Acton, the Trail passes a monument at "Perspiration Point," commemorating the men of the CCC who in 1934 built fire trails across this parched land. Stark and isolated, the monument looks over a bleak desert where plants thicken their leaves to fight evaporation and cacti grow spines to protect their stems from the burning sun.

Beyond Acton and *State Highway 14* the Trail blazes off into the Mojave Desert, 25,000 square miles of lava, ashes, and the beds of dried-up lakes. For desert lovers this stretch of the PCT is a

Christmas tree of biological inventions. Living here are the territorial creosote bushes, which drop chemicals to prevent the seeds of other plants from germinating and competing. Cat's claw thickens its leaves to save water, and in the dryness lizards, as an adaptation to the blowing sand, have developed a membrane like a windshield wiper for ejecting sand particles in their eyes.

For miles the PCT parallels the Los Angeles Aqueduct, then heads north around Cross Mountain to the border of Sequoia National Forest. Deep in the dry forest beyond *State Highways 178 and 155*, the PCT arrives at the Siberian Pass. The air freshens and cools, and to the north snow-clad Mt. Whitney (14,494 feet), the tallest mountain in California, looms like white marble. Its appearance lures the walker across a sweeping terrain where monkey-flowers bob and mountain lakes sparkle between gray granite rocks. Chickadees sing as they hang upside down on pine cones, and the way is cool and pleasant.

Where the Trail drops into ravine bottoms, the Western winter wren warbles his song from tangles of plants. This stubby-tailed bird identifies itself by frequent bobs and bows and hides its nest of moss and twigs in the roots or rock crevices.

For forty-five miles the Trail takes to the top of the Sierra Nevada. Alpine meadows with views of unglaciated mountains lead into quiet forests and finally to Big Whitney Meadow. The surrounding mountain peaks are sawteeth in the sky.

On the side of Mt. Whitney at 13,560 feet the Pacific Crest Trail joins the famous John Muir Trail. This 212-mile footpath begins in snowfields, passes through some of the grandest scenery on earth, and terminates in Yosemite Valley.

Explorer, naturalist, and writer, John Muir (1838–1914) lived in this region for six years. The great granite walls of Yosemite, the giant trees and plume-like waterfalls inspired him to write *The Mountains of California, Our National Parks*, and *Yosemite*. Such sayings as "Leave only your footsteps" and "Any fool can kill a tree" are among the Muir quotations posted by the National Park Service. Muir was instrumental in persuading Congress to make Yosemite a national park, and it was he who urged Theodore Roosevelt to place 148 million acres of redwood forest in permanent trust to the government. As a geologist he was the first to realize that Yosemite Valley was the art work of the glaciers.

On into Kings Canyon National Park the PCT and Muir Trail weave past the Castle Dome and up through basins and canyons to see the work of ice in sculpting the Sierra Nevada. Polished walls of granite and rock bowls stand on exhibit.

To the west, in a complex of conifers at altitudes between 5000 and 8400 feet, stand those colossi among forest trees, the giant sequoias. They occur naturally in no place on earth except this well-drained interacting community of plants, animals, and weather. The trees rise over the forest canopy to a height of more than 250 feet and many have trunks 20 feet in diameter. Leaves from one-eighth to one-quarter of an inch long, and their half-inch cones are in sharp contrast to the huge trunks. So admired are the sequoias that some have been given human names. The oldest and largest of these, about 4000 years old, 273 feet tall, and 115 feet in circumference, is the General Sherman Bigtree.

Striking up toward timberline, the PCT seeks out the rare fox-tail pine, a tree that has adapted to the rocky slopes at the upper limits of tree growth, at around 8000 feet. It grows only in the Rocky Mountains of Colorado in southern Utah, the San Francisco Peaks of Arizona, and here on the southeastern slopes of the Sierra Nevada. The tree is easily identified by grabbing its cones. Unlike those of any other pine, their in-curved spikes will pierce the skin.

The Trail drops sharply into alpine meadows to wind across the deep sand of Guyot Flat, which supports only scattered sedges and screaming winds. Here the back side of Mt. Whitney is seen, streaked with lanes carved by avalanches.

The next 146 miles of mountain passes and tundra to the famous Red Meadows in Yosemite are the essence of the PCT. No highways intersect the wilderness. Swag saddles bind peaks together and snow patches fracture the sunlight into sparks along this alpine stretch. Then the PCT descends to the northern border of Kings Canyon National Park and into timber again at 10,000 feet.

On down the Trail, at the headwaters of the South Fork of the Kings River are the Vidette Meadows, a famous high Sierra campground where Joseph Le Conte (1823–1901), geologist, author, physician, and friend of John J. Audubon, found inspiration for his many writings. It was here in the meadow that he died during a trip in 1901 with the Sierra Club which he helped found. One of

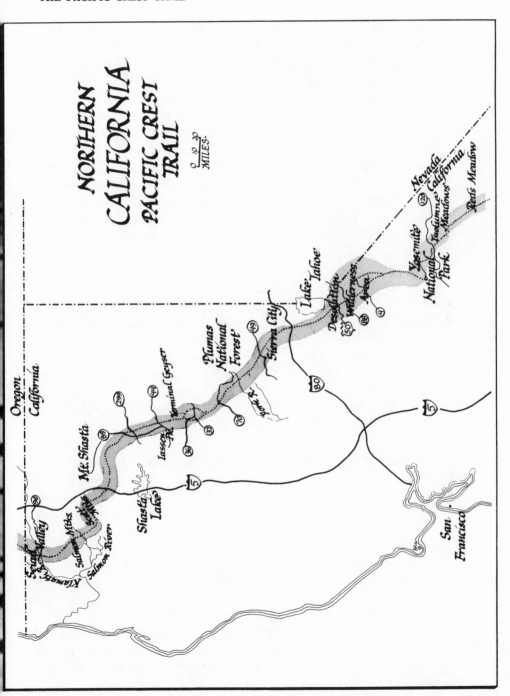

the most joyous and popular writers of his days, he came West after
the Civil War and unraveled the geological history of the California
and the Sierra Nevadas in particular.

The climb out of the meadow is steep all the way to Wanda and
Helen Lakes, named after the daughters of John Muir. Here a
stone hut protects the walker from the constant blasts of wind and
the cold night air. The Trail drops down to Evolution Lake (10,850
feet) where marmots whistle beneath peaks named for Charles
Darwin and other evolutionary scientists. Everywhere the hardy
lichens raise thoughts of survival. Along the downward-zagging
switchbacks water splashes from cracks, and the view is of Silver
Divide, which spreads from horizon to horizon. Finally the Trail
eases into flower-spangled Red Meadows, where supplies are
available.

On down the Trail, Devils Postpile, a towering rock 865 feet
high, looms into view. This massive pinnacle of dark feldspar was
volcano-born. As it cooled, it fractured into hexagonal columns
which the glaciers smoothed and broke into mammoth "posts."
Because of its uniqueness, Theodore Roosevelt in 1906 named the
Postpile as the first U. S. National Monument.

For the next three miles the volcanic ridge is spangled with stone
rubble three million years old. Vistas appear between forest trees
as the PCT circles the top of the great glacial bowl that is Yosemite
National Park. On this crest the Muir Trail and the Pacific Crest
part.

The Muir Trail leads to Tuolumne Meadows, the largest subalpine meadow in southern California. Freckled with white yampa
and yellow cinquefoil, it is edged by a palette of blue harebells and
the red-orange and gold of the Indian paintbrush. Rocks as big as
houses, known as "erratics" or "wandering boulders" have been
dumped here by the glaciers, geological strangers to the rocks on
which they rest. Near by is a natural soda spring where walkers mix
its waters with fruit juices and sugars to make thirst-quenching
drinks.

The PCT goes north out of Yosemite, crosses *State Highway 120*,
and climbs to Bond Pass (9400 feet). In this treeless alpine country
there are distant views of mountains and intimate ones of flowers.
Tucked in the crevices of rocks beside blue Dorothy Lake are
patches of yellow stonecrop, a strange plant with star like flowers,

which can survive dry conditions by simply not growing. When water returns the stonecrop begins growing again.

Winding downward, the Trail enters White Canyon and tests the patience of walkers, who must ford the Carson River six times within a very few miles. The effort is worth making; along the way are aspens and lodgepole pines carved into grotesque shapes of men and women by lonely Basque sheepherders some time around the turn of the century. Beyond the river the groves of aspen are mixed with red fir, the perfect-pointed Christmas tree of the West Coast, shading the Trail until it arrives at *State Highway 4* and the Silver Creek Campground.

On the fifteen miles to *Old State Highway 88*, the PCT winds out of the forest for a view of Raymond Peak, a volcano of star-tlingly colored rocks—brown, red, pink, purple—to which the plant kingdom has added green ribbons of grass and clumps of yellow buttercups. It is fortunate that Raymond Peak is there to keep a walker's eyes lifted above the crowded campgrounds, where trail bikes roar down lanes and campers yell and shout.

North of *Old State Highway 88* lies Benwood Meadow, a garden of blue, red, yellow, and purple alpine flowers—mountain bluebell, columbine, corn lily, larkspur, and yampa. Each has its place in a complex of soils, temperature, and animal life. For instance, the yampa, a member of the parsley family, puts hibernating fat on the grizzly bears, who in turn, weed it and add to its vigor. The Indians, who realized that what was good for the bears was good for human-kind, also harvested the yampa. Lewis and Clark, wise enough to learn from the Indians who learned from the bears, made yampa their staple food in the West. Today the interaction between plant and animal has been upset by the elimination of the grizzly; as a result only remnants of the once vast yampa gardens remain in the area.

Beyond *U. S. Highway 50* the PCT wanders into Echo Lake Resort and the Desolation Lake Wilderness, an area that is pitifully misnamed. The most man-invaded wilderness area in California, it is a clutter of camps, motorboats, trash and people.

In keeping with the PCT policy of avoiding well-used areas, the Trail passes to the west of Lake Tahoe. It is unable, however, to avoid using the overrun "staircase" up the side of Mt. Tallac (9800 feet), which is just as well, since the top rewards walkers with a view of Crystal Range and its mirror-like glacial polish. Campers who bed down for the night awaken to a sunrise that lights the red rocks, gray granite, and snowfields like the facets of a chandelier.

On ahead, lakes and spilling creeks, snowmelt and flowers inspire the walker to the border of Tahoe National Park. The Trail climbs up onto a high saddle from which a glance back reveals Lake Tahoe lying like a blue jewel among the mountains. Underfoot lie marine sediments that were changed into near-marble by a flow of hot lava a million years ago.

A stench of auto fumes overtakes the walker as the PCT goes under *Interstate 80* into Crystal Valley, up through a parking lot, and finally over Castle Pass to the Sierra Club hut. Several miles farther along, the warm waters of Paradise Lake invite swimming under boughs of mountain hemlock, Western juniper, and water birch, trees that signal a change from the biotic area of the southern California forests to that of the Northwestern Coniferous Forest. The moisture from the Pacific now touches the mountains.

The Trail crosses *State Highway 49* a mile east of Sierra City, parades up the side of a roaring cascade, and then strikes out along Old Gold Lake Road, where miles of dense manzanita grow on the rocky moraine deposited by a vanished glacier. Sparrowhawks hunt from dead tree stumps, finches call to keep in touch with one another, and in the distance the weather-altered volcanoes are humped like sunning turtles.

Along the next stretch the campsites are some of the best in California, set as they are beside streams, spring-fed creeks, and ponds where ducks, herons, and rainbow trout intermingle. Fishermen flash rods as they try to lure up America's most beautiful fish— the rainbow trout. A native of California, the rainbow is now raised in hatcheries all around the country and is stocked in streams throughout the United States and Europe. These fish are coveted for their beauty, flavor and size—they weigh up to 26 pounds and may reach 42 inches in length.

A side trek down from the ridge to Packer Lake Lodge offers the walker home cooking, showers, and supplies. Back on the Trail, the colorful Sierra Buttes support a new biotic community—pine, incense cedar, black oak, white fir, and broadleaf maple. On the trailside grow thimbleberries, delicious relatives of the raspberry with prickerless stems and leaves.

For the fisherman, the long hike into Deer Lake is rewarded with cold, clear water and trout that leap to the fly. Near the lake the Western goshawk and long-eared owl sit close to the cinnamon-red trunks of the incense cedar.

Large patches of bark yanked from dead conifers belie the presence of the Arctic three-toed woodpecker with its solid black back and barred sides. On the ground, the pert blossoms of red-stemmed dogwoods tell walkers they are in the rain belt.

Around a bend is Franklin Canyon and the toothpick-fragile suspension bridge that spans its gorge. After an unsteady crossing. the walker reaches firm ground and acres of manzanita with its tough leaves and little, apple-like fruits. Above the plants glows the distant peak of Bucks Summit.

Ferns dapple the floor of the white fir forests; then the PCT tips downward, crosses the main Feather River, and arrives at *State Highway 70*.

Huge California red firs, with cones that stand up like candles, shade roaring Chips Creek. At Sunflower Flats the view is of white snowfields, dark manzanita, and Lassen Peak, a graceful volcano that seems to float over the acres of grass. The Trail crosses a lava bed that in eons past flowed out of volcanoes in the distant Cascades.

Now everywhere flowers prevail. Daisies, asters, and buttercups dance in the wind all the way to *State Highways 32* and *36*. The through-walkers trek off to Deer Creek on *State Highway 32*, for this is the last place for supplies in fifty-two miles.

North of *State Highway 36* the Trail enters Lassen Volcano National Park—and rain. Meadows are strung with beads of water, mosses thrive, and moisture-loving ferns spring out of cracks in the rocks, tree roots, limbs, and stumps.

Near the Warner Valley campground, Terminal Geyser boils up from the earth at 203°F. and forms a misty cloud over grass and forest. Through the steam, Mt. Lassen is a distant stage set for the nearby Painted Dunes, Fantastic Lava Bed, and Cinder Cone, all eerie creations of the volcanoes. And here the Sierra Nevada ends.

Across *State Highway 44* ten miles of dusty, shadeless trail bring the walker to the cool waters of Hat Creek River and the beginning of the Cascade Range. In ravines the black bears dig for insect larvae and chase their cubs up trees. Mule deer pause in tall groves and screaming jays shatter the silence.

Passing *State Highway 299* and *State Highway 89*, the forest on the north of the Trail is wet and that on the south is dry for the next seventy-five miles; for the ridge is the moisture break for the clouds moving in from the ocean. Finally the ridges and red fir forests bring the walker to Grizzly Peak with a view of Mt. Shasta. The rest of the way to *Interstate 5* is moderately moist.

At *Interstate 5* the Trail heads off into the Scott and Salmon mountains. Water is scarce all the way to Eagle Pass, where a cold spring quenches the walker's thirst. More dry miles lie ahead before the Trail comes into the Northwestern Coniferous Forest, the rain forest of the coast.

Up over Big Ridge to Buckhorn Mountain, the PCT cuts through miles of whortleberries or huckleberries, plants of acid soil that grow at altitudes from 6000 to 9000 feet. The fruits are sweet and delicious. The Trail passes isolated campsites where the varied thrush sings and nests. Farther on, robins hop along the grassy streamsides of the clear Klamath River. After crossing miles of blue serpentine and granite rock, the footpath arrives in the luxuriant Seiad Valley. Regal ponderosa pines with their downward-sweeping branches dominate the landscape.

The Trail drops from about 6000 to 1375 feet at *State Highway 96* and the town of Seiad Valley.

The valley floor marks the end of the California trek. Although the border is still about forty miles north, most walkers consider Seiad Valley the end of the southern and the beginning of the northern PCT.

Heading for the California–Oregon border, the Trail winds up Kangaroo Mountain, past pungent elk wallows where these lordly animals roll and coat themselves with insect-repelling mud. Then it goes on through park-like storybook forests of huge trees all the way to the boundary. Near the state line grows one of the rarest trees on earth, the weeping spruce. A graceful tree about 100 feet high, it is furnished to the ground with needle-crowded branches. The name is derived from the pendulous lower branches, which have numerous whip-like twigs seven to eight inches long. The trees form small groves at about 7000 feet in just two places in the world, here in Siskiyou National Forest and in the coastal range of

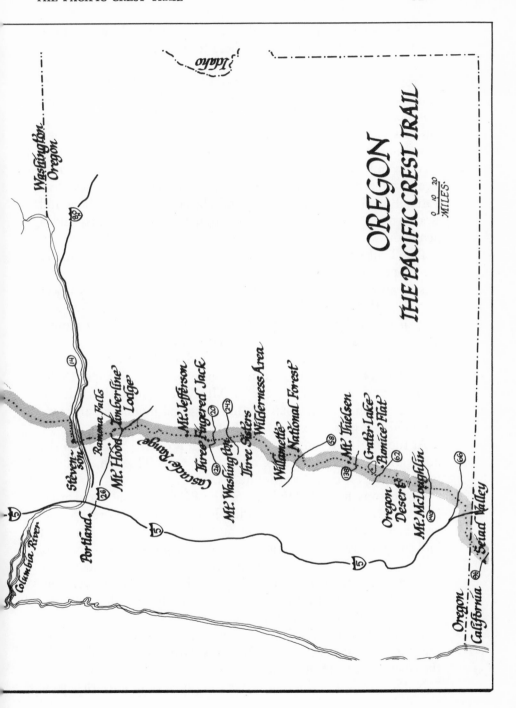

southwestern Oregon. Although the trees are rain-lovers, surface water is scarce. A running tap is here to fill canteens for the long dry climb to Mt. Ashland.

Crossing *Interstate 5* for the second time, the PCT heads north into Douglas fir, incense cedar, and Oregon oak. On slopes and switchbacks, where the trees are thin, the majestic Cascade Range can be seen rising beyond the valleys, luring the walker on through forests of red fir to Wrangle Campground.

A few miles beyond *State Highway 66* lies rainbow trout country, recognizable by fast-running streams, shaded banks, and icy clear water. Beavers dam the streams and elk bed down in willow and aspen groves. Their beds are recognized by flattened grass and a rich odor.

The Trail weaves up to a basalt waterfall near Fish Lake where the dipper or water ouzel, a sleek gray bird of the high country, flies in and out of booming cascades. This bird also hunts insect larvae on the bottoms of fast streams, where it floats, dips, and sings like a nightingale. Beyond the waterfalls dusky blue grouse, so tame they can be almost touched, walk beside the Trail.

The PCT passes *State Highway 140* and winds through stands of huckleberries, gooseberries, currants, and the Oregon grape. Douglas firs frame the conical peak of Mt. McLoughlin (9510 feet). Clouds and snowstorms play around this regal mountain, and over the Trail as it twists west and climbs to the summit.

At the top the rolling view to the south is of Mt. Shasta. To the north are aquamarine-blue Crater Lake, Mt. Thielsen, and the snow-draped Three Sisters Mountains.

On the way to *State Highway 62* the PCT seeks out the densest forests of the Rogue River Wildlife Refuge. In aspen groves mule deer bed down, and to the right and left lakes lie like shards of broken glass. Everywhere the thin volcanic soil supports the cup-shaped pasqueflower that typifies the western wilderness. The PCT goes up open slopes and through clouds along the very rim of the West as it traverses some of the nation's grandest country, the forests and mountains of Oregon.

The climb to Devil's Peak is laborious; but the descent is a free ride for glissaders, who can take the snowfields down, almost to the edge of the Oregon Desert.

Not a true desert, this flat area is composed of pumice that blew out of a volcano to the north some 6000 years ago. The desert is timbered with lodgepole pine; although there is no water for hikers, the trees find it deep in the soil.

At the edge of the desert the Trail drops into the twilight of a mountain hemlock forest where fallen needles hush the footsteps. Many of these trees are five feet in diameter and more than a hundred feet tall. If there were a Northern tree of the PCT it would be this stately hemlock, whose soft leaves stand out from all sides of its branches. It is easily recognized by the three-inch-long cones that decorate the tips of the new twigs, and by bark that is deeply divided into dark cinnamon scales with blue or purple edges. Primarily, however, the mountain hemlock is identified by the places where it grows—the exposed ridges and mountain slopes, up with the winds and endless views. This slope-loving tree shades the saw-whet owl, the black bear, and the busy red squirrel. Flitting through its foliage is the western crossbill equipped through evolution with a beak that acts as a pair of pliers for prying open the cones.

At *State Highway* 62 the PCT crosses into Crater Lake National Park and descends onto a pumice flat furnished from the guts of ancient Mt. Mazama, the 12,000-foot mountain that once stood on the present site of Crater Lake. About 6000 years ago a series of violent eruptions blew up the mountain and collapsed it into its own hole. Slowly the dust descended, shrouding Pumice Flat and laying down a three-inch deposit on Mt. Rainier. Then what was left of the mountain subsided into the huge blowhole, which filled up with the blue water that is the hallmark of Crater Lake.

The PCT lies far west of the rim of Crater Lake, avoiding crowds in accordance with Trail policy. However, no PCT walker can resist wending up to the edge of this vivid lake, which lies 900 feet below the crater's rim (7100 feet). The deepest lake in the United States (11,932 feet), it is one of the most stunning natural wonders of the earth—a turquoise in a setting of dark brown and bright yellow stone. Wizard Island in the center was formed by a small eruption that followed the major one.

The PCT crosses *State Highway 138* a few miles beyond Crater Lake National Park and heads for the summit of Mt. Thielsen. This is one of the steepest climbs on the Trail that can be made without ropes. Going almost straight up a pumice slope, the footpath noses to the top of Mt. Thielsen (9173 feet), where distant

Crater Lake is but a blue circle in the forest. Magnificent Mt. Shasta and Mt. Jefferson rise on the northern horizon.

Whitebark pines, which lie down and creep when confronted with ice and wind, spill down the windy mountain top. Wildflowers entertain hosts of butterflies and on the descent are green-backed tree swallows that dart over the trail as they feed on clouds of insects. The Oregon junco smacks out a warning to its nestlings, who hide in the ferns and moss. The black head and pink bill of the male distinguish this bird from all other juncos.

The Trail passes underneath Sawtooth Ridge, a veritable shark's mouth of a pinnacle, then descends to flats of pumice.

Between Mt. Thielsen and *State Highway* 58 stretch great stands of Douglas fir, sprinkled with bright lakes and with gardens of phlox, lupine, and bluebells. The Northern belted kingfisher hunts in the pools of White Fish Creek, and above it volcanic Diamond Peak flashes in the sun. Diamond View Lake mirrors this unique mountain on its still surface.

State Highway 58 is the jump-off for a true wilderness adventure. Ahead lie 140 miles of rocks, ice, and forest before the next road and supplies. The blue lupine, the trail flower of the northern PCT, edges the path all the way to Willamette National Forest, a land of lakes, snow-capped peaks—and drizzling rain. The moisture-loving oxalis proliferates in the wetness, clouds sweep in and out of the trees like ghosts.

The PCT leaves the forest and moves out upon great slabs of rock with a view of serene Waldo Lake and Diamond Peak. Shining in the distance are the white peaks of those ancient volcanoes, the Three Sisters.

In the Three Sisters Wilderness the PCT becomes a crest trail in the fullest sense. It follows the ridges above lakes, teeters among buttes, and switches high above elk meadows; here it has in fact merged with the famous Oregon Skyline Trail. This section takes the walker over cinder cone and crackling pumice into campgrounds where trout flash in pools and sandpipers run along lake shores.

On the high ledges may be seen for the first time the mammal of the cliffs and peaks, the regal Rocky Mountain goat with its snowy fur, and its black eyes, nose, hoofs, and horns.

The PCT ascends to Le Conte Crater and a view of the South Sister, which harbors the famous Clark and Lewis Glaciers where ice-fiends love to climb. The Trail winds over the crater's pumice soils in which the friendly Columbia gopher digs its own subterranean PCT among the knotweeds. This attractive member of the ground squirrel family has a large brushy tail and a tawny face, and is the source of a sharp whistle that is repeated several times.

Along the Trail leading to the Middle Sister is a mountain hemlock six feet in diameter, which halts all who pass. The tree is so distinctive that it seems to be an ancient person looming in the wilderness and walkers often greet it with "Hi, Tree." The Middle Sister (10,470 feet) is covered with huge erratic boulders and splotched in summer with colorful Indian paintbrush and white pasqueflower. Pink heath glows in avalanche trails and the yellow-bellied marmot whistles his single human-sounding note from the gray rocks.

The Trail circles the Middle Sister and heads for the North Sister (10,094 feet), the only one of the peaks that can be safely climbed without ropes and mountaineering skills.

A few miles north, near Yapoah Crater, the peaks of Mt. Washington, Three Fingered Jack, Mt. Jefferson, and Mt. Hood rise above the dark conifer forests. Hummingbirds buzz the Trail, investigating bright backpacks for possible sources of nectar. Defying all the laws of aerodynamics, these little buzzers, with their needle-like bills and metallic feathers, move up, down, forwards or backwards, and even roll, having adapted their movements to slip inside the bell-, platter-, and horn-shaped flowers. These darters are the ruby-throated, rufous, and on rare occasions the Calliope. This last species is the smallest hummingbird of the United States, marked with purple-red rays on a white throat.

Just beyond the border of the Three Sisters Wilderness Area, after zigzagging the Yapoah Lava Flow, the Trail comes to *State Highway* 242 and the base of Belknap Crater (6872 feet). Ahead is one of the most dramatic stretches of the PCT, marked as it is with lava flows, ice, and flowers. The lava from Belknap Crater is quite young, perhaps 200 years old, and is dark and fire-pitted. Jagged black clinkers contrast with the white bands that are snowfields. On the skyline the wind and ice have carved grotesque stone creatures where thousands of toads hop. These are the boreal toads, relatives of the common toad of California, and they live in forested sections under rocks. They breed in swift cold mountain streams and come out on the lava beds to hunt for insects that hide in its crevices.

Santiam Pass, *State Highway 20 and 126*, brings the walker to the Mt. Jefferson Wilderness. The pass was first crossed in 1859 by Andrew Wiley, a trapper who sought the beaver along an old Indian trail beside the Santiam River.

The Trail passes the Cathedral Rocks, a bizarre landscape of volcanic glaciation, and crosses numerous "milk" streams, so called because they are white with the dust the glaciers have scoured from the rocks. At Scout Lake is a magnificent view of Mt. Jefferson, named by Lewis and Clark in honor of their President on March 30, 1806.

Many fishermen angling for trout in cool, green Scout Lake catch the twelve-inch Pacific giant salamanders that dwell here mute and silent. These creatures are stout of body, have large mouths, and live only in the rain country of the Northwest. Their larvae develop in lakes and as adults they hide on land under logs. The fishermen who catch them are so startled by their prehistoric-looking eyes and lumpy bodies that many anglers return to civilization with tales of the Scout "Loch" monster.

Mountain hemlock, Douglas fir, alder, vine maple, rhododendron, and coralroot line the Trail on the way to a series of ridges where Mt. Hood, the prince among volcanic mountains, rises in its white beauty. Leaving the ridges and winding gently downward, the Trail arrives at Olallie Lake, its name an Indian word for huckleberries. There is a last view of Mt. Jefferson to the south.

State Highway 26, at Wapinitia Pass, and *New State Highway 35*, bring the walker into Mt. Hood National Park. At bends and openings the steep-sided volcano can be seen, a lordly dragon of a mountain that blows steam.

Across the Salmon River the Timberline Lodge, constructed as a WPA project in the 1930s, offers refuge and rest. Ambitious hikers climb Mt. Hood for a spectacular view of the entire Cascade Range, but most walkers follow the less strenuous path up the banks of Lost Creek. Lupine, monkeyflower, bistort, corn lily, yarrow, and Indian paintbrush abound in fields, and mariposa lilies bloom in the moist niches. Overhead, flycatchers loop after insects and call to their mates.

Rushing creeks cross the Trail all the way to the veil of water,

Ramona Falls, a favorite rendezvous for guitar-playing walkers. Beyond the falls, a steep switchback goes up Bald Mountain to a view of Mt. Hood, then down through patches of gooseberries and thimbleberries to the north ridge of Lost Lake. Ahead stand magnificent Mt. St. Helens, Mt. Rainier, and Mt. Adams.

Benson Plateau commands a fine view of the Columbia River and the basalt flow that was spewed across the ancient landscape eons ago when vents in the Cascades blew up.

The Trail leads through Douglas fir forests to Cascade Locks, the Columbia River and *Interstate 80N.*

In the middle of the Bridge of the Gods, which spans the Columbia, the Trail enters Washington State. *State Highway 14* lies on the other side of the river. Two miles east is Stevenson, a supply town for the long, 132-mile trek to the next highway.

The Trail teeters along rocky bluffs for a last view of the Columbia, then plunges into a forest of Douglas fir and mountain maple all the way to Table Mountain. Almost invariably it rains or has just stopped raining on this section, and drops from the bushes perpetually soak the walker's clothing.

Twenty-three miles north, Big Huckleberry Mountain brings the PCT to lava beds again. Conclaves of mountains rise to the southwest, and deer, bear, and coyote cross to the flower-splashed mountainside and Trail. Occasionally mountain lions look down from rocky crests, and everywhere bees and butterflies are on wing.

At the foot of Sawtooth Mountain, where the Trail enters the Mt. Adams Wilderness, a lumber operation violates the primeval stillness for many miles. The climb up the mountain (12,326 feet), on the gentle south ridge, goes past abandoned sulfur mines, restoring one's serenity with constant views of the glistening White Salmon Glacier on distant Mt. Rainier.

On the downward trek off Mt. Adams, a waterfall of glacial ice hangs on the mountainside like an azure pendant and dazzles the eye on the long dry miles to a spring of crystal water, said to be the best tasting of the entire PCT.

Split Rock, where conifers grow in volcanic ash and storms blow in and out like autumn leaves, is a weather mark. Beyond it, snow blocks the Trail until mid- or late summer, and both land and air are always cold. Nearby Goat Lake (6450 feet) is perpetually frozen. Mountain goats crop forbs and grasses, and the way is al-

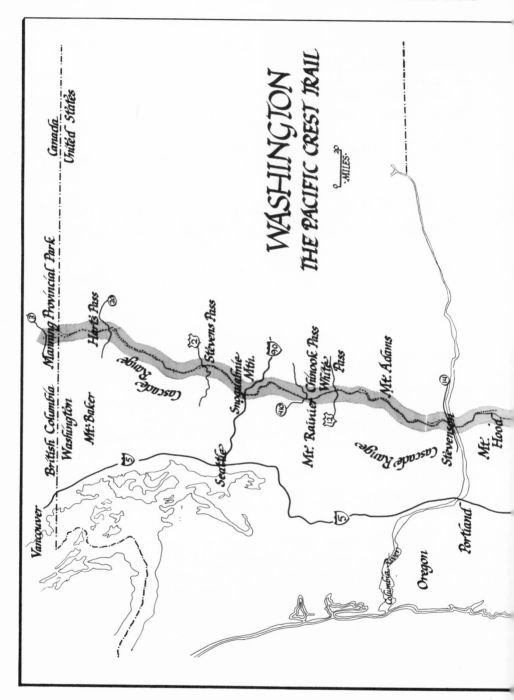

WASHINGTON
THE PACIFIC CREST TRAIL

most straight up to the highest point on the PCT, Upper Lakes Canyon (7620 feet). Here in the snow-filled saddle, where the wind screams constantly, and the trees lie tight against the rocks, are hoofprints of elk. The long tilt downward brings the Trail to the White Pass ski area and *U. S. Highway 12.*

The next supplies are 98 miles north. Along the route is some of the finest timber of the Northwest: forests of Douglas fir and Engelmann spruce.

Farther up the Trail, at Buesch Lake, the rare Canadian elk crop the grasses and blue lupine dominates the scene from Crab Mountain into Chinook Pass. Beyond, the rocky route is hazardous, icy but dramatic all the way to *State Highway 410* and the border of Mt. Rainier National Park. One of the oldest parks in the nation, it was established March 2, 1899.

The PCT sneaks into this permit-cursed park (you need them for fires, camping, fishing, and so on) at its eastern edge, climbs a ridge for a view of Mt. St. Helens, Mt. Adams, and the impressive Mt. Rainier, then hastily leaves, passing miles of mountain-ash on the way to the heather-lined Dewey Lake.

At Chinook Pass the water flows east and west, marking the divide of the Cascade Mountains. Here sego lilies with their little clown faces look up from the grass. Warblers sing in the dense bushes.

At Crown Point, a distinctive intrusion of blue dacite mixed with quartz forms a knife edge on which the Trail teeters before snaking down to Maggy Creek Canyon. Avalanche trails to the right and left are dark with false huckleberries and yew, tough plants that have adapted to the violence of sliding snow and ice.

The Trail crosses Government Meadow, a memorial to the first wagon trail to cross the Cascades, in 1853; then it climbs Pyramid Peak (5715 feet) for a startling view of the North Cascades. Farther ahead an occasional elk wallows along the steep pull to the top of Blowout Mountain.

Down a zigzag path through a forest of mountain-ash, the PCT opens onto a logging scar. Eroded and bare, the slopes are slowly being healed by clusters of bunchberry and Oregon grape. The wind that rips across the unprotected land will delay the healing for perhaps a century longer.

Beyond Yakima Pass, Mirror Lake, which reflects the handsome profile of Tinkham Peak, is a favorite spot for campers and fisher-men since it lies but a mile from the road. Surrounding the area are many tarns, small mountain lakes so called because they have no visible source of water, but which were dug by ice chunks. Rocks, snow, and black peaks wall the Trail for the miles to Olallie Meadow (3650 feet), a flowered carpet beneath Mt. Catherine.

Past acres of fireweed and huckleberry, the PCT goes over a railroad tunnel, edges beside several foxglove-lined beaver ponds, and comes down into Snoqualmie Pass. Here, at the bus terminal on *Interstate 90*, walkers arrive and depart the Cascade section of the Trail. The last supplies for the next 68 miles can be purchased at North Bend on *Interstate 90*.

Past condominiums and ski trails, up roads and through forests, the PCT goes northward onto miles of arch-breaking talus slopes. Near timberline grow bracken and maidenhair ferns. Winter wrens and wood thrushes sing constantly in rain and sunshine.

At the Middle Fork of the Snoqualmie River, mining is in progress, primarily for hydrogen sulphide but also for gold. Otter run the shores of the river, ravens call, and storms break along the steep, snowy Trail as it heads out for Burnt Boot Creek and Dutch Miller Gap.

Beargrass and lupine, bluebirds and ground squirrels cheer the walker to Skeeter Creek and a peaceful campsite in a forest spangled with white trillium.

The climb up steep Cathedral Rock (6100 feet) pains the lungs, but brings the walker into a hanging glacial valley resplendent with waterfalls and streams where trout lurk behind fallen logs. Here the eye lifts to the peaks and rocks.

Next the Trail zags to Glacier Lake, a green-blue pool at 5000 feet, zigs up to Trap Lake (5800 feet) and finally slabs out to an all-encompassing view of Thunder Mountain and the forests around it.

Past shooting-star flowers, white heather, oceans of bluebells and swamp whiteheads, the Trail descends to *U. S. Highway 2* and Stevens Pass, named for John Stevens, an explorer for the Great Northern Railroad. He spent years in this wild country, hunting for a railroad route through the treacherous Cascades, and settled on this pass in 1893.

Between Stevens Pass and the terminus of the PCT in Manning

Park, British Columbia, lie two weeks' walk over rugged trail. Just off U. S. 2 the walker comes upon a meadow of shooting-star and cinquefoil, patches of blue aster and red columbine, cascades of Indian paintbrush and golden coneflowers, where photographers and painters are at work. Dark Lichtenberg Mountain looms ahead, the wind sharpens and the cold settles in.

On the way up Union Peak, clouds weave across the Trail all the way to Lake Janus, where tree frogs sing and evening grosbeaks pry open fir cones.

Wenatchee Pass, Frozen Finger Gap, Grizzly Peak: the names reflect the fury of this land where, paradoxically, the fragile tiger lily blooms.

Cady Pass, a deep cut in metamorphic rock, brings the PCT into bleak country, plunges it on to Skykomish Peak, down snowbound trails, and into the soggy soils of Dishpan Gap.

The landscape is deeply glaciated, the air crystalline. Many of the snowfields are permanent and the flowers are dwarfed by the harsh environment. The way is difficult, discouraging and bleak right on up to the top of Kodak Peak, where the incomparable Mt. Rainier stands on the horizon.

Icy winds drive the walker to the shelter of the rocks and monoliths as he then descends through a maze of glaciers to Kennedy Hot Springs. This warm earth-spa, a short distance off the Trail, provides a reviving hot bath before the long climb up Glacier Ridge for a view of the ice rivers on Glacier Peak: Kennedy, Scimitar, Ptarmigan, and Vista glaciers. Seven hundred and fifty-six glaciers, half of the total in the U. S. outside Alaska, lie in the North Cascades. They grind the mountains to dust in cold silence all through the year except July. During that month they rest. In early August the clouds roll over the mountain, blocking out the sun, and the trickling water turns to ice. Then the glaciers move and grind once more.

On the Trail the biotic community has changed again. The Northwestern Coniferous Forest is behind and the twisted, gnarled spruce and firs of the Canadian Coniferous Forest dominate the landscape from here to the Arctic Circle.

Farther down the Trail, in Cloudy Pass, doors on old mining shacks bang and shutters creak to announce the beginning of the final trek north.

At Stokehen River and *State Highway 20*, the PCT enters great forests of tamarack, the deciduous pine whose soft needles fall in September and October. From Porcupine Creek to Cutthroat Pass grow scrub pine and mountain-ash, and tough heather tears at walkers' pants and shoes.

On the downward slope of the Tatie Peak (7386 feet) the Trail comes upon the remains of abandoned gold mines, now visited by bears and mice. The way is peaceful, and in the remote back country the work performed by these miners seems superhuman. In Hart's Pass civilization returns with a bang. Tourists gather in campgrounds and cluster at the Forest Station with its exhibit of antiques from the mining days of the 1890s.

The Trail edges the side of State Creek, keeping in view Mt. Baker, a dormant volcano until the summer of 1974, when it became active, melting snowfields, sliding tons of mud toward campgrounds, and forcing the evacuation of a town.

Windy Pass earns its name every inch of the way to the Pasayten Wilderness Area. Now the walker quickens his step: the end of the Trail is near. He arrives on Lakeview Ridge for a last breathtaking view of the Cascade Range, such as turns practical men into poets. Then the walker follows the path gently downward through alpine gardens, across streams and up a short slope to Monument 78 and the Canadian border.

Not far ahead, in the forest of white-bark birch and tamarack on Windy Joe Mountain, the sounds of traffic rise up from *Canadian Highway Route 3* and the din brings this great walk to an end.

Highways Crossed by the Pacific Crest Trail, south to north

California:
    State Highway 94
    Interstate 8
    State Highway 78
    State Highway 79
    State Highway 71
    State Highway 74
    Interstate 10

State Highway 38
State Highway 173
State Highway 138
Interstate 15
Angeles Crest Highway
State Highway 14 (U. S. 6)
State Highway 138
State Highway 58 and 14

State Highway 178
State Highway 155
State Highway 120
State Highway 108
State Highway 4
Old State Highway 88
U. S. Highway 50
Interstate 80
State Highway 49
State Highway 70
State Highway 32
State Highway 36
State Highway 44
State Highway 299
State Highway 89
Interstate 5
State Highway 96

State Highway 140
State Highway 62
State Highway 138
State Highway 58
State Highway 242
State Highway 20 and 126
State Highway 26
New State Highway 35
Interstate 80N

Washington:
  State Highway 14
  U. S. Highway 12
  State Highway 410
  Interstate 90
  U. S. Highway 2
  State Highway 20

Oregon:
  Interstate 5
  State Highway 66

Canada:
  Highway 3 in Manning Park,
    British Columbia

Bibliography and Maps

BISHOP, SHERMAN C. *Handbook of Salamanders.* New York: Hafner Publishing Company, 1962.

CRAIGHEAD, J. J., F. C. CRAIGHEAD, and R. J. DAVIS. *A Field Guide to Rocky Mountain Wildflowers.* Boston: Houghton Mifflin Company, 1963.

MUNZ, PHILIP A. *California Mountain Wildflowers.* Berkeley and Los Angeles: University of California Press, 1969.

Pacific Crest Trail, The. Volume 1: California, by Thomas Winnet, J. P. Schaffer, J. W. Robinson, J. W. Jenkins, A. Husari, *Volume 2: Oregon and Washington,* by J. P. Schaffer, B. and F. Hartline. Berkeley: Wilderness Press, 1973, 1974.

PALMER, R. S. *The Mammal Guide: Mammals of North America North of Mexico.* Garden City, N. Y.: Doubleday and Company, Inc., 1954.

PETERSON, ROGER. *A Field Guide to Western Birds.* Boston: Houghton Mifflin Company, 2nd rev. ed. 1961.

SARGENT, CHARLES S. *Manual of the Trees of North America* (2 v.). New York: Dover Publications, Inc., 2nd ed. 1965.

U. S. DEPARTMENT OF AGRICULTURE. *Trees: The Yearbook of Agriculture.* Washington: Government Printing Office, 1949.

U. S. DEPARTMENT OF THE INTERIOR, BUREAU OF OUTDOOR RECREATION. Maps of the National Scenic Trails are available on request.

U. S. FOREST SERVICE. A detailed map of the Pacific Crest National Scenic Trail is available on request. Write for the Federal Register of January 30, 1973 (Vol. 38, No. 19).

4

T H E   L O N G   P A T H   *

The Long Path, extending from the George Washington Bridge in New York City to the Adirondack Mountains upstate, is in some ways the most delightful of all the American trails. Unlike any of the others, it is a bushwhacking trail, to be followed by map and compass, challenging each walker to reach the scenic sites, using only maps and his own decision whether to go over the mountain or around it, across the meadow or along the streamside, down an old road or off through the woods. No one need follow anyone else's footsteps on the Long Path, and the walk can be as easy or difficult as the walker chooses.

The idea for this singular trail originated with Vincent J. Schaefer, a professor at the State University of New York Atmospheric Sciences Research Center, at Schenectady. On a summer day in the early 1930s, as he walked home from an outing with the newly formed Mohawk Valley Hiking Club, he was thinking about the hours he had just spent bushwhacking through a trailless forest to a tor, using a Geological Survey map. It was a time of major trail-blazing. In Vermont the Long Trail had been completed, the Appalachian Trail was famous around the world, and hikers in Oregon and California were painting blazes on trees down the Cascades and Sierra. That day Schaefer, who was later to discover how to make rain by seeding clouds, conceived of a path that would be a ten-mile-wide corridor of wilderness from the edge of New York City to the spruce–fir forests at the top of Mt. Marcy in the Adirondacks. Within the corridor the route taken would depend upon the mood, curiosity, and ingenuity of the walker.

* For information about biotic communities along this trail see pages 260–261, 272–274.

Schaefer went with his idea to three men: Harvey Broome, who had worked on the Appalachian Trail; Ed Fogarty of the New York Hiking Club; and William Carr, the creator of indigenous zoos such as the ones at Bear Mountain and in the Arizona Desert. Wrote Schaefer to Carr:

I see the Long Path as a compass and map walk. A wide corridor marked on a topographic map through areas that are likely to appeal to a bushwhacking hiker. The on-paper-only route would spot ice caves, cracks and fissures, high tors, valleys, forests and meadows. There would be no cutting or blazing, for this trail would be a truly wild walk that wouldn't erode the land or scar the solitude . . . and each found site would be an adventure in orienteering.

Carr gave his enthusiastic support to the new concept and trail authorities in New York concurred. A few months later, Schaefer met with W. W. Cady, a biologist and back-country hiker, and between them they laid out the Long Path. Cady mapped the route from New York City to Gilboa, Schaefer the one from Gilboa to Mt. Marcy. Before the summer was over, the Path was in existence; all they had to do was to draw it on a map. For shelter along the Path its creators mapped routes to Forest Service and conservation cabins or to good tenting areas along creeks or in shadowy glades. The Mohawk Hiking Club, sponsor of the trail, built one lean-to.

Most of the Long Path's southern section no longer adheres to the original intent, most of it since having been blazed and marked. Thanks to the current interest in orienteering, which is now taught by hiking clubs and university physical education departments, anyone who wishes will be able to follow the original route after less than an hour's instruction. Orienteering compasses, specifically designed to make bushwhacking simple, can be bought from any camping outfitter and topographic maps may be obtained by writing the U. S. Geological Survey. With every topographic state index, the Survey includes a brochure that enables one to learn quickly the symbols indicating foot trails, roads, creek beds, graveyards, power lines, houses and churches, elevations, etc.

The geology encountered along the Path ranges from the Piedmont red shale of the Appalachian Ridge to the gneiss of the rugged Hudson Highlands. The Path crosses fertile valleys to reach the

Catskills and Adirondacks, a circular mountain region where the granite is perhaps the oldest in the western hemisphere.

The Long Path penetrates three biotic areas: the Chestnut oak–tulip-tree, the beech–birch–maple–hemlock forest, and finally the Northeastern Coniferous Forest of spruce and fir.

The Path begins in the din of traffic on the George Washington Bridge and crosses to the chestnut oak–tulip-tree community in the Hudson Highlands in New Jersey. Going N8° E on the east side of the *Palisades Parkway*, the Path treks through fields of daisies and yarrow above the Hudson River gorge. Overhead in autumn and spring a spectacular assortment of hawks, buteos, and golden eagles migrate down this flyway. For those who do not want to go down to Englewood Landing on the Giant Stairs, a jumble of gargantuan boulders, there is a footpath. The climb out of the river bottom brings the walker to the grassy *Palisades Parkway*, which runs all the way north to the New Jersey–New York line. From there it twists to the top of Snake Hill and enters Blauvelt State Park, heading down to Bradly Hill Road, across *Interstate 87* into Nyack. This river town with its mixture of Victorian and modern houses is to be explored at each person's discretion, following whatever streets one may choose along the river or through town—on a northward course toward Hook Mountain State Park.

A bearing of W324° brings the walker to Bear Mountain—Harriman State Park and a web of established trails. In addition to blazes on mountain maples and red oaks, signposts and arrows mark the way to Highland Falls across *U. S. Highway 6*. The Long Path walker bushwhacks. Paralleling 9W through West Point to the south side of Storm King Mountain, the walker can take a shady country road through meadows and forests to Cornwall. Camping and lodging are available all along the first seventy-five miles of the Long Path.

West of Cornwall, at Orr's Mills on Moodna Creek, a due north bearing brings the bushwhacker to Newburgh. Cross *Interstate 87* and *84*, and bear N 35° west to the Catskill Aqueduct and Bloomingburg on *State Highway 17*. Here lie the toes of the Shawangunk Mountains, famed for the cliffs where alpine climbers practice their nerve-tingling art. The Path goes through the towns of Walden and Allard Corners and takes *State Highway 52* to the white cliffs of the Shawangunks. An alternate choice is along

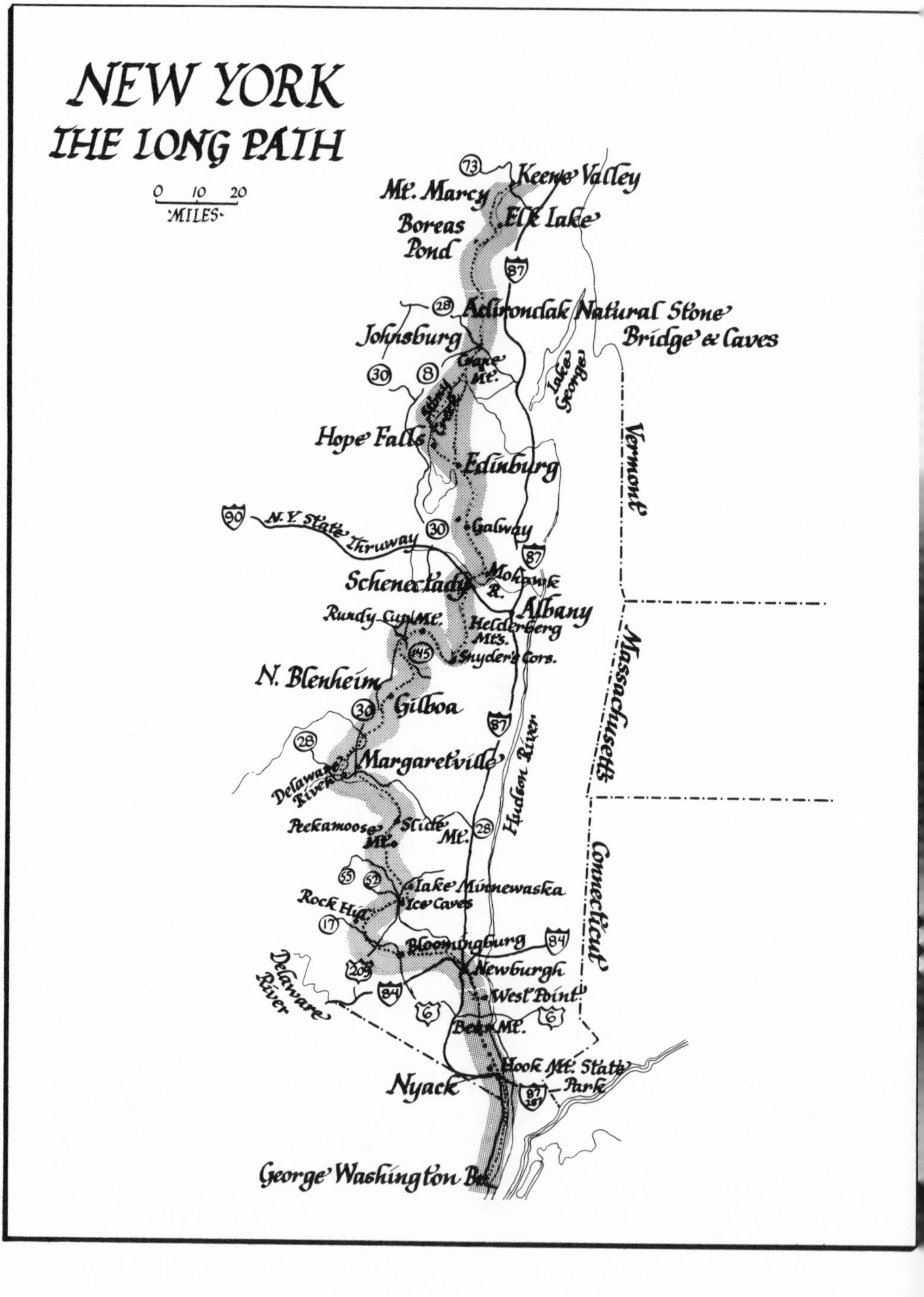

NEW YORK
THE LONG PATH

0   10   20
·MILES·

Mt. Marcy
Boreas
Pond
73
Keene Valley
Elk Lake
87

28
Adirondak Natural Stone
Bridge & Caves

Johnsburg
30   8
Grace
Mt.

Hope Falls

Edinburg

Lake George

Vermont

90
N.Y. State
Thruway
30
Galway
87

Schenectady
Mohawk R.
Albany

Rundy Cup Mt.
Helder-berg
Mts.
Snyder's Cors.
145

N. Blenheim
30
Gilboa
87

28
Margaretville
Delaware River

Peekamoose
Slide Mt.
28
Hudson River

55   52
Lake Minnewaska
Ice Caves

Rock Hg.
17
Bloomingburg
84

Delaware River
209
Newburgh
6W
West Point
6

Bear Mt.
6

Nyack
9W
Hook Mt. State Park

Massachusetts

Connecticut

George Washington Br.

Interstate 17 to Rock Hill and across field and woods to Spring Glen.

The shale layers that underlie the Shawangunk Mountains make up the floor of the Great Valley immediately to the east. Originally a mud deposit in an extensive sea, the area was folded down and uplifted during a crustal revolution that occurred about 400 million years ago. Then it was eroded, and submerged again by a shallow sea, whose waves laid down a layer of fine beach sand and gravel which are now the "white stones" of the Shawangunks. Another upheaval about 280 million years ago titled these strata into their present position. Eons later glaciers, rain, and wind carved them into their present shapes. Bits of quartzite scattered through the metamorphic gneiss make handholds and toeholds for the mountaineers who come from all over the nation and world to scale the "Gunks' " sheer walls.

Not far away, to the north of Sam's Point, are subterranean fissures that are the Ice Caves. Even in July cold air billows up from the dark hollows, and adventurous hikers climb down into the cold chambers to chip ice for their canteens.

Traveling northeast for about five miles, the bushwhacker arrives at serene Lake Minnewaska and a large stand of virgin hemlock that cast feathery shadows on needle-strewn paths. The lake is on the famous Mohonk Estate, one of the most beautifully preserved natural areas in New York. In 1869 two Quakers, Albert E. Smiley and his twin brother Albert H., bought three hundred acres, including an abandoned inn, from John Stokes. The brothers were schoolmasters and not having sufficient money to support the acreage they reopened the old Mohonk Inn on Lake Mohonk, and built another hotel on Lake Minnewaska. Over the years the brothers constructed carriage roads and paths, banned autos, smoking, and drinking, and welcomed walkers and climbers. To these inns came people who had simple values and respect for nature. In 1963, after the death of the brothers, the Smiley family set up a trust fund to maintain their property according to their ideals. Eventually the rising taxes forced the family to put the land up for sale. In 1970 New York State took over part of the quiet wilderness, but as costs spiraled, sadly, the Minnewaska Hotel was sold at auction in 1976 and burned down in 1978.

Beyond the Mohonk Estate the Long Path skirts Rondout Reservoir, passes Vernooy Kill, goes over the Brownsville Bridge through a woods to Sholam Schoolhouse, and eventually comes to Catskill Park. A compass and map reading here should seek out Peekamouse and Slide mountains (4204 feet). A route should be found up and over Mt. Tremper (3760 feet), and down and around the town of Big Indian. For lack of wild land, the Path now parallels *Highway 28*, crosses it, and arrives at Margaretville. By going almost due north on the Delaware River watershed near *State Highway 30*, the bushwhacker can study the remarkable geology of the Catskills. Here the massive rocks and cliffs look like parts of the Rockies.

From this valley to Gilboa Dam the walker can pick either a route through fields of strawberries that ripen in June or one along the mountainside. Yet another way is through a hardwood forest of birch, maple, and beech. In Gilboa, at the New York State Museum across the bridge below the dam, is an exhibit of eastern fossil tree stumps.

At this point, Schaefer's section of the on-paper-only path begins. He leads the bushwhacker from Gilboa up the western side of a long ridge, with fine views, and down to Blenheim and the longest single-span wooden covered bridge in the world.

Schaefer suggests the walker take the covered bridge and climb toward the falls of the Keyser Kill, past Breakabeen Cemetery to Schoharie Creek with its cool swimming holes and good trout fishing. A few miles on is Panther Creek. "A short distance up Panther Creek," Schaefer wrote in his original description of the Long Path, "the beautiful cascade known as Bouck's Falls will be seen as it tumbles over a shale cliff." Natural gargoyles are carved in the rock by the rushing water. At Bouck's Falls the Long Path goes up a steep bank, through a patch of old red pines, and continues along the stream for a mile and three-quarters on an old Indian trail. All along the way are views of the Schoharie Hills and Panther Creek Valley. Eventually the bushwhacker arrives on the road from Watsonville to Petria and descends into quaint Holly Hollow where Lime Creek, a famous trout stream, flows under hemlocks.

The Path leads to the peculiar escarpment called Vrooman's Nose, a high cliff of shaly rock containing several fossiliferous layers. "On a flat rock on the summit," Schaefer writes, "are some exceedingly fine glacial scratches." Another outstanding feature on Vrooman's Nose is a large stand of dwarf hackberry clinging to the southern face, one of the few places this interesting tree grows in eastern New York. Covering the ridge top is a heavy mat of bearberry, making a perfect bed for the camper. "Awaking from sleep," Schaefer wrote, "the walker sees the sun peeking over the high summits of the Helderbergs and lighting the patchwork of farmland far below, with the Schoharie winding through in long sweeping curves."

From Vrooman's Nose the Long Path loops through parks, quarries, and historic towns to Witches' Hole in the Helderberg Mountains. The Hole can be entered by descending on a 20-foot rope into a wide chamber, from which a narrow, tortuous way leads north out of the Hole into an evergreen forest in Witches' Hollow.

In the immediate vicinity are many queer caverns occupied by porcupines, bats, cave crickets, and daddy-long-legs. Places to be found are ancient flint quarries used by the Indians, great springs that rush out of hidden passageways, and fossil coral reefs in the limestone ledges.

The Long Path goes into John Boyd Thatcher Park and follows Mine Creek along four miles of stunning cliffs known as Indian Ladder because, the story goes, the Indians climbed the cliff by means of a great tree set close to them. Today a wooden ladder leads to a narrow, winding way, the Bear Path, that lies on a weathered seam in the rocks. The treacherous route leads to Minelot Falls, Tory Cave, and Haile's Cave, the largest cave in the vicinity. Its high vaulted rooms can be explored after a trudge through mud, water, and low passageways.

A route north should go by way of Sutphen's Sink on the way to Spooky Hollow, where several caves can be explored. The Long Path heads west from the Hollow on an old dirt road and climbs over grassy hills past farms where cattle graze to a pine plantation, the Christmas Wildlife Sanctuary, which is also the outdoor headquarters of the Mohawk Valley Hiking Club. The sanctuary comprises more than 100 acres, with many labeled nature trails, bird feeding stations, and a host of wildflowers. Emerging from the Sanctuary, the Path combines a cross-country route with a tame but pretty path along wooded roads and lanes. This is bumpy country that has been cut by the glaciers into rounded hills of all sizes.

Staying west of Albany, the Long Path goes through Altamont, treks northwest to Duanesburg, then curves northeast through the edge of Schenectady and across the Mohawk River to the *New York State Thruway, Interstate 90.*

Having passed schoolyards and along streams, the Path, as Schaefer routed it on the U. S. Geological Survey map of the Amsterdam Quadrangle, fords a stream, goes under a railroad, and takes to farm roads on the way to Wolf Hollow, a remarkable feature of the Mohawk Valley, lying north of the crossing of the New York State Barge Canal at Lock 9. This hollow was formed millions of years ago when a great convulsion caused a vertical slippage of more than a thousand feet along the fault line. At the point where the Chaughtanoona Creek flows away from the road, the sharply tilted strata record the drag occasioned by the movement. The Long Path now enters the narrow crack of Wolf Hollow and continues for three-quarters of a mile to its northern end. "One of the great Indian trails descended to the Mohawk through this narrow, deep ravine," Schaefer wrote, "and many quenched their thirst at Johnnie's Spring which lies on the left shortly after entering the hollow."

The first great battle between the Iroquois–Mohawks and the Algonkin–Mohicans was fought near the spring and on the rocky nose of Kinaquariones, above the river. Farther along, the trail arrives at a quarry that supplied limestone rocks for the Erie Canal more than a century ago. The Path continues north over the hills of quartz crystal to Consaulus Bog, an ancient post-glacial lake. In this tamarack swamp grow the ingenious meat-eating pitcher plants, which lure insects to their sweet lips where they plunge to their deaths in water pockets at the bottom of the plant's tube-like leaves. There the insects rot and are absorbed by the plants.

The Long Path moves down a country road to the Kayderosseras Range, the first ridge of the Adirondacks. Ahead lies the village of Galway on Glowegee Creek, a fast-flowing, spring-fed trout stream. Taking a northerly and then a northeasterly direction, the bushwhacker finds himself on the old Frenchtown Road in almost forgotten country, where stone fences run under dark trees that have reclaimed the once cultivated farmland. Clumps of roses and lilacs mark abandoned cabin sites. The Path winds on to Lake Desolation, named by a British Army officer who during the Revolution was forced to winter here. Even today it is a grim place surrounded by cold glacial meadows and dark alder swamps.

The Long Path enters the forgotten village of Mount Pleasant, a glass factory town of the early 1800s. Nothing remains of this once busy community save a few grassy mounds that are old glass dumps, where bits of glassware can still be found.

Heading over bridges and down the road for about six miles, the Path comes to Edinburg on the mouth of the enormous Sacandaga Lake, almost as large and even more beautiful than Lake George. Near the bridge is one of the military roads through the Adirondacks that date back to the Revolution, for walkers to explore.

The country beyond Edinburg blends romance with history, wilderness with backwoods industry, and easy travel with rough. Several miles out of town an old road leads over Mason Hill to the nearly forgotten village of Hope Falls. Extending for many miles the forested valley of East Stony Creek gives the walker his first real taste of the Adirondacks.

A road of gravel and dirt follows the rushing, boulder-strewn Stony Creek to Brownell's Camp, where the Long Path takes the route along which British troops retreated following the Revolution. It then climbs a spur of Tenant Mountain where a giant hemlock tree bears a blaze dating back to 1788. Tenant Mountain's streams are stocked with trout for the fisherman. The top makes a good place to map a route up either side of East Stony River to Round Pond, a clear, blue lake in an old hardwood forest. Cut with coves, rimmed with sandy beaches, and haunted by huge pike, it is what Schaefer called "an ideal spot to tarry."

From Round Pond the Path leads into a quasi-civilized section of the mountains with beautiful scenery, and log cabins inhabited by native mountaineers. Vireos and ovenbirds sing in the tops of the tall sugar maple and beech trees, and hawks watch the fields for mice. The Path then cuts across Breakneck Ridge and takes an old road around Crane Mountain, crossing State Highway 8 and 28. Finally it emerges in a long mountain meadow below Ives's Dam near North Creek. "At this pretty village," Schaefer wrote, "the high peak country starts to beckon the hiker. In every direction lakes and streams, wild mountains and great stretches of unbroken woodland can be found."

The Long Path winds along the headwaters of the Hudson River to the Adirondack Natural Stone Bridge and Caves. After passing through private land for a considerable distance, it reaches state land in the depths of Panther Gorge. A long northerly trek to Boreas Pond includes the crossing of five mountain streams; then the Path follows Casey Brook upstream to the Conservation Department's Blue Trail out of the town of Elk Lake. The Long Path has now left the watershed of the Hudson; almost all the streams ahead from now on drain to the St. Lawrence River.

Following the Blue Trail for three rough miles, the Path takes the hiker to the tumbling, ice-fed waters of Marcy Brook under a cathedral-like roof of primeval spruces. Schaefer called it "one of the most charming spots in the world."

Leaving the shadowy brook behind, the Path follows a blazed trail to the summit of Mt. Haystack (4918 feet). The climb is one of the hardest in the Adirondacks, ". . . but the sheer beauty of the exposure to vistas and clouds make it well worth the effort," wrote Schaefer.

From the summit the bushwhacker heads down to the Little Haystack and the Blue Trail, then climbs Basin Mountain. "At this point," in Schaefer's words, "the tramper has tasted the charm of this wild country and may now understand the reasons why so many heed the call of the rock-clad summit of Mt. Marcy, the cloud splitter." He recommends the ascent.

After Mt. Marcy the bushwhacker sets his compass for the town of Keene Valley, on *State Highway* 73, and public transport back to civilization.

Highways Crossed by the Long Path

9W and Interstate 87
  (Palisades Interstate
  Parkway)
U. S. Highway 6
Interstate 87 and Interstate 84
State Highway 17
State Highway 52
U. S. Highway 209
State Highway 55A
State Highway 28
State Highway 30

State Highway 23
State Highway 145
U. S. Highway 20
State Highway 7
Interstate 90 (New York
  State Thruway)
State Highway 147
State Highway 28
State Highway 8
State Highway 73

Bibliography and Maps

BROCKMAN, C. FRANK. *Trees of North America: A Guide to Field Identification.* New York: Golden Press, 1968.

KJELLSTROM, BJORN. *Be Expert with Map and Compass: The Orienteering Handbook.* La Porte, Indiana: American Orienteering Service, 1967.

NEW YORK–NEW JERSEY TRAIL CONFERENCE AND AMERICAN GEOGRAPHICAL SOCIETY. *New York Walk Book.* Garden City, N. Y.: Doubleday/Natural History Press, 1971.

ROBBINS, CHANDLER S., BERTEL BRUUN, and HERBERT S. ZIM. *Birds of North America: A Guide to Field Identification.* New York: Golden Press, 1966.

TORREY, R. H. "The Long Brown Path," *New York Post,* Feb 23–weekly to July 31, 1934. A weekly series following in detail the route mapped by Vincent Schaefer and W. W. Cady. (Note: Original maps of the route may be obtained from Vincent Schaefer, Box 36, Schermerhorn Road, Schenectady, N.Y. 12306.)

U. S. GEOLOGICAL SURVEY. Topographic maps needed by the orienteering walker for West Point, Schunemunk, Newburgh, Ellenville, Slide Mountain, Neversink, Phoenicia, Margaretville, Hobart, Gilboa, Schoharie, Berne, Amsterdam, Broadalbin, Saratoga, Stone Creek, Thirteenth Lake, North Creek, Newcomb, Schroon Lake, and Mt. Marcy can be ordered from this source, at 1200 South Eads Street, Arlington, Va. 22202.

5

THE CONTINENTAL

DIVIDE TRAIL *

The Continental Divide Trail, along the roof peak of the Rocky Mountains, extends from the Mexican to the Canadian borders, passing through New Mexico, Colorado, Wyoming, Idaho, and Montana. On one side of the Trail the rain and snowmelt rush eastward to the Atlantic; on the other they roll to the Pacific. The parting line is the Trail itself, a path both real and imaginary. No one has ever walked its more than 3000 miles and only a few have followed it for more than a few hundred, for the sawblade trail is upstairs with the stars and ice, the lightning and thunder, and with the scarce living things that have adapted to intense light, scant oxygen, and the frozen dryness of mountain peaks. It is the toughest and wildest trail in the nation, and much of it is impossible to follow.

Nevertheless, many thousands of people have enjoyed the spectacle of its strange two-way waterflow in short walks off the more than twenty highways and roads that intersect the Continental Divide. To see the splitting streams, the dazzlingly brilliant flowers covering the Western Alpine Tundra, the repetitiveness of the lodgepole and subalpine forests and of the sagebrush desert, makes this trail an exhilaration for even those who do no more than park and sit.

The history of the Trail dates back to the mountain men who noticed that the water flowed in two directions from this divide. Over the past hundred years it has been mapped by the U. S.

* For information about biotic communities along this trail see pages 258–259, 264–267, 287.

86

Geological Survey and is now on all highway maps, a line running through a series of national parks, forests, and state lands.

The mountains that support the Continental Divide Trail extend 3000 miles and are a thousand miles wide in places. The rugged peaks are primarily granite carved by glaciers, wind, and rain. On the mountainside are limestone and sandstone, and the southern half of the Trail is in old volcanoes.

The Trail has its beginning on Triple Peak in Glacier National Park, a spot that can be reached by climbing Gun Sight Pass Trail. This geological showpiece sits in a wilderness of snowfields, rocks, tilted monoliths, and hanging glaciers. This is the very top of the North American continent. A pot of water poured into a pool here spills three ways—to the Atlantic, the Pacific, and the Gulf of Mexico. Around the pool colorful lichens thrive, and the highland rush grows like a picket fence around chunks of ice. The soundscape is a blare of wind and the crackling of frost. The view is across the mountains, down into valleys, and endlessly up into clouds and stars. No trees grow at Triple Peak, for it lies in the dominant biome of the Continental Divide Trail above timberline, the Western Alpine Tundra with its snowfields, rocks, mountain goats, and grasses. Although the tundra is the essence of the Continental Divide Trail, the walker goes through a series of communities as he treks up and down the line of the Divide.

In a typical situation in the northern section, the walker leaves the cedars and firs at the bottom of the mountains to enter the subalpine forest community, a boundary forest between the tall trees down-mountain and the alpine world above. The trees here are primarily subalpine fir, a tree with blistered bark and flat needles, together with the white-barked pine, Engelmann spruce, and yellow cedar. The subalpine floor is heavily needled.

Beyond this forest grows the elfin timber or krummholz (German for "crooked timber"). This contorted but beautiful timber is composed largely of subalpine firs and Engelmann spruce, and is shaped by wind and cold. A seed will start to germinate in the shelter of a boulder and grow upward. As it meets wind coming over the rock, it sends its limbs downward. They take root and thrust up twigs that also stop at the wind's arc, eventually taking the shape of the air current. Now the tree acts as a shelter just as the boulder once did; the limbs migrate out, and eventually the crooked little forest has moved out and away from its shelter. An old krummholz can end up a hundred yards away from the original rock.

Around the elfin forests wander ptarmigan, the chickens of the mountain peaks. Two species live on the Continental Divide Trail, the rock and the white-tailed ptarmigan. During the winter the sexes separate, the males remaining above timberline, the females flocking to the willow thickets down-mountain. Pairs form a life bond even though they are only together briefly during the breeding season. The mothers raise the chicks alone. The birds blend softly into the grasses in summer, then moult and match winter snow.

Between the krummholzes are rock slides, boulder fields, and talus slopes, the junk piles of avalanches and glaciers. Pikas, soft-eyed rabbits of the mountain peaks, run between the boulders harvesting wildflowers and grasses. With them dwell three species of marmots, the whistling, the yellow-bellied, and the rare hoary marmot. Above the krummholzes the tundra begins, a biome of adaptation and specialization. Many of the plants survive by producing, early in the spring, a red pigment that protects them against the fierce alpine light. Others thicken and dwarf their leaves as desert plants do, to stave off thirst in an environment in which water turns to ice for most of the year.

The next zone up is the snowline, a thermal zone in which the average temperature is 32°F. during the warmest month of the year. Snow accumulates and forms permanent snowfields behind boulders and in cirques to survive, just as living things do. The summer sun glazes these fields with an ice crust that throws back the light and thus protects the snow beneath. Nevertheless, the warmth penetrates and the melting can be heard as a low gurgle inside the crusted mass.

At snowline dwells the gray-crowned rosy finch, with its brown back and breast, gray head, and pink tail coverts. Its call note is a sweet "cheeeeeecheeeeee," its nest a grass cup in the crevices of rocks.

The snowfields themselves support yet another plant community of algae that grow on their surfaces. Walkers here are often astonished to look back and see their footsteps printed red on the snow. Many think they have been struck with altitude fever, whereas in fact they have crushed the red protective coat of the algae, exposing their red pigment. These miniscule plants grow precisely at the freezing point, 32°F., not above and not below. They survive the intense radiation by concentrating the X-rays of the sun. This was discovered by a uranium prospector who heard his geiger counter begin to tick while boiling snow water on the Continental Divide one evening. The ticking was loudest near his bucket and he carried the water to his lab. Tests showed the "treasure" to be simply the radiation from the sun.

Above the snowline is the aeolian zone, a territory named after the Greek wind god Aeolus. Here live only those plants that can take their nutrients from the wind—algae, lichens, and liverworts. More than twenty species of lichens (half fungi, half chlorophyll or algae) account for the brilliant swatches of apricot, apple-green, red, and orange on the gray rock faces. As these plants transpire, the carbon dioxide they give off combines with the water to make a weak carbonic acid. The acid slowly etches away the granites, sandstones, and shales, eroding the mountains over the eons.

Although the Continental Divide's southern terminus in the United States is the spine of the Animas Mountains at the New Mexico–Mexico border, the first access to a footpath is west of Silver City, on U. S. Highway 180, where a rough trail winds to the roof peak. An easier start is north of this at Pinos Altos on State Highway 15. The Trail leads over Black Peak (9025 feet) in Gila National Forest, the first federally established wilderness area. The concept originated with Aldo Leopold, naturalist, in 1925 while he watched a road crew cut into magnificent Gila National Forest. "Our tendency is not to call things resources until the supply has run short," he said to a friend. A year later he persuaded the Forest Service to establish a section of Gila as an area never to be cut, mined, or developed, a roadless land to be entered only on foot, horse, or skis or by canoe. Forty years later the importance of Leopold's concept was acknowledged by Congress in passing the Wilderness Act of 1964, to preserve other wild areas as a natural resource for future generations.

In Gila National Forest the Continental Divide Trail climbs through junipers and pinyons and several species of evergreen oak. It passes trout streams and the bedding-down groves of white-tailed and mule deer. Spotted and round-tailed ground squirrels

NEW MEXICO
THE CONTINENTAL DIVIDE

""" along the Continental Divide - no actual trail
..... trail

0 10 20 30
MILES·

chirp as they defend their territories. The Trail comes to *State Highway 78*, and crosses into the Tula Rosa Mountains. The climb to Elk Mountains leaves the hiker without a trail north; a map and compass are necessary to find the Forest Service roads and old mining trails that lead to the roof peak and the New Mexico–Colorado border.

In Colorado's San Juan National Forest a good trail lies along the Divide; it can be picked up at Wolf Pass on *U. S. Highway 160*. After a walk through San Juan and Rio Grande National Forests, the Trail threads into windswept, thin-soiled fields of gravel, sand, and boulders. The barren land lacks snow cover in winter, and only the hardiest plants grow here, such as the cushion plant that huddles out of the wind in cracks and crevices, and the alpine forget-me-not that grows in micro-habitats created by patches of dwarf clover.

As the Trail climbs, the plants become ever more ingenious. They grow close to the ground and develop food-storing roots, as well as flowers that turn to follow the path of the sun, storing heat in their petals.

The Trail passes Rio Grande Pyramid (13,830 feet), circles Pole Creek Mountain, and heads northeast above the wild Saguache River. It crosses *State Highway 114* at North Cochetopa Pass, where drive-and-walkers can teeter along the Divide for a mile or two in either direction.

The Trail here is in the Subalpine Forest. It then goes up again to the Alpine Tundra. In the meadows grows the snow buttercup, an ingenious flower found only at timberline and above, which exudes heat and melts its way up through the snow to bloom. The heat given off during respiration is sufficient to melt a hole an inch or so in diameter. The generic name of this buttercup, *Ranunculus*, means "little frog," a fitting one since it is found beside the mountain pools in summer.

From Cochetopa Pass northward the moss campion dominates the scene. A moss-like cushion, it is starred with pink flowers. The plant is circumpolar, having been pushed around the globe by the Pleistocene glaciers. High in the Rockies it is often seen in a patch with blue forget-me-not and white phlox like a miniature U. S. flag.

Turflike meadows of grasses, sedges, and forbs also appear in the alpine community, and in the avalanche tracks grows the mountain

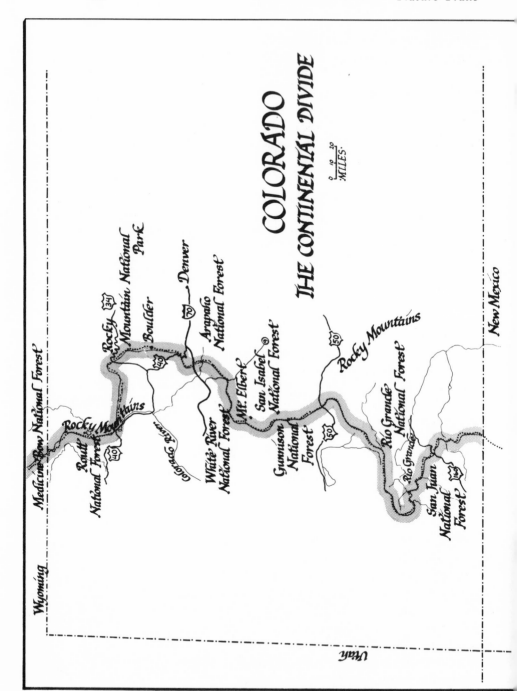

heath, a small and treelike plant with cones. The leaves are foils against the dryness and intense light. They not only thicken and curl to reduce water loss, but also manufacture a pigment that blocks the sun's radiation. From late June through August, bright pink, urn-shaped flowers appear on the long slender stalks.

Walking the Continental Divide Trail here becomes largely the feat of hopping dwarf willow forests. These diminutive trees, barely two inches high, are more than five hundred years old. One step can fell a willow grove for some twenty generations, and so Divide walkers avoid them judiciously.

Age and slow development is another trait of the plants of the Alpine Tundra, as typified by the dryad, an alpine member of the rose family. It requires fifteen years to develop the roots that hold it on the exposed gravel slopes before beginning to bloom. A few blossoms decorate it at first; then, as the plant ages, there are more and more, so that ancient plants can be recognized by their pro-fusion of big white flowers.

From North Cochetopa Pass the Divide Trail goes through a chain of National Forests to *Interstate* 70 and *U. S. Highway* 401. The distance from here to Rocky Mountain National Park as the crow flies is thirty miles.

In the Park the Divide Trail is nonexistent, although many roads cross over it and a few run beneath it. A Park ranger observed: "To follow the Divide in Rocky Mountain Park you'd have to be, at the least, a mountain goat, and probably you couldn't even follow it then. It's a sawblade of a line."

Handsome substitute routes are Mountain Trail and North Inlet Trail, which meet on the Continental Divide and follow it for sev-eral miles. The two trails form a loop about fifteen miles long, but six miles on either will bring the walker to Tyndall Glacier on the Divide and into the land of the pipit, the bird that represents the spirit of the Trail. About the size and color of a sparrow, it has a streaked buffy beak and bobs as it walks on the ground. The pipits arrive in the open turf country above timberline as soon as the snow is gone in late June and make their small nests in thick clusters of grass. Nestlings remain in the nest three weeks, but fly well upon departure. They join their parents in large flocks that wing and flash over the meadows. Pipits feed on the larvae of the caddisfly which live in rushing streams. These creatures make tiny houses of sand grains, so after prying the creature out of its sandy home the pipit dips it into the swift water to wash off the sand.

In Wyoming the Continental Divide Trail descends from the lodgepole pine forests in Medicine Bow National Forest to the Desert Shrublands in Great Divide Basin north of *Interstate 80* and south of *U. S. Highway 287* in Sweetwater County.

The Great Basin breaks the continuous line of the roof peak, for it is a flat uplifted circle off which the water flows in all directions. This dry table consists largely of sand dunes that support rabbit-bush, yucca, and clusters of saltbush. Most walkers follow the eastern rim of the circle, beginning north of Lamont on *U. S. State Highway 73*, a back-country, dirt road that crosses and recrosses the Divide to within a few miles of West Alkali Creek. A compass and map are needed to follow the Trail from Picket Lake up Continental Peak (8431 feet) and down to the dirt road where the table ends and the single watershed begins again. About ten miles farther on is South Pass, the famous niche in the Rockies through which the Oregon Trail emigrants, the Mormons and mountain men funneled to the West Coast.

The road through the pass is on the Continental Divide all the way to the foothills of the Wind River Mountains, those wild peaks where mountaineers climb with the Rocky Mountain sheep. In the foothills of the range, the Trail follows the water bench above Little Sandy Creek, goes up Wind River Peak and on into some of the most sublime country in the United States. In these mountains lodgepole and Douglas fir guard alpine gardens, snow-fields, and the aeolian zone. Glaciers shine like chrome against dazzling blue skies and, a few minutes later, disappear under black clouds and snow. In cracks and crevices lie miniature gardens, some of which have adapted to water, others to drought, depending on their exposure. Waterfalls roar down these mountains, trout leap in the lakes, and marmots pause on rock pinnacles as if to admire the spectacular views. The Divide Trail in the Wind River Range is primarily for young men and women with a great deal of mountaineering experience, for the route is extremely rugged. Most people follow the less strenuous trails that thread below the ridge line.

More than a hundred miles northwest the entrance to the Trail in the Wind River Mountains, the Divide Trail crosses *U. S. High-*

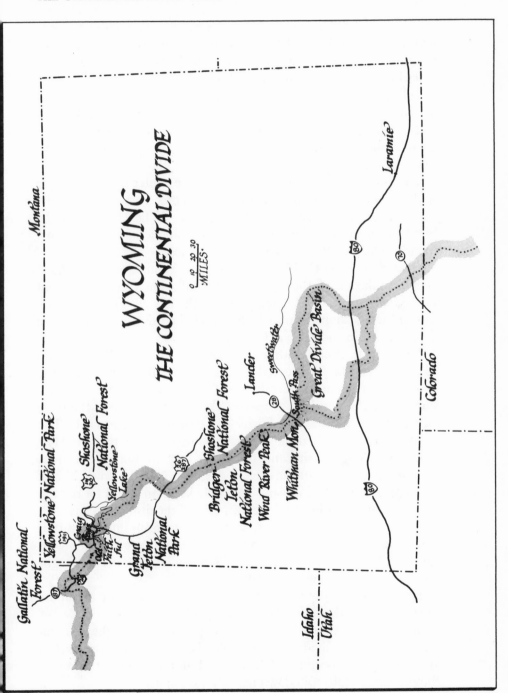

way 26 and 287 at Togowotee Pass. Every year thousands of people park here and walk the Trail to see, off in the mist of distance, the magnificent Grand Teton range where the highest peak, 13,770 feet, looks like the Matterhorn of the Alps.

Yellowstone National Park and Montana are reached by cutting northward to Crescent Peak (12,165 feet) and Hawks Rest (9750 feet), then taking to the roof peak through and out of the park.

Only one person has traversed these two hundred miles of saw-toothed ridge—Woody Marmore of Mammoth, Wyoming, the son of a Yellowstone Park ranger. He was 18 the winter he followed the spill line on cross-country skis from Togowotee Pass to Cook City, Montana. The trip took twenty-three days. "When I came off the beautiful ridge I could not speak for a day and a half," he said to a friend. "The Divide Trail stuns you to silence."

Since there is no Divide Trail as such in Yellowstone Park, most people walk one of the several paths out from Geyser Basin on U. S. *Highway* 89 *and* 287 that lead over the Divide. The most beautiful is the Shoshone Trail, which crosses the ridge line twice, once at Geyser Basin and again at Craig's Pass.

The Divide itself heads off across the Madison Plateau into Idaho but can be intercepted on the Belcher River Trail and the Old Faithful–Boundary Creek Trail. On the east side of U. S. *Highway* 89 *and* 287, the Trail at Lewis Lake circles the base of the ridge on which the Continental Divide lies, but does not reach it. The spirit of the watershed nevertheless dominates this path to Hart Lake and Geyser Basin, and from Overlook Mountain it can be seen on the skyline. For the drive-and-walker, U. S. *Highway* 89 *and* 287 passes beside Atlantic and Pacific Lake, a still pond on the top of a hill that drains in two directions toward the distant oceans.

Snaking out of the Yellowstone, the Trail climbs into the Bitter-root Range on the Idaho–Montana border and enters Montana at Lost Trail Pass, where Lewis and Clark came upon a long-sought stream that flowed west toward the Pacific.

The Divide goes up the Lewis Range and into a dense subalpine forest that extends all the way to Glacier National Park.

In Glacier National Park the Going-to-the-Sun Highway *is* on the Continental Divide, for five miles between park headquarters and the visitors' center at Clemmes Mountain. Along the way a thousand waterfalls spill down in a silver curtain.

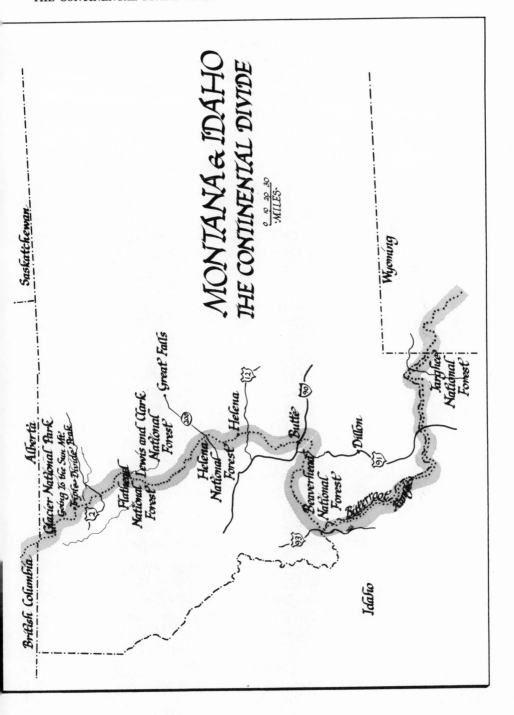

MONTANA & IDAHO
THE CONTINENTAL DIVIDE

0 10 20 30
·MILES·

The McDonald Creek Trail, which goes north to Waterton Creek Trail, follows the Divide 2000 feet below its jagged crest, but northward from the visitors' center skilled mountaineers can walk the Divide. Most walkers take the Nyack Creek Trail at Red Eagle off *Highway 2*, which runs close to the Divide through Mt. Stimson Pass, around Mt. Philip, to Elk Mountain, and out of the Park into Canada.

High along this trail, Rocky Mountain goats and their kids cavort on steep ledges, pipits sing, and the chickweeds that bloom here are so white that they compete with the snow. Douglas Chadwick of Pole Bridge, Montana, who explored much of the Divide country in Glacier National Park, calls this trail the philosopher's footpath. "Looking down on mountains, glaciers, valleys and rivers from the Divide," he said, "I can see how earth and man and beast and plant all fit together, and I understand my place in the scheme of things."

Highways Crossed by the Continental Divide Trail

New Mexico:
  Gila National Forest
  State Highway 180
  State Highway 78

Colorado:
  San Juan National Forest,
    U. S. Highway 160
  Rio Grande National Forest,
    State Highway 149 or 114
  San Isabel National Forest
    and Gunnison National
    Forest, U. S. Highway 50
  State Highway 82, Snowmass
    Winter Sports area
    (Aspen), Mt. Elbert (highest mountain in Colorado)
  White River National Forest,
    U. S. Highway 24

  Arapaho National Forest,
    Interstate 70
  Rocky Mountain National
    Park, U. S. Highway 34
  Routt National Forest, U. S.
    Highway 40

Wyoming:
  Medicine Bow National
    Forest, State Highway 70
  The Great Divide Basin,
    Interstate 80 and U. S.
  Highway 287 and U. S.
    Highway 3
  Shoshone National Forest,
    State Highway 28
  Bridger–Teton National
    Forest, U. S. Highway 26
    and 287

Yellowstone National Park,
U. S. Highway 89 and 287

Montana–Idaho border:
Targhee National Forest and
Gallatin National Forest,
U. S. Highway 191
Beaverhead National Forest,
State Highway 87 and
futher on Interstate 15
Salmon National Forest,
State Highway 29

More Beaverhead National
Forest, U. S. Highway 91
Deerlodge National Forest,
Interstate 90
Helena National Forest, U. S.
Highway 12
Lewis & Clark National
Forest and Flathead
National Forest, State
Highway 200
Glacier National Park, U. S.
Highway 2

Bibliography

ARMSTRONG, PATRICIA. "I'm in Love with Tundra," *Backpacker Magazine,* June 1976 (Vol. 4, No. 3).

CRAIGHEAD, J. J., F. C. CRAIGHEAD, and RAY DAVIS A *Field Guide to the Rocky Mountain Wildflowers.* Boston: Houghton Mifflin Company, 1963.

FROME, MICHAEL. *Rand McNally National Park Guide.* Chicago and New York: Rand McNally, 1967.

KJELLSTROM, BJORN. *Be Expert with Map and Compass: The Orienteering Handbook.* La Porte, Indiana: American Orienteering Service, 1967.

PETERSON, ROGER TORY. A *Field Guide to Western Birds.* Boston: Houghton Mifflin Company, 2nd rev. ed. 1961.

SARGENT, CHARLES S. *Manual of the Trees of North America* (2 v.). New York: Dover Publications, Inc., 2nd ed. 1965.

SIERRA CLUB, THE. *Hiking the Yellowstone Backcountry.* San Francisco: Sierra Club Books, 2nd printing, 1975.

SWINGER, ANN H., and BEATRICE E. WILLARD. *Land Above the Trees: A Guide to American Alpine Tundra.* New York: Harper and Row, 1972.

U. S. DEPARTMENT OF THE INTERIOR, NATIONAL PARK SERVICE. A good map of the entire Continental Divide Trail, both existing and proposed, is available from the Shadow Mountain National Recreation Area, Estes Park, Colorado 80517.

Note: Most road maps of the region show the Continental Divide.

6

T H E   P O T O M A C

H E R I T A G E   T R A I L *

T he Potomac Heritage Trail lies on both the Virginia and
the Maryland sides of Chesapeake Bay in the historic Tidewater Country. It comes into the streets and avenues of
Washington, D. C., up the Chesapeake and Ohio Tow Path in
Maryland to Harpers Ferry, West Virginia. There it branches;
one arm goes west and south into the Allegheny Mountains, the
other north into Pennsylvania. The Trail is level and easy, with the
exception of a few tough climbs in West Virginia.

The Potomac Heritage is the first trail to be blazed and conceived by the Bureau of Outdoor Recreation after Congress set up
the National Scenic Trails System. The names of its originators are
lost in the jumble of government bureaucracy; whoever they are,
they created an imaginative and interesting trail, and millions of
people walk parts of it every year.

The Trail's geology varies from the sedimentary rocks of the
Coastal Plain to the band of igneous intrusive rock in the Alle-
ghenies, a range in the Appalachian mountain system.

At this writing only 320 of a proposed 874 miles are marked,
including trails through Spruce Knob, Seneca Rocks, and the Dolly
Sods in the Monongahela National Forest, West Virginia, plus
184 miles along the C & O towpath. Along Chesapeake Bay in
southern Maryland and Virginia, the Trail is still on paper but
can be walked by taking to roads, streets, and town parks. Old
plantations, Revolutionary houses and churches, a mixture of

* For information about biotic communities along this trail see pages 260–261,
275.

100

Indian relics and gracious living are features of the Tidewater sections of the Trail.

The eastern part of the Trail lies in the Eastern Mixed Forest of white and scarlet oaks and shortleaf pine, one of the forests of the temperate deciduous region. At its western end the Trail is shaded by a sycamore and red-maple forest along the river bottomlands, and by beech–birch–maple–hemlock and spruce–fir forests in the Allegheny Mountains.

On the map the Trail looks like a stick man lying on its back. Its left leg lies on the Maryland side of the Chesapeake, its toe is the starting point in the salt-marsh grasses at Point Lookout, Maryland. Here birds wheel and flash above the bay estuaries and crabs scurry sideways. Grebes, loons, and scoters flock to the salt marshes to stalk fish and crustaceans in the shallows and along watery trails made by muskrats and rice rats. The water shrew dives among the reeds, and fairly seems to walk on water, and Virginia deer hide their fawns in the bushes above the tide line. Raccoons hunt the vast acres of *Spartina* marsh grass, which in winter become a port for the ducks, geese, and swans that move down the Atlantic flyway. Behind the marshes grow oaks and pines and thick groves of white cedar. Willows, alders, and sycamores line the streams and the higher ground of the Chesapeake Bay region.

The Trail starts in an old Union Army prison camp, now Point Lookout State Park, and shaded with oaks and planted maples. Wide and sandy, the Trail winds into the old Indian village of Piscataway, renamed St. Mary's City by the colonists. This seacoast town, the first permanent settlement in Maryland and its one-time capital, was named for Henrietta Maria, the consort of King Charles I.

The town today is not far different from the time of its settlement in 1634. A seventeenth-century state house still looks out upon the St. Mary's River, and the old Clocker's Inn has not been altered since the days when St. Mary's was a busy frontier town.

Crossing *U. S. Highway 301*, the Trail follows a stream valley beyond Leonardtown and Charlotte Hall into two fresh-water swamps, Allen's Fresh and Zekiah. These watery platters of reeds, arrowhead, and spadderdock lie along the streams above high tide and support the swamp trees, red maple and buttonwood. Cranes, egrets, and frogs make their home here. Cattails grow in almost pure stands,

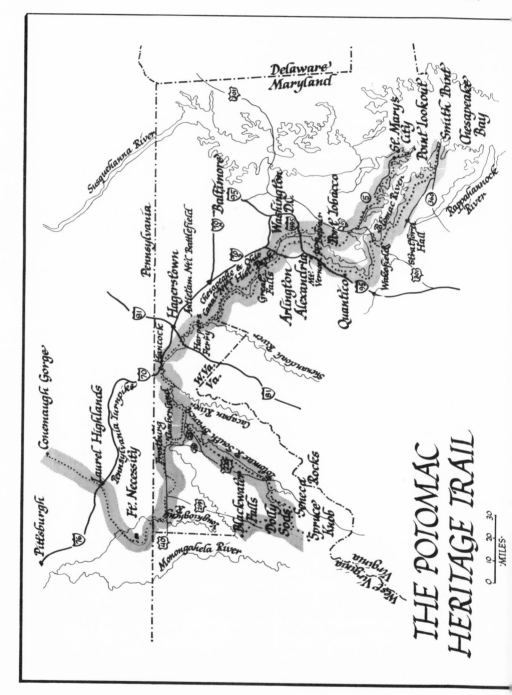

sheltering otter and muskrat. Clapper rail, willet, and Wilson's plover explode into flight over hardwood swamps where the osprey seeks out the tall trees and the long-billed marsh wren sings from the rushes.

Leaving this primitive environment, the Trail turns west and enters the historic town of Port Tobacco, one of the busiest seaports of the New World in the seventeenth century. The town, originally the Indian village of Potobac, was visited in 1608 by Captain John Smith, founder of the first permanent English colony in America, Jamestown, Virginia.

In Port Tobacco the Trail becomes a personal excursion to old houses and old buildings, which should include St. Ignatius' Church, an exquisite example of early American architecture. Rosehill, the handsome eighteenth-century home of George Washington's personal physician, Gustavus Brown, sits among boxwoods and magnolias.

A few miles beyond Port Tobacco, Doncaster and General Smallwood State Forests provide a trail that leads to a fine stretch of the original oak and pine forest of this biome in Piscataway Park-on-the-Potomac. Eventually the Heritage Trail will run north to Washington, D. C., through pine flatwoods, national forests, and game refuges, but at this writing the route is along country roads, where fields on all sides are planted to sweet potatoes, soybeans, corn, wheat, and barley. The land, which never reaches more than a hundred feet in elevation, is crossed by many broad, shallow valleys and cut by widely meandering streams that pour into Chesapeake Bay.

On this coastal plain between the ocean and the District of Columbia the valley soils are wet sands and old tidal marsh loam of unclassified organic minerals which make one of the richest farming areas in the East.

At Washington, D. C., the Potomac Heritage Trail crosses the Anacostia River Bridge and proceeds down Pennsylvania Avenue. It passes the Library of Congress, the Supreme Court, the U. S. Capitol, the Washington Monument, the White House, and the Lincoln and Jefferson memorials to present the cityscape and living history. Tracing its way to the Chesapeake and Ohio Canal, the PHT passes the Watergate Inn, where former President Nixon's career began to unravel.

The south leg of the Potomac Heritage Trail lies on the Virginia side of Chesapeake Bay and passes through a different era of history and a somewhat different biotic area. At Smith Point, Virginia, on the bay, the Trail begins at an estuary. Oysters, clams, and crabs abound, and commercial fishermen tie up at the docks with tons of shad, herring, and striped bass. Since much of this area is private land, the Trail follows a road to the headwaters of Nomini Creek near Stratford Hall. Built in the 1720s by Thomas Lee, a forefather of General Robert E. Lee of the Confederate Army. This 30,000-acre eighteenth-century plantation is reminiscent of a way of life that produced many of our nation's early leaders.

From here to Mt. Vernon, *U. S. Highway* 3 is the Trail, a picturesque route through plantations and the small towns of Westmoreland County, the birthplace of George Washington, of James Monroe, and of Richard Henry and Francis Lightfoot Lee. Fields roll out to meet forests of dogwood, maple, oak, honey locust, birch, and tulip-tree. The mockingbird and cardinal dominate the songsters in the formal gardens and the meadowlark holds forth in fields and on grassy lawns.

Off to the right, Westmoreland State Park, established in 1936, offers swimming, boating, and picnicking in a biotic area that supports the original trees and flowers of the coastal plain. Mountain laurel shades violets, trillium, and bloodroot all the way to Wakefield, George Washington's birthplace.

At about every quarter-mile on *U. S. Highway* 3 a plaque marks historic sites of early Tidewater Virginia: Richard Henry Lee's grave, the home of his brother John, and Nominy Church, built in 1755 and attended by the first President. Beneath this culture lies another, that of the American Indian. The museum at Westmoreland displays artifacts of the people who lived in this area more than a thousand years ago.

In spring the fuchsia-pink flowers of the redbud, one of America's most vivid native trees, brightens the woodlots and roadsides as well as the extensive gardens at Wakefield, where George Washington's father, grandfather, and great-grandfather are buried in the family cemetery.

Taking to the road, the Trail passes through the grounds of Quantico Marine Corps School and arrives at Mason Neck for a view of Gunston Hall, the plantation home of George Mason, author of the Virginia Declaration of Rights. The mansion faces a National Wildlife Refuge where the bald eagle once nested, and where in spring and fall thousands of migrating birds, including loons and warblers, raise their voices above the sound of automobiles and tractors.

Less than five miles down the Trail is Mt. Vernon, George Washington's Potomac River plantation and a major attraction of the Potomac Heritage Trail. A wide path suitable for biking and hiking begins at Mt. Vernon and follows the Potomac north to Washington, D. C. Not far off the Trail is Woodlawn Plantation, given by Washington to his nephew Lawrence Lewis and his ward Eleanor Parke Curtis on their marriage. Down this paved portion of the Trail the historic houses and towns reflect the sophistication of the men who wrote the Declaration of Independence and the Constitution of the United States. As the Trail enters Alexandria, Virginia, it becomes diversified, and each walker chooses his own route.

Christ Church, built between 1769 and 1773 of native brick and stone, in the style of an English Country church, contains George Washington's pew and still has an active congregation. The Friendship Fire Company of 1774, which claims Washington as a member, displays some of the earliest engines in America. The house where Light Horse Harry Lee, the Revolutionary War hero, lived while his son Robert E. Lee was attending school, is furnished with rare antiques and preserves Lee family pictures and letters. The old Presbyterian Meeting House and two imposing blocks of town houses dating back to the eighteenth and nineteenth centuries, Gentry and Captain rows, are open to the walker. On King Street, two blocks west of the planned trail, sits the Ramsay House (1724), the home of William Ramsay, a Scottish merchant and city's first Lord Mayor. Next door stands the Carlisle House, Alexandria's "grandest home," built in 1752 by John Carlisle. Surrounding these museums are houses of comparable age, many now occupied by Washington officials. Beyond the town, long-abandoned farms have grown up to luxuriant stands of Virginia pine.

The Trail runs along a narrow corridor to Memorial Bridge, where the Lincoln Memorial and the Washington Monument dominate the landscape on one side of the river, and Arlington Cemetery and the Tomb of the Unknown Soldier on the other.

The right leg of the Trail on the Virginia shore now parallels *State Highway* 7 and the Potomac River, and winds through the fashionable hunt country. Rugged bluffs, deep tributary streams, and deciduous hardwood forests give a natural freshness to the Trail as it comes in to Great Falls. Here in 1750 the 76-foot drop of the Potomac River was circumvented by the Potowamac Canal, surveyed by the young George Washington. This assignment gained him insight into both the natural history of the new country and its growing commercial needs. The canal was used for fifty years by river boatmen bringing agricultural goods from West Virginia into Alexandria and the other Potomac towns. Only a few vestiges of the canal remain, at Matildaville near Great Falls.

Westward through Fairfax County the Trail was not yet complete at the time of this writing, but will cross *U. S. Highway 15* and follow the river through the agricultural countryside north of Leesburg and Oakhill. As of 1977 it could be resumed at Balls Bluff National Cemetery, a Civil War monument near the home of President James Monroe. Crossing the river at Harpers Ferry, the Virginia branch joins the Chesapeake and Ohio Canal towpath.

Back at Watergate Inn, the Maryland Trail takes to the Chesapeake and Ohio Canal towpath in Georgetown. The Canal was planned at the end of the 1700s to connect the Atlantic seaboard with Pittsburgh and the Ohio River. The enterprise went no farther west than Cumberland, Maryland, however, for even as it was dedicated it was obsolete. On July 4, 1828, the same day that President John Quincy Adams broke ground for the canal, merchants in Baltimore were launching the Baltimore and Ohio Railroad. Outmoded at its birth, the canal nevertheless served the nation for almost a hundred years before its closing in 1924. Forty years later the serene waterway that wends through sycamore and red-maple forests was again serving the nation. It is the core of the Potomac Heritage Trail and a National Historic Park. Many of the locks that regulated the water level are still functioning, and a few lockhouses where keepers and their families lived are open to visitors. The towpath, once trod by mules and drivers as they hauled rope-pulled barges up the canal, is now the centerpiece of the walk.

From Georgetown to Harpers Ferry the towpath is shaded by hickory, maple, walnut, tulip-tree, and ash, a vegetation characteristic of the Northern coastal plain. Occasionally the trees reflect the deep South in a pure stand of Virginia pine, complete with the Good-God (as the pileated woodpecker is known here) that screams through the long shiny needles. The cottontail rabbit, gray fox, red fox, mink, and raccoon hunt along the canal at night, and the Virginia deer and an occasional bobcat roam the shadows at dusk and dawn. A potpourri of Northern and Southern birds are to be seen along the towpath: summer tanager, Louisiana water-thrush, Kentucky warbler, hooded warbler, yellow-breasted chat, Carolina wren, tufted titmouse, Carolina chickadee, and blue-gray gnatcatcher.

The towpath Trail begins at the Tidewater Lock in Georgetown, at the mouth of Rock Creek, where canal barges once entered from the Potomac River. From this lock to Seneca, Maryland, twenty-two miles to the west, the locks have been largely restored and the forest and flowers are undisturbed. Beside the path Virginia blue-bells, columbines, and dog-tooth violets bloom in spring, and bouncing bets flower in summer.

State Highway 112 leads down to the canal on Tschiffley Syca-more Landing and Edwards Ferry roads. Here stores are open all year round and canoes and bicycles can be rented. Thirty-seven miles along by pedal, paddle, or boot is Marble Quarry where the columns were cut for the statuary hall in the U. S. Capitol. Miles 40 through 50, out of Georgetown, bring the walker to White's Ford where Robert E. Lee's army waded into Maryland in September of 1862.

Several miles along is Lock 27, a red sandstone structure and in 1831 a sensation, for it could raise or lower a 92-foot-long canal barge with a cargo of 128 tons. Mosses now grow in its stonework and the resurrection fern clings in the cracks waiting as a seemingly dead leaf for the rain to revive it.

On down the towpath is Point of Rocks, a narrow right-of-way and once the source of a dispute between the C & O Canal Com-pany and its rival the B & O Railroad. Locomotives ran so close to the canal that mules fled before the roar of the engines, rocking and tossing their barges. The Canal Company sued, and a long-drawn-out case was settled by a ruling that a fence must be erected between the railroad and the canal.

Ten miles west is Lock 29, which canoeists enjoy using. They pull ashore and drain the lock by opening the iron paddle gates at the bottom of the big wooden doors. When the water reaches the

level of the canoe, the big doors are opened, the canoe is paddled
in and the doors are closed. The iron paddle gates on the upper door
are opened next, the lock fills, and the canoe rises to the level of the
upper canal. The process can be repeated only 74 times a day, as
compared to the 605 times that were possible in 1880.

Between miles 60 and 70 is the site of the New Armory Dam,
once a power source for the Harpers Ferry Arsenal, established by
George Washington. The dam was destroyed during the Civil War
and never repaired.

At Harpers Ferry the focus of interest is on the October 1859
raid by the abolitionist, John Brown, whose attempt to free slaves
cost several lives and led indirectly to the Civil War. Brown was
born in Torrington, Connecticut, where as a youth he helped fugi-
tive slaves escape to Canada. Later, in Springfield, Massachusetts,
he organized a league among Blacks to protect them from slave-
catchers. In 1855 he followed five of his sons west and helped prevent Kansas from becoming a slave state. After a number of small
but bloody battles John Brown, now known as "Old Osawatomie
Brown," considered an invasion of the South and collected arms
and men for the raid. An outlaw, he nevertheless received aid from
many sympathizers "to take over the Federal Arsenal and Armory
at Harpers Ferry" and bring an end to slavery. On October 16,
1859, Brown and eighteen followers captured and entered the arsenal. The following day Brown, with his dead and wounded, was
surrounded by the militia. At dawn Colonel Robert E. Lee forced
the doors open and captured the protestors. Lee delivered Brown
to a trial at which, though he conducted himself with intelligence
and courage, he was convicted of treason. He was hanged on December 2. At his death Ralph Waldo Emerson wrote, "Brown has made
the gallows as glorious as a cross." Two years later the Civil War
began, with Union troops marching to war singing "John Brown's
body lies a-moldering in the grave, but his soul goes marching on."

The region around Harpers Ferry is salted with battle sites. One
of these, Antietam, is the site of "the bloodiest single day of the
Civil War." On September 17, 1862, a four-hour battle left more
than 12,000 dead and wounded. Near by at Fort Frederick, thousands died during the French and Indian Wars, between 1689 and
1763, part of the long struggle between France and Great Britain

for possession of North America. During this conflict both foreign nations tried to buy help from the Indians but succeeded only in promoting turmoil, misery, and battles.

South of Oldtown, Maryland, which is on the Potomac Heritage Trail, stands one of the engineering wonders of the 1840s, the 3020-foot Paw Paw Tunnel, drilled through the limestone of the Allegheny Mountains.

The right arm of the Trail leaves the canal and winds into the birch–beech–maple–hemlock forests of West Virginia. A clearly marked path leads to Seneca Rocks, Spruce Knob, and Blackwater Falls. The ridge tops are crowned with spruce and fir, typical of the far North, whereas the bottomlands along the South Branch of the Potomac support "cove hardwoods," slender yellow poplars, and silver and red maples. On well-drained dry hillsides grow oaks and shagbark hickories. Quail, grouse, and turkey run through the dense cover, and white-tailed deer, cottontails, squirrels, fox, and a few black bears move through shadows and light. The Trail crosses many clear, cool mountain streams where rainbow, brook, and occasionally brown trout dwell, and where, in sunnier waters, small-mouth bass abound.

Running parallel to *State Highway* 28 the Trail comes into the Dolly Sods, a unique area of many water gaps that frame dramatic vistas. This country is a high plateau, wild and uninhabited. Winds scream over a tableland that is patched with yellow-green sphagnum bogs and blue-purple mats of heath shrub. The Sods are haunted by owls that scream from thickets of young spruce growing near the many waterfalls. From the depths of strangely carved canyons rise the shrieks of woodpeckers.

A puzzling geological feature of the Dolly Sods is the "rock glacier," a tongue of boulders that have fallen off a sandstone and conglomerate outcrop uphill and spilled down the mountainside. Such rock glaciers appear in the glaciated land near the Arctic Circle, but since the glaciers never came closer to the Dolly Sods than central Pennsylvania and Ohio, geologists do not understand how these formations came to be.

The wildlife is also mysterious. On these high plains is an abundance of that far Northern species the snowshoe hare. No scientist can say how these animals got there. Ruffed grouse, wild turkey, and fox mix with black bear and white-tailed deer. Beavers are numerous; their ponds, dams, and lodges entertain walkers and photographers.

The Trail splits once again at the mouth of the Seneca River and one finger leads southwest to Spruce Knob (4862 feet), the highest point in West Virginia. Out from the summit stretches a panorama of forests, mountains, clouds, rivers, and rocks. Plans are in progress to complete the route from Dolly Sods to Blackwater Falls in the Allegheny Mountains through the geological break known as the Allegheny Front.

The left arm of the Potomac Heritage Trail continues along the Chesapeake and Ohio towpath to Cumberland, Maryland. This quiet town is the terminus of the Chesapeake and Ohio Canal. The Trail is not marked through the town, but can be found on Braddock Road, which leads to the Cumberland Narrows, a spectacular natural cut in the Appalachians through which the pioneers funneled to settle Pittsburgh and what is now Ohio. The Historic Braddock Road leads on to Frostburg (so named because it is the coldest spot in the snow belt). The road was built in 1775 by an army of Americans under the British General Edward Braddock, and was used to move military supplies across the Allegheny Mountains during the French and Indian Wars. At the end of hostilities it was quickly adopted by settlers heading west to the Ohio frontier.

Beyond Frostburg the Potomac Heritage Trail comes into the primitive Savage River State Forest and crosses the tumbling Savage River where the national championship whitewater canoeing contests are held annually. The roar and whiteness of the water contrast with the quiet and dark of the hemlock forest.

Beyond *U. S. Highway 219* the PHT bends northward at Friendsville, and follows the Youghiogheny River to the Mason–Dixon line, the boundary between Maryland and Pennsylvania. It was named after two British engineers, Charles Mason and Jeremiah Dixon, who surveyed the border in 1713. As events leading to the Civil War evolved, an imaginary lengthening of this line came to be thought of as the boundary between free and slave states.

Upon rounding the Youghiogheny Reservoir, the Potomac Heritage Trail strikes west once more along Braddock Road to Fort Necessity National Battlefield, another blood-bathed site of the French and Indian Wars. Here in the fields George Washington surrendered with honor in July 1754, the first and last time he surrendered to an enemy.

The Trail runs northeast over the Youghiogheny River Bridge into Ohiopyle State Park at the foot of Pennsylvania's Laurel Ridge Highlands. Here it crosses the *Pennsylvania Turnpike* and terminates in Conemaugh Gorge, where hemlocks overhang white water.

Bibliography and Maps

AMERICAN YOUTH HOSTELS, INC. A *Collection of Maps of the Chesapeake and Ohio Canal*. Washington Potomac Area, American Youth Hostels, 3rd printing, 1967.

U. S. DEPARTMENT OF THE INTERIOR, BUREAU OF OUTDOOR RECREATION. *Final Environmental Statement: The Potomac Heritage Trail*. Washington: FES 75–34, 1975.

———. *The Potomac Heritage Trail*. Washington: U. S. Department of Interior, Bureau of Outdoor Recreation, 1974. This pamphlet contains an excellent map of the trail.

WEST VARGINIA HIGHLANDS CONSERVANCY. *Dolly Sods Area—32,000 Acres in and Adjacent to the Monongahela National Forest, West Virginia*. West Virginia Highlands Conservancy, 4th ed. 1973. 6202 Division Road, Huntington, W. Va. 25705.

7

T H E   F L O R I D A   T R A I L   *

The Florida Trail is the flattest footpath in the nation. With an elevation of only 90 feet at its highest point, it runs northward through the state of Florida, beginning in the Big Cypress Swamp and passing through Ocala and Osceola National Forests. Then it turns westerly, takes to the bank of the Suwannee River for seventy-five miles and, passing south of Tallahassee, winds through Apalachicola National Forest to terminate among pelicans, willets, and gulls at Panama City on the Gulf of Mexico. The Florida Trail covers almost the entire length and breadth of the state, a distance of more than a thousand miles, and goes through two distinct life zones—the Subtropical and Southeastern Pine Forest.

Though the Trail is easy to walk, it is best traveled in December, January, February, and March, when the temperatures are a pleasant 60 or 70°F., the air is crisp, and the dry season is upon the land. From April to October, when rains are frequent, water covers much of the southern section of the Trail and the heat and insects make foot travel difficult.

When the sun shines, however, and the waters recede, the Florida Trail is a glistening and fascinating path. It wends past cypress swamps and over bright "islands"—elevations in the terrain. A rise of no more than twelve inches will support an entirely different community of plants. On some of these "islands" grow willows; on others, pine or cypress, laden with ferns and flowers. The hardwood islands called "hammocks" support mahoganies, oaks, gumbo lim-

* For information about biotic communities along this trail see pages 271, 289–291.

112

bos, and pond apples. Orchids bloom, bromeliads erupt like fountains from the ground and from tree limbs, primitive birds shriek and rasp.

The southern end of the Florida Trail goes through an ecosystem unique to North America, where life has adapted to excess water, excess sunlight and warmth—the Subtropic Biome. North of Lake Okeechobee the Trail strikes out across tall grasslands and then into slash and longleaf pine country. This, the great Southeastern Pine Forest, also has its islands of hardwoods: ash, red maple, red bay, willow, persimmon, water oak, magnolia, and gum. Near the Georgia border the islands in the pines support live oak, cherry, and chinquapin. In low pockets of water all along the Trail, baldcypress flourishes.

All the land over which the Trail passes is ecologically young, having lifted out of the sea approximately 10,000 years ago. Its relative youth is evident in the poor drainage that creates swamps, shallow lakes, and ill-defined streams. The underlying rock is a porous limestone, that leaches out to make vast holes, sinks, and mysterious subterranean rivers.

The Florida Trail is also young, and at this writing, was still being built. Walkers who wish to can join crews in blazing and cutting this sunny footpath. Although approximately 400 of the proposed one thousand miles have been completed, walkers must join the Florida Trail Association to obtain maps, because much of this trail is and will be through private land. Landowners are more likely to give permission to trail-builders when they understand that access is limited to those who care enough to write and pay a small fee. The Trail was also, as of 1977, being considered by Congress for addition to the National Scenic Trail System.

The history of the Florida Trail dates back only to 1964. That was the year a young man from New Jersey, James A. Kern, arrived in Florida and bought a house. In a few months he had become enthralled with the birds, sun, and water of his new surroundings. As he watched the evening sky fill with wood storks and glossy ibis, he began thinking of a magazine devoted to photography and nature, to be called *Florida Trails*. The magazine never came to be, but the Trail did. Within a year the dream of a wild footpath had so burgeoned that Kern dropped the idea of a magazine to concentrate on the trail. Bird-watchers, walkers, and conservationists supported him, and in 1966 they completed marking the first 57 miles of trail through Ocala National Forest. Today the Florida Trail Association not only builds the trail but promotes hikes, canoe trips, and courses in natural history and photography.

The Florida Trail starts in the Subtropical Zone, which lies between Florida Bay and Lake Okeechobee. Going north, the first orange blaze is on *U. S. Highway 41*, known as the Tamiami Trail, just north of Everglades National Park. The blaze is painted on the gate at Bill Mitchell's Oasis Airport, which opens onto a pine island, typifying one of four plant communities found in the cypress swamps. In the subtropics, plant communities vary with a rise of a mere foot in elevation because of their differing tolerances of water. The water-loving cypress is found in the low spots. Stretching across higher ground is the grass prairie, which requires less water. A slightly higher elevation supports the pines, which can take some wetting and a large amount of winter dryness. Within the pine islands, a further rise in elevation supports the hardwood hammocks. Throughout the area are sloughs and ponds, the home of waterlilies and arrowhead, plants that have adjusted to total wetness. Pine, hammock, and grass prairie each support animal communities unique to themselves.

The walker who likes to identify trees will be glad to know that the pine islands have but one species, slash pine. Beneath them grow quantities of saw palmetto, the attractive fanlike plant that dominates much of Florida's wild land. At the edge of the pine islands and throughout the grass prairie rises the round, lollypop-like cabbage palm, Florida's state tree. The heart of its fronds is a delicious vegetable and the leaves are useful for shelter and clothing —almost all man's needs. It is this palm that gives the state its tropical appearance.

On the pine islands, Florida red-tailed hawks are the builders of the large stick nests. Raccoons, marsh rabbits, gray squirrels, and even bear raise young in the pale shade of these long-needled trees. Over the fans of the saw palmettos flit clusters of pink day-flying moths, while two other species, the dogface and pearl crescent, hover among the grasses. Gathered around thistles are Hunter's butterflies and the small reddish-brown Southern metal marks. Since insects tend to stay near their food supply, by knowing the plant the insect can be identified, and vice versa.

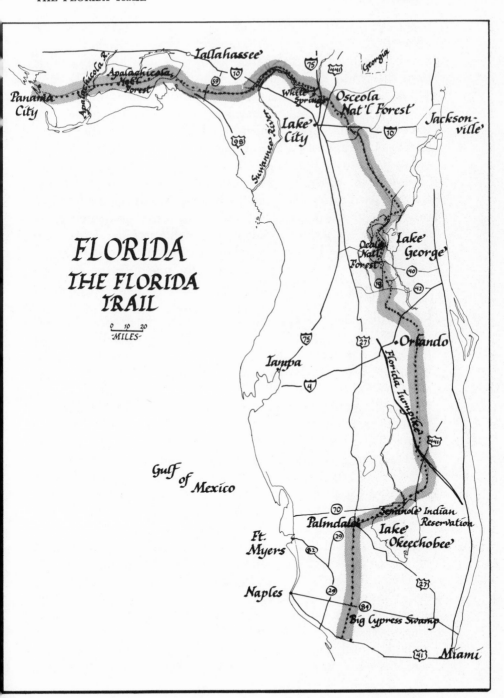

FLORIDA
THE FLORIDA
TRAIL

0 10 20
MILES

At mile one-and-a-half the path plunges into a small hammock of water and scrub oaks. Pineapple-like bromeliads that live on nutrients in the air decorate their limbs, and quantities of warblers from the North flit through the trees and then vanish like rain. Monarch butterflies that have migrated from as far away as Canada drift over the Trail. Blue lupines color the island floor and the Florida opossum, an occasional gray fox, and the crackling armadillo walk the animal trails. Into this refuge comes the great horned owl.

Beyond the oak hammock the Trail enters the grass prairie, a zone speckled with cabbage palms, palmettos, and about a hundred varieties of grasses and sedges. One of these is the versatile sawgrass, actually a sedge, which has adapted to both water and drought. In the grass prairie the leaves of the bright-green "alligator flag," a long-stemmed, big-leafed plant, infallibly announce the presence of 'gators whether it be pond, slough, or cypress heads. During the dry season these jagged-backed reptiles, using teeth and tail, dig out the weeds and muck that fill the numerous limestone holes and sinks. Fish, turtles, and frogs increase and are fed upon by birds and mammals that frequent these holes, particularly in winter when the water is low. Before their role in the ecology of the Everglades was recognized, the alligators were shot almost to extinction, and along with them went most of the wood storks, ibises, and spoonbills that fed at their holes. Today these birds are making a slow comeback, for the alligator is now protected.

Across the grass prairie the Trail meanders through stands of dwarf cypress, the same species as the large baldcypress, but stunted because of the poor and shallow soil. Though no more than ten feet high, most of these trees are a hundred years old.

After a few miles the Trail winds into a wetland known as the Big Cypress Swamp. Eerie light filters through swatches of Spanish moss, casting prickly shadows behind them. Jutting up above the water are the "knees" of the cypress that bring oxygen to the roots. Growing on top of many of these are gardens of very specific mosses and ferns. Beneath the plants small creatures dwell. Orchids cling to the trunks of the trees, and all around grow the massive strap and royal ferns. The pop ash of southern Florida flourishes here. Between the trees a golden spider spins its enormous web, which sometimes spans a twenty-foot area. Twisted together, the threads make a strong twine which the Indians wove into cloth.

The Big Cypress Swamp harbors spectacular birds: the vanishing wood stork (distinguishable by its black bill and black wingtips), the snowy and great egrets, great blue and little green herons, and in the deeper ponds the primitive fish-eating anhinga. Unlike other diving birds, it has no oil glands to prevent its feathers from becoming soaked. When seemingly it has become so wet it almost drowns, the anhinga climbs onto a bush and lifts its black and white wings, as though hanging itself out in the sun to dry.

On top of the cypress trees sit the black and turkey vultures looking like huge dried prunes. These massive birds roost at night in the large trees and remain humped there until the morning sun heats the land and thermal currents begin to rise. Without these updrafts the huge birds cannot easily get airborne, so they must wait until about 10 A. M. to begin cruising the sky. Then they spread their wings, are lifted up and over the swamp to hunt dead and decaying animals.

For a botanist, the sloughs and ponds are an orderly affair. On their shores grow the sedges. In the shallows are the emergent water plants: arrowhead, bullrush, and alligator flag. In deeper water float waterlilies, spadderdock, and insect-catching bladderworts, and their associates, the alligator, soft-shelled turtle, Florida spotted gar, sunfish, and mosquito-fish. Like stars on the landscape are the flowers of the spider lily with their long tendril-like petals that are pure white. The moonflower vine climbs vigorously over willow and cypress, blooms at dawn, and polka-dots the swamp with huge white and yellow blossoms.

The southern section of the Trail terminates seven miles north of *State Highway 84*. Eventually it will head through Palmdale around Lake Okeechobee, skirt the edge of the Seminole Indian Reservation, and plunge north through the Tall-Grass Prairie of Florida which is now rich cattle and farming country. Paralleling *U. S. Highway 441*, the Trail will wind among the midland lakes, serpentine west of Orlando and arrive at Ocala National Forest, where at this writing the Florida Trail resumes in an ecological niche as different from the the Big Cypress Swamp as the top of a high mountain is from the prairie.

The first blaze is at Clearwater Campground on *State Highway 42*, where many walkers swim in the glaucous spring and relax on the white beaches.

The Trail leads under live oaks and glossy-leaved magnolias, and here the tupelo or sour-gum tree of song and folklore makes its first appearance. In spring the pungent flowers of the tupelo attract so many bees and insects that each tree seems to be alive and dancing.

Ocala, our first and southernmost national forest, was established in 1908. It was the heart of the Seminole Nation when in 1539 Hernando De Soto passed through the Indian village of Ocala, now known as Juniper Springs. The many wild orange trees scattered through the hammock on which the modern village sits are a reminder of the Spaniards who brought the orange to North America.

Many nature lovers on the way north or south camp in this forest, where birds and wild things are so friendly each newcomer is welcomed by flocks of birds, bold deer, or by squirrels and raccoons.

In 1832 Osceola, an Indian who is to the South what Geronimo is to the West, rose to fame when he opposed the U. S. government's plan to drive all Seminole Indians out of Florida. When the order to leave was read, Osceola speared it with a dagger and shouted, "There! This is the only treaty I will make with the whites!" He refused to move, and the United States government sent troops to Ocala. Osceola and his braves killed every U. S. soldier in the battle of 1835, which began the Seminole War, a war that in a sense has never ended. In 1837, after two years of seeking vengeance, the United States government captured Osceola and confined him to a dungeon at Fort Moultrie, South Carolina, where he died in 1838, a few days after his now celebrated portrait by George Catlin was painted. Today there is no sign of the village of Ocala; Juniper Springs has erased it. However, the Florida Trail follows an old Indian trail to Juniper Creek, which winds in the shade of magnolias, black jack and water oaks, along a natural contour that the Ocalas and Osceola once followed.

The Trail leaves the hammock and emerges in the dominant plant community of Ocala, called locally the Big Scrub, a vast stretch of sand pine, palmetto, and grass. In this harsh environment, where only the hardiest plants survive, the small-leafed sand pine has adapted to nearly sterile soil. Its seeds must be opened by fire before they can germinate. Today fire protection has retarded new growth of the sand pine; ecologists are experimenting with controlled burning to bring it back.

Other plants of this desolate soil are the scrub oak, rosemary, and palmetto overtopped by islands of longleaf and loblolly pine, whose foot-long needles shimmer when the sun strikes them. Below them needle palms burst from the earth like green rays.

Along the Trail in the Big Scrub, holes are evidence of the Florida gopher, not a mammal but a burrowing turtle, and host to the curious gopher frog which leaves the tunnel only to breed.

Dawns in Ocala National Forest are almost invariably foggy and mysterious. Mist washes out the details of the pines, and the sawgrass becomes a phantom sea rolling against elf-like stumps and bushes. Many walkers come to the forest simply to spread their sleeping bags and awaken to this other-worldliness. When the sun strikes the mist, it becomes a silver curtain behind which the forest voices wail and cry. Fish hawks glide in and out of the fog, and the rare white ibis circles above feathery water holes. At sunup the cloud lifts, trees stand clear and the curved-billed limpkin sobs the call that gave it the name of "crying bird."

In the tall grass off the Trail walks the rare Ocala deer, a three-foot-high relative of the Virginia white-tailed deer. It has adapted to the poverty of this sterile land by dropping its fawns throughout the year, so that no single spring crop of young descends on the struggling plants and grasses.

In the Big Scrub the black bear finds a home and the endangered Florida panther stalks deer, rabbit, and bird.

The Trail comes to the shore of Lake Kerr and crosses over into an island of longleaf pine. No plants grow under these great trees, where fallen needles lie many inches deep. The footfall of the walker is hushed all the way to Lake Delaney and the Osceola National Forest. Bayous, the marshy inlets of lakes and rivers, appear for the first time.

The Trail comes into the little town of White Springs and there takes to the magnificent Suwannee River bank for seventy-five miles. Passing the stone Stephen Foster Memorial it goes out of town, passes bubbling springs, sinkholes and quiet grottos where live oaks, draped almost to obscurity with Spanish moss, shade the footpath.

Not far from White Springs, the river cuts into a limestone layer known as the Ocala uplift. Deep trenches are carved into this limestone and into the dolomite of the Oligocene and Eocene ages. Fossil-filled rocks tell the history of an ancient life that once dwelled here. Here the Suwannee River becomes clear and free of biological and chemical pollutants. In these waters dwell fifty species of fish. Bluegills, redbreast sunfish, warmouth, flier, largemouth bass, and channel catfish are favorites of fishermen. Living with them are such non-game fish as the chub-sucker, spotted sucker, American eel, yellow bullhead, bowfin, Florida gar, mosquito-fish, pirate perch, dollar sunfish, and banded sunfish.

Ducks abound in the Suwannee River. Some common winter residents are the redhead, lesser scaup, red-breasted and American mergansers, baldpate, pintail, and bufflehead. Black duck, mallard, and gadwall are year-round residents. The beautiful harlequin wood duck comes to this silvery river whose banks support three species of amphibians, 73 of reptiles, 232 of birds, and 42 of mammals. The rare and endangered species here are the wood stork, Southern bald eagle, American osprey, Southern red-cockaded woodpecker, Florida panther, Florida water rat, and the Florida manatee, that old seacow of the brackish waters that sometimes comes up the Suwannee almost as far as White Springs.

At Indian Flint Quarry is a unique outcrop of flint rock. Here, where the Alapaha joins the Suwannee, underground rivers bubble to the surface and then disappear.

The Trail enters Apalachicola National Forest, a flat region of slash pines. The sandy soils are fine and deep, supporting a shrubby undergrowth interspersed with many shallow swamps. The trees are a Southern gathering: longleaf pine, pond cypress, slash pine, black gum, sweetgum, red maple, shortleaf pine, water oak, tuliptree and magnolia. Here the holes in the sand belong to a "salamander" that is in fact no amphibian but a ground squirrel much like the Western ground squirrel. The so-called glass snake and the swift, both in fact lizards, dart over the low plants; loggerhead shrikes post themselves on bare limbs above bushes to hunt prey. The Trail crosses the Apalachicola River, wends past the Dead Lakes, and terminates in Panama City on the Gulf of Mexico, ten feet above sea level.

Insects along the Florida Trail are more abundant, more varied, and zanier than on any other national trail. The giant water tiger that comes to the flashlight at night is a cause for horror. The sicklelike jaws of the larval stage injects a chemical that breaks down the innards of frogs and fish into a soup which the insect sucks up through its straw-like beak. Flying all along the Trail are armadas of dragonflies, a welcome army for walkers since they swoop and devour clouds of mosquitoes. In spring thousands of love-bugs hatch, seize mates, and flock over the Trail, never letting go until death. Locusts, katydids, and walking-stick insects are numerous on the Trail, and the mole cricket makes long tunnels in the sandy wetlands. Butterflies here are easily recognized by the plants they live upon.

In the swamps near Panama City the water is so black with tannin that its surface becomes a silver mirror reflecting water-lilies and the clouds overhead. Primitive voices call, owls hoot, and the Florida Trail ends in a land that seems like the beginning of the world.

Highways Crossed by the Florida Trail

U. S. Highway 41
State Highway 84
State Highway 80
U. S. Highway 27
State Highway 70
Parallel along U. S. 441
Interstate 4
Florida Turnpike
U. S. Highway 441

State Highway 42
State Highway 40
U. S. Highway 301
Interstate 10
U. S. Highway 441
Interstate 75
Interstate 10
U. S. Highway 98

Bibliography and Maps

BARBOUR, THOMAS. *That Vanishing Eden: A Naturalist's Florida.* New York: G. P. Putnam's Sons, 1944.

CRAIGHEAD, FRANK C., SR. *Orchids and Other Airplants.* Miami: University of Miami Press, 1963.

———. *The Trees of South Florida: The Natural Environments and Their Succession.* Miami: University of Miami Press, 1971.

FLORIDA TRAIL ASSOCIATION, INC., 4410 N. W. 18th Place, Gainesville, Florida. Maps covering the Florida Trail are available from this source.

GEORGE, JEAN CRAIGHEAD. *Everglades Wildguide.* Washington: National Park Service, Office of Publications, 1972.

HOTCHKISS, NEIL. *Common Marsh, Underwater and Floating-Leaved Plants.* Toronto: General Publishing Company, 1970.

MCILHENNY, E. A. *The Alligator's Life History.* Boston: Christopher Publishing House, 1935.

PETERSON, ROGER TORY. A *Field Guide to the Birds.* Boston: Houghton Mifflin Company, 1968.

SIMPSON, CHARLES TORREY. *Florida Wildlife.* New York: Macmillan, 1932.

WRIGHT, ALBERT HAZEN, and ANNA ALLEN WRIGHT. *Handbook of Frogs and Toads.* Ithaca, N. Y.: Comstock Publishing House, 1949.

8

O ne of the longer trails, the North Country Trail forms
the first transcontinental footpath by leaving the Adirondack Mountains in New York, looping around the Lake
States and joining the Lewis and Clark Trail in North Dakota,
thus linking together over 6000 miles of foot trail that will eventually go from ocean to ocean.

In the near future the Trail will traverse parts of Maine, New
Hampshire, and Vermont. At present it goes through New York,
Pennsylvania, Ohio, Michigan, northern Michigan, Wisconsin and
Minnesota, meets the Lewis and Clark Trail in North Dakota, thus
tying Montana, Idaho, Washington, and Oregon to the cross-
country path. (The Lewis and Clark Trail is described in Part Two,
Historical Trails.)

The concept of the North Country Trail originated in 1920 in
the offices of the Lake Central Region of the U. S. Bureau of Outdoor Recreation at Ann Arbor, Michigan. A green strip 200 feet
wide and 3246 miles long, it links many old logging roads, footpaths, ski and hunting trails that lace through the boreal forests
of the north country.

The Trail passes within fifty miles of a total of thirteen million
people living in Syracuse, Rochester, Buffalo, Youngstown, Pittsburgh, Akron, Columbus, Lansing, Grand Rapids, Traverse City,
Marquette, Duluth, and Fargo, furthering the dream of Benton
MacKaye, "to bring beauty to people confined to the mechanized
cities."

* For information about biotic communities along this trail see pages 260–261, 270,
272–274, 283.

The North Country Trail is moderately tough to walk although not as difficult as the Pacific Crest, the Continental Divide, or the Appalachian, but it does seek out points of interest and outstanding scenery that may demand short spurts of effort. Since the route is almost entirely through glaciated country, it is rocky and cumbersome to walk in places. Geological Survey maps give the best information on the roughness of the terrain.

After leaving the Adirondack Mountains in New York the Trail goes over sedimentary sea beds that are 500 million years old. Out of this rock the glaciers have carved the Finger Lakes; the Allegheny Mountains of Pennsylvania have buckled up to expose more of it, and it also rims the Great Lakes. In Wisconsin, Minnesota, and eastern North Dakota, the sedimentary layers give way to igneous and metamorphic rocks.

The biotic areas, however, are what give the North Country Trail its special flavor. It winds among spruces and firs, the pointed trees of the Northeastern Coniferous Forest that are the hallmark of the North Country Trail. It also penetrates the Eastern Pine Forest, a biome that supports one of the earth's rarest birds, the jack pine warbler, which nests only in jack pines in Roscommon County, Michigan. In Ohio, the oaks and hickories of the Midland Broadleaf Forest shade the Trail, and in North Dakota the Tall-Grass Prairie surrounds it.

At this writing a volunteer group of people were walking the Trail for the first time. Since the Trail is not continuously blazed, a compass and map from the Bureau of Outdoor Recreation are required to get from point to point.

The North Country Trail begins as of this writing at Crown Point on Lake Champlain in the Adirondack Mountains, off *State Highway* 22, and meanders across *Interstate* 87 and *State Highway* 30 through birch, beech, hemlock, and sugar-maple forests floored with partridgeberry, ferns, and orchids. The mountain summits are tipped with balsam fir and spruce. The Trail seeks out clear trout streams, where black bears walk and white-tailed deer pause to drink. Wild turkeys are numerous, and along the high parts of the Trail in the Adirondacks the fisher and pine marten dart along tree branches.

Walkers in spring and fall may spot golden eagles soaring overhead as they climb Mt. Marcy to the Lake Tear-in-the-Clouds, the

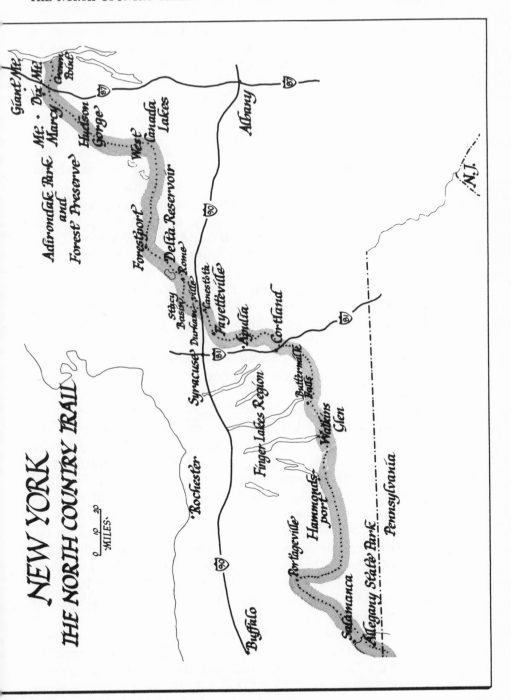

NEW YORK
THE NORTH COUNTRY TRAIL

source of the Hudson River. The Trail leaves the Adirondacks on the Old Black River Canal Trail, crosses *State Highway 12*, passes through Rome, New York, and takes the Erie Canal Towpath to Fayetteville.

Just beyond this summertime town the NCT joins the Finger Lakes System of paths, crossing *U. S. Highway 20*, and plunges into the soft light of the hemlock forest that grows along the Trail from Buttermilk Falls to Taughannock to Watkins Glen and *State Highway 14*. In summer the veeries and thrushes sing almost continuously around the cascades in these gorges of shale.

West of the Finger Lakes Region the North Country Trail winds for about fifty miles through several small parks before it enters Allegheny State Park on the south side of *State Highway 17* near Salamanca, a good place to pick up the Trail for a walk among stately trees.

After approximately twenty miles, the Trail crosses the Pennsylvania line and the Allegheny National Forest, as well as *State Highway 59*, to meander down the east side of the Allegheny Reservoir. A one-mile side trip to Tionesta for the sight of 400-year-old hemlocks and a 300-year-old beech, remains of primitive America, becomes a breathtaking experience. The Trail here is easy and refreshing.

Leaving the Allegheny National Forest, the Trail passes near the village of Maple Creek and enters Cook Forest State Park on the existing Baker Trail. It comes to the largest stand of virgin white pine and hemlock remaining in Pennsylvania, a fragment of William Penn's primeval woods that is now a National Natural Landmark. The Trail edges the Clarion River, crosses *Interstate 80*, and reaches the confluence of the Clarion and Allegheny rivers. At Parker, off *State Highway 58*, it enters Moraine State Park on the forested Allegheny plateau, and follows the Glacier Ridge Trail. Continuing west, the NCT crosses *State Highway 8*, winds along Slippery Rock Creek through McConnell's Mill State Park, and arrives at the spray-slippery rocks that give the rushing white-water creek its name.

The Trail now enters Ohio, crossing *Interstate 76* and *State Highway 31* along Little Beaver Creek, a wild river that should be part of the National Wild and Scenic Rivers System. This is the only unglaciated part of the Trail and can be recognized by its

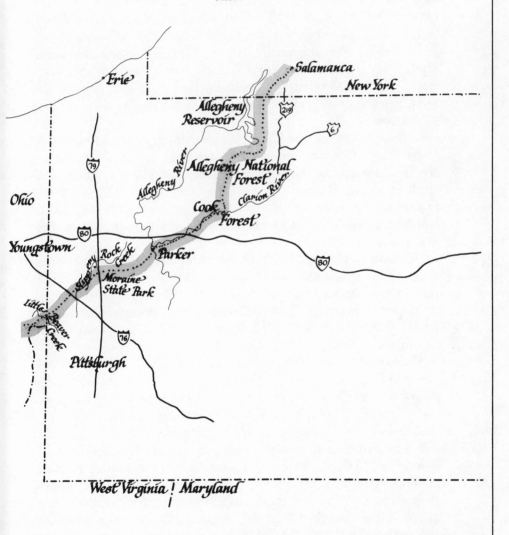

PENNSYLVANIA
THE NORTH COUNTRY TRAIL

0   10   20
·MILES·

Erie

Salamanca

New York

Allegheny
Reservoir

219

6

Allegheny River

79

Allegheny National
Forest

Clarion River

Ohio

Cook
Forest

80

Youngstown

Slippery Rock Creek

Parker

80

Moraine
State Park

Little Beaver Creek

76

Pittsburgh

West Virginia | Maryland

steep valleys and narrow ridges. Several niches of vegetation are to be found in the rollercoaster terrain: beech–maple on the slopes, oak–hickory on the drier ridges, maple–elm–sycamore in the flood plains. Hemlocks will be found on their favored site, a steep slope with rock outcroppings in a ravine with flowing water.

A restored grain mill and covered bridge are located in Beaver Creek State Park, on *State Highway 7*. Along the Creek are remnants of the Sandy and Beaver Canal, a feeder channel to the Ohio–Erie Canal. The Trail follows the canal to Zoar, an easy and picturesque walk, where many restored houses and stores depict the Zoar of 1817, when it became the first communal settlement in the United States. Here the North Country merges with the Buckeye Trail, which unfortunately spends much of its length along highways. Most walkers prefer to take the Ohio–Erie Canal from Zoar to Zoarsville.

Leaving the canal, the Trail meanders through the Muskingum Conservancy District—one of the oldest such districts in the country. The forests are speckled with lakes; wildflowers, birds, and small mammals abound. On down the Trail at Leesville, on *State Highway 212*, is a station of the underground railroad which, before the Civil War, sheltered escaped slaves en route to freedom in Canada.

Continuing through lakeland and hills into Wayne National Forest and across *State Highway 78*, the North Country Trail follows the Little Muskingum River to the Ohio River, then swings north across *Interstate 77* to Marietta; the first permanent settlement in Ohio, dating to 1788, it was named after Queen Marie Antoinette of France.

Through Wayne State Forest (*State Highway 13*) the Trail crosses *U. S. 33* and enters Hocking Hills State Park, traversing deep gorges cut by waterfalls and passing underneath old sycamores and hemlocks. The massive rock formations are riddled with caves that shelter ants, snakes, bears, and salamanders.

A localized climate of high rainfall that makes this area unusual dramatically affects the forest cover. In the cool, moist ravines, hemlocks and yews dominate and ferns grow verdantly. The slopes support hardwoods, and the hilltops are covered with plantations of red, white, and Scotch pines. Conkle's Hollow is a spectacular spot with walls of rock 250 feet high enclosing a narrow canyon.

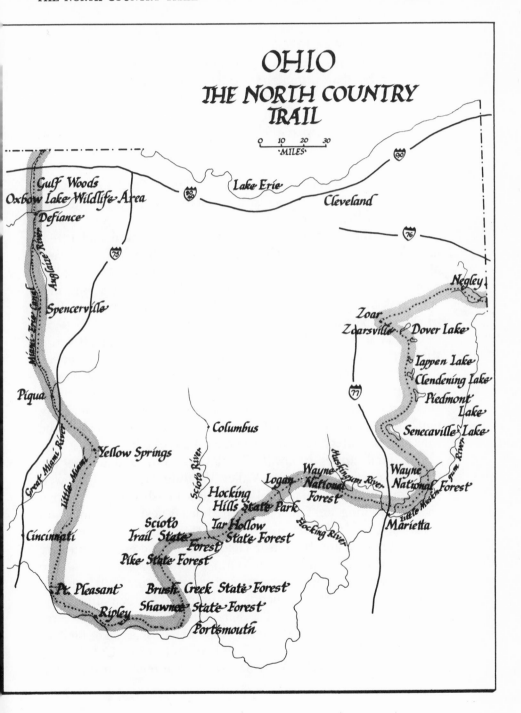

OHIO
THE NORTH COUNTRY TRAIL

0 10 20 30
·MILES·

Gulf Woods
Oxbow Lake Wildlife Area
Defiance

Lake Erie
Cleveland

Auglaize River
Miami-Erie Canal

Spencerville

Negley

Zoar
Zoarsville Dover Lake

Piqua

Tappen Lake
Clendening Lake
Piedmont
Lake
Senecaville Lake

Great Miami River
Little Miami River

Yellow Springs

Columbus

Scioto River

Muskingum River

Wayne
National
Forest

Wayne
National Forest

Little Muskingum River

Logan

Hocking
Hills State Park

Cincinnati

Scioto
Trail State
Forest

Tar Hollow
State Forest

Hocking River

Marietta

Pike State Forest

Pt. Pleasant

Brush Creek State Forest
Shawnee State Forest

Ripley

Portsmouth

The Trail takes the walker through Tar Hollow, Scioto Trail Park, and Pike State Forest, then on to Shawnee State Forest, the largest contiguous woodland remaining in Ohio. This rugged, densely forested area, sometimes called "Ohio's Little Smokies," is alive with birds and deep-forest wildflowers.

The bluffs above the Ohio River beyond *State Highway 125*, with their broad view of the river valley and of the distant hills of Kentucky, are cut into rugged unglaciated hills and descend to a gently rolling land called the Flats.

About midway across the Flats is Point Pleasant, General Ulysses S. Grant's birthplace, a state memorial, off *U. S. Highway 52* near New Richmond.

Leaving the Ohio River, the Trail juts northward and comes into Perintown, on *U. S. Highway 50*, where beside the east fork of the Little Miami River the Cincinnati Nature Center displays plants of the Midland Broadleaf Forest. Squirrels, raccoons, and opossums live in this flood plain together with woodpeckers, jays, hawks and sparrows.

The Trail follows the Little Miami National Scenic River, a stream that flows alternately through deep gorges and steep wooded slopes past pleasant farmlands and small towns. Near Lebanon is Fort Ancient Indians where a prehistoric people constructed three-part earth enclosures in which the dead were buried. A museum, much like those to be found on the Natchez Trace, displays the tribe's tools, pottery, ornaments, and methods of burial.

The Trail crosses *Interstate 71* at Glendower and follows the Little Miami into the Spring Valley Wildlife Area, a natural wetland containing a semi-natural lake and a marsh where waterfowl abound in spring and fall. The footpath leads next into John Bryan State Park, off *U. S. Highway 68*, then to the Clifton Gorge State Nature Preserve and the Great Helen Nature Preserve. From here it passes through gently rolling farm country on sections of the Miami–Erie Canal, which served as the main route of transportation until the mid-1800s, when it was outdated by the railroads.

The Trail crosses a region of flat, fertile farmland where corn, wheat, oats, and hay are the main crops, then passes lakes built to provide the old canal with water, and comes to Deep Cut Park, at Spencerville off *State Highway 81*. Now a National Historic Landmark, this 6600-foot-long excavation was dug by hand as part of the Miami–Erie Canal project in Ohio's Great Black Swamp.

A post-glacial swamp, it came into existence as part of the Glacial Lake Maumee which occupied much of northwestern Ohio and the eastern edge of Indiana about ten thousand years ago. Once thickly forested and dotted with bogs and pools of water, this was the last area in Ohio to be settled, after extensive drainage and timber cutting made it tillable.

The Trail continues northward, crossing U. S. Highway 30 and State Highway 613, into the Oxbow Lake Wildlife Area northwest of Defiance, on U. S. Highway 24. Here cattails and rushes make habitats for frogs, turtles, snakes, and waterfowl. Near Stryker, south of the Ohio Turnpike and close to the Ohio–Michigan border, the path enters foreboding Goll Woods, a virgin swamp–forest of oak and cottonwood, where toads and mushrooms abound.

The Trail comes into Michigan along Bean Creek in rolling farm country. Originally this area was heavily forested, but by 1870 most of the handsome hardwoods had been logged. Today the land is planted mainly to corn, wheat, and hay. U. S. Highway 12 meets the Trail at Jonesville, follows the St. Joseph River for about five miles, and then heads south.

Near Albion and Interstate 94, the Trail crosses the Kalamazoo River to enter a lush farming valley that produces celery, onions, apples, and grapes as well as wheat and barley. At first soft, open, and rolling, the terrain becomes more rugged as it reaches the forested Barry County State Game Area and Yankee Springs Recreation Complex (State Highway 37). Along the Trail is an active sugar bush where maple sap is collected in February and boiled into syrup and candy.

Heading northward along the Thornapple River, the North Country Trail (reached here from Interstate 96) stays east of Grand Rapids, Michigan's second largest city, following the Thornapple to the magnificent Rogue River and then crossing U. S. Highway 131 into Manistee National Forest. The Muskegon River is crossed at Croton, in an area rich with logging history and Paul Bunyan stories. Then the Trail crosses State Highway 20 and enters an area known as the Big Prairie. Once covered by forest, then cleared as farmland, the soil has now been rendered useless for

several square miles by wind-driven sand. The blowing sands have killed trees, covered houses, and even buried fences installed to control them. Despite reforestation efforts in hope of controlling the sand, most of the area remains simply as a vivid object lesson on the effects of the axe and plow.

From the Big Prairie, the Trail leads through roadless miles to the headwaters of the White Water, a river of dashing ripples and falls freckled with canoes in spring and summer. Then it heads northwest to Ludington, north of whose Pump Storage Project it begins to parallel the shoreline of Lake Michigan, finally taking to the sandy beaches and dunes off *U. S. Highway 31*. On the landward side, picturesque fruit orchards and pastureland are intermixed with woodland all the way to Bear Lake reached from *U. S. Highway 31*. Here the Trail enters an inland area once forested with majestic white pines, which elderly people in the area still talk about. Today jack and red pine have replaced the stately trees that were logged off in the early 1900s.

For a short distance the North Country Trail joins the Shore-to-Shore Riding and Hiking Trail, which crosses the state from east to west, to enter the deciduous Kalkaska State Forest, off *U. S. Highway 131*. To the north about thirty miles, the Trail passes several ski areas near Boyne City and Boyne Falls, near the range of the only elk herd in Michigan. The walker should be on the alert for the musty odor that betrays the presence of the big deer.

Striking into the Michilimackinac Wilderness, the NCT comes to the five-mile-long Mackinac Bridge familiarly called the "Big Mac," which connects the lower and upper peninsulas of Michigan. Once a year, on Labor Day, it can be crossed on foot. On any other day the walker must board a shuttlebus, or take a ferry via Mackinac Island. On the other side of Lake Michigan, entering the Hiawatha National Forest at the *U. S. Highway 2* and *Interstate 75*, the walker comes upon clear Brevoort Lake in which dwell pike, bass, and panfish. The Trail goes around marsh areas, over sand dunes, and into a second growth of Northern hardwoods, jack and red pines. Then it crosses *State Highway 28*, skirts Whitefish Bay, and arrives in Tahquamenon State Park, noted for two dramatic waterfalls. The Upper Falls cascade to a forty-foot drop along a sweeping two-hundred-foot semicircle framed by huge sandstone walls. The Lower Falls form a dancing lacework of cascades that flow

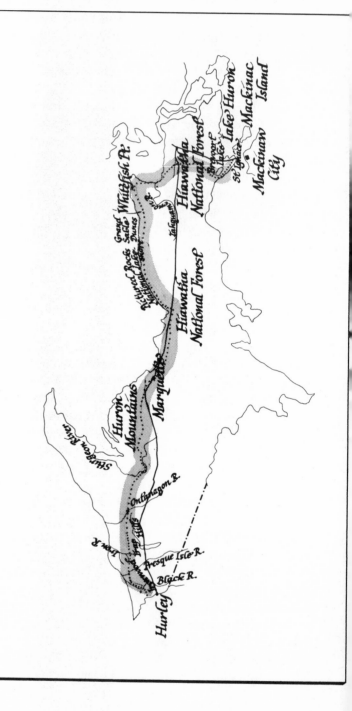

UPPER MICHIGAN
THE NORTH COUNTRY TRAIL

0 10 20
MILES·

around a jade-green island. *State Highway 123* leads to this splashing wonder.

Cutting across Whitefish Point, the North Country Trail now follows the southern shore of Lake Superior to the Pictured Rocks National Lakeshore, where a series of multicolored cliffs rise straight from the cold blue water. The view from the top of water, rocks, and pointed trees is the North Country at its most dramatic. From here the walker is plunged into devastation at Kingston Plain, once a cathedral of virgin white pine but now reduced to stumps.

Traversing high ridges with intermittent views of Lake Superior, the Trail wanders through open fields in a Northern hardwood forest of maple, beech, ash, basswood, yellow and canoe birch. Mixed in thickly with the hardwoods are the trees of the northland, white and black spruce, balsam fir, and Northern white cedar. Gradually, the vegetation changes to Northeastern Coniferous Forest as the Trail wends north.

The landscape is all primeval as the Trail winds southwest of Marquette and takes off, with barely a road to cross, for the Sturgeon River. Along the way are lakes, streams, and swamps inhabited by goshawk, bald eagle, ruffed grouse, gray jay, raven, hermit thrush, golden-crowned kinglet, various warblers, and many species of waterfowl.

Taking to the banks of the Sturgeon River for about ten miles, the Trail winds through stands of jack pine, on the flat and sandy Baraga Plains to Ontonagon River in the Ottawa National Forest. On down the path lies Victoria, a ghost town now, but a lively copper mining town in the 1800s.

The reddish-brown Iron River is crossed as the Trail skirts the southern edge of Porcupine Mountains Wilderness State Park, which contains some of the wildest country in the Midwest. Glacial dumps rising 1500 feet interspersed with deep scourings make the Trail a rollercoaster whose streams and rivers are the walker's reward for traversing it. The Trail now cuts through stands of white pine, hemlock, and Northern hardwoods. Here the North Country unfolds in all its primeval beauty. There are stands of virgin timber in several places, and salmon rise to the fly near the mouths of the streams.

From the Porcupines the Trail crosses the Presque Isle River, proposed as a State Wilderness river, and heads east, skirting the

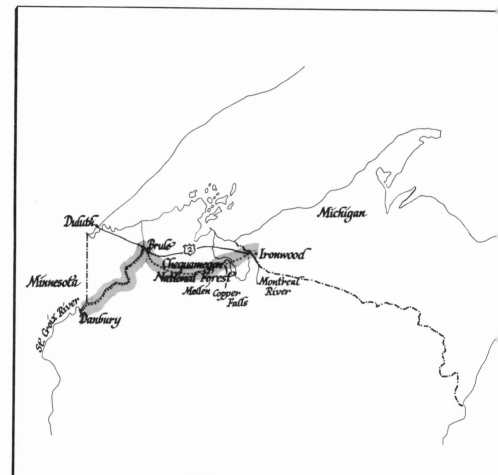

WISCONSIN
THE NORTH COUNTRY TRAIL

0   10   20
MILES·

Black River. The last section of the Trail in Michigan follows the ridges of Gogebic Mountain Range, then crosses *U. S. Highway* 2 into Ironwood and over the Montreal River into Wisconsin.

It takes off again north of Hurley, beyond *U. S. Highway 51*, teetering along the Gabbro–Panokee–Gogebic Iron Range, eighty miles long and half a mile wide; it passes waterfalls, sheer gorges, cliffs, and rock outcrops that churn the water into ribbons and lace. At Copper Falls State Park, off *State Highway 169*, the footpath comes into Mellen, at *State Highway 13*, and seeks out two glorious waterfalls in the rocky gorge of Bad River.

The next sixty miles are in the dense Chequamegon National Forest, where the terrain is rolling-to-rugged, off *U. S. Highway 63*. Here on the Penokee Mountains some of the grades are long and steep, and in places, must be scrambled up. Radiant as these woods are in late spring and early summer with wildflowers, and alive with birds, to avoid being eaten alive by insects it is best to wait until summer or fall to walk this part of the Trail. The hardwoods along the path are primarily sugar maple, which together with the aspen and birch set the forest aflame with a red, yellow, and orange in September and October. By November winter has set in, and with the onset of the snow this section of the North Country Trail becomes a paradise for cross-country skiing and snowshoeing.

Beyond the Chequamegon National Forest, on a high rocky point off *U. S. Highway 2* from which there is a broad view of the valley, the Trail meets the Brule River. Passing an old copper mine near Brule, it enters what was in the 1700s a Chippewa-Sioux battleground where the Chippewa (or Ojibwa) won their claim to the territory. Arrowheads, spearheads, and musket balls can still be found near the community of Winneboujou.

Going south on an ancient Indian footpath along the Bois Brule River, the North Country Trail crosses the St. Croix Portage, made famous by the voyageurs at *U. S. Highway 53* near Solon Springs. From here it takes to the north bank of the beautiful St. Croix River. Managed by the National Park Service, this wilderness river area is a dramatic series of high rock bluffs, low marshes, and sandy hummocks. The trees change from a mix of conifers and Northern hardwoods to one of swamp species. In the river swirl trout, smallmouth bass, muskelunge, and sturgeon. White-tailed deer, moose, black bear, cottontail rabbit, snowshoe hare, raccoon,

MINNESOTA
THE NORTH COUNTRY TRAIL

gray squirrel, coyote, red and gray fox, mink, muskrat, otter, and beaver haunt the shallows. As with all of the Northern lake country, the upper St. Croix has a history of Indian presence, logging, farming, and fire.

Crossing the St. Croix River at Danbury, on *State Highway 35*, the walker comes into Minnesota on a northward course through Nemadji State Forest and the Nemadji River. Wandering through the Jay Cooke State Park, one of the largest state parks in Minnesota, east and south of *Interstate 35*, the Trail passes around the Fond du Lac Indian Reservation and comes upon the Savonna and Sandy Lake Fur Post, used by the voyageurs of the eighteenth century.

The Trail arrives at the Mississippi River and looks down on a route once used by steamboats, off *State Highway 232*. Old landings, locks, and a lock-keeper's house are still in existence at Sandy Lake, where the Trail follows the Mississippi north of Ball Bluff, then heads west for Hill River State Forest, famous for its scenic timber, and the Moosewillow Wildlife Area. Here moose, cows, bulls, and calves stand hock-deep in lily-pads, geese graze, and ducks dabble.

Around numerous lakes the NCT skirts the edge of the Chippewa National Forest and Leech Lake Indian Reservation, once the home of the Chippewa Indians. A sophisticated people and one of the largest Algonquin tribes, they hunted, planted crops, gathered wild rice, and lived in loosely federated villages, occasionally warring with their neighbors the Sioux and Fox. In the eighteenth century trappers, loggers, and settlers all but eliminated the Chippewa. A few live here today near the burial mounds and battlefields of their ancestors.

Crossing the forested hills, the North Country Trail crosses *State Highway 371* and loops north through Paul Bunyan State Forest across *U. S. Highway 71* to Lake Itasca, the source of the Mississippi River. During the migratory seasons the lake is dark with waterfowl menaced from the sky above by hawks and falcons. The trail crosses *State Highway 34*, east of the town of Detroit Lakes, proceeds to Frazee, crosses *U. S. Highway 10*, and winds for more than sixty miles around glacial lakes in wild boreal country.

On its way to the North Dakota border the NCT passes the Bradbury homestead and a ghost town, three miles west of Fergas, on *Interstate 94*. Then it strikes out along the Otter Tail River and across the open prairie, now extensively farmed. It crosses into North Dakota at Breckinridge on *U. S. Highway 75*. Almost instantly the North Country Trail becomes open and flat. The path goes up the Red River Valley, crossing the bed of ancient Lake Agassiz, which millions of years ago was larger than all the Great Lakes combined, filling the entire region of the Northern Plains. Today the area is planted to sugar beets, grain, potatoes, and giant sunflowers. Here the Trail is ancient and brand-new both at once.

For thousands of years this area west of the Red River of the North had been Sioux land. With the arrival of white settlers, the Army built a series of forts from St. Paul to Montana. One of these, Fort Abercrombie, on *Interstate 29*, was constructed in 1858 and marks the gateway to the Great Plains. Everywhere now the Trail is haunted by the tragic extinction of the great Sioux tribes. Beyond, the route works its way through wooded glacial valleys to the Anselm and takes to the bank of the Sheyenne River, where sycamores and maples thrive in a sandhill setting.

In a magnificent 50-mile stretch between Kindred and Anselm basswoods grow to vaulting heights, along with many shrubs and grasses unique to North Dakota. All are threatened by the proposed Kindred Reservoir.

The Trail cuts across the Sheyenne National Grasslands, one of the last remnants of the Tall-Grass Prairie in North Dakota. The grasses are the big and little bluestem and, on the uplands, needlegrass and dropseed.

Beyond the National Grasslands, the North Country Trail rejoins the Sheyenne River, runs past the old Fort Ransom Historic Site, and arrives at Clausen Springs. Here along the Sheyenne in 1853 the prairie Indians held a council to protest the white man's trespass on their treaty rights.

The Trail continues up the Sheyenne River into Hobart Lake National Wildlife Refuge and through Valley City, on *Interstate 94*. Some fifty miles to the north, south of Devils Lake, the largest natural lake in North Dakota, it enters the Fort Totten Indian Reservation. Here dwell blue geese and snow geese, the waterfowl of the north. Herds of elk, deer, and buffalo are tended at Sully's Hill National Game Preserve adjacent to the lake; then the Trail comes into Fort Totten, reached by *State Highway 57*,

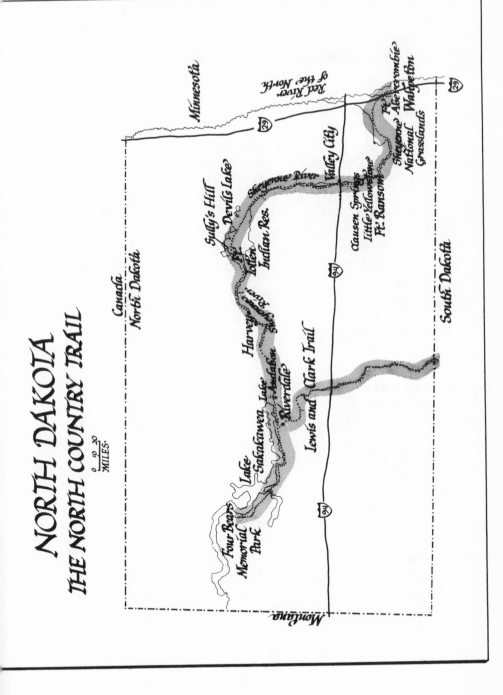

NORTH DAKOTA
THE NORTH COUNTRY TRAIL

0 10 20
MILES.

Canada
North Dakota

Montana

South Dakota

Minnesota

Red River of the North

Four Bears Memorial Park

Lake Sakakawea

Riverdale

Lewis and Clark Trail

Harvey

Fort Totten Indian Res.

Sully's Hill

Devils Lake

Sheyenne River

Valley City

Clausen Springs

Little Yellowstone

Ft. Ransom

Sheyenne National Grasslands

Ft. Abercrombie

Wahpeton

29

94

94

29

which has the only preserved original cavalry square in the United States.

Heading west, the North Country Trail passes through Harvey and leaves the Sheyenne River to cross miles of prairie and to circle Lake Audubon, in the Riverdale Game Management Area. Crossing *U. S. Highway 83* it meets the Missouri River at Garrison Dam, which formed Lake Sakakawea. Here in the shade of the cottonwoods is the eastern terminus of the North Country Trail as proposed, but most walkers continue along the lake to Four Bears Memorial Park, a roadless natural landscape at the western end of the lake, off *State Highway 23*. Deer and antelope nibble the grasses; ducks, geese, swans, and pelicans dabble in the water. The rugged buttes, home of the Indians for centuries, are pitted with old villages, burial grounds, and battlefields.

For the cross-continental walker, at this quiet spot the Lewis and Clark Trail begins as he points his boots west toward the Pacific Ocean.

Interstate Routes Crossed by the North Country Trail

New York:
  Interstate 87
  Interstate 90
  Interstate 81

Pennsylvania:
  Interstate 80
  Interstate 76
  Interstate 79

Ohio:
  Interstate 70
  Interstate 77
  Interstate 71
  Interstate 75
  Interstate 80

Michigan:
  Interstate 69
  Interstate 94
  Interstate 96
  Interstate 75

Wisconsin:
  None

Minnesota:
  Interstate 35
  Interstate 94

North Dakota:
  Interstate 29
  Interstate 94

Bibliography and Maps

BROCKMAN, FRANK C. *Trees of North America: A Guide to Field Identification.* New York: Golden Press, 1968.

KORTRIGHT, FRANCIS H. *The Ducks, Geese and Swans of North America.* Harrisburg, Pa.: The Stackpole Press, 1942.

ROBBINS, CHANDLER S., BERTEL BRUUN, and HERBERT S. ZIM. *Birds of North America: A Guide to Field Identification.* New York: Golden Press, 1966.

U. S. FOREST SERVICE, EASTERN REGION, 633 West Wisconsin Avenue, Milwaukee, Wisconsin 53203. Maps showing trails in New York, Pennsylvania, Ohio, Michigan, Wisconsin, and Minnesota are available from this source. (Note: State Departments of Recreation in the respective capital cities of these states will also supply maps on request.)

U.S. DEPARTMENT OF THE INTERIOR, BUREAU OF OUTDOOR RECREATION. *Final Impact Statement: The North Country Trail, A Potential Addition to the National Trails System.* Washington. Available from the Bureau's Lake Central Regional Office, 3853 Research Park Drive, Ann Arbor, Michigan 48104.

9

In northwestern Arizona the Colorado River has cut a 900,000-acre chasm, one mile deep and twenty miles across. This is the Grand Canyon of the Colorado River. Between the two rims lies a paradise for walkers in search of spectacular vistas. Round towers of rock are carved into temples; mammoth anvils sit on blue plateaus; staircase cliffs and slopes descend a thousand feet at one drop. Here panoramas begin at the edges of cliffs and unfold almost beyond the reach of comprehension.

The trails are moderately hazardous not because of the elevation, which is flat on the plateaus and graded into 10° inclines on the developed trails in and out of the canyon, but because of the heat. In summer the temperature of the Inner Canyon is often more than 110°F. Dehydration, heat exhaustion, and sunstroke befall many people who walk the Grand Canyon trails without suitable precautions. At least a gallon of water per day is needed by a walker in this desert. Springs, streams, and water pipes are spaced along the developed Bright Angel Trail; but water must be carried on approximately twenty-five other trails, including the Hermit Trail, the Louis Boucher Trail, Grandview and Horseshoe Mesa trails, the Bass Trail, and the one to the Havasupai Indian village. These all start on the rim. Inner Gorge hikes are for the experts.

Ruins of adobe houses deep in the canyon date back to the 1200s. The Grand Canyon was first seen by European man in 1540 when a Spaniard, García Lopez de Cardenas, was sent from Zuñi, New Mexico by Francisco Vásquez de Coronado, his commander, in

---

* For information about biotic communities along this trail see drawings on pages 281–282.

144

search of a mysterious "large river" to the west that had been reported. Guided by Hopi Indians, Cardenas and his twelve men reached its rim and fell on their knees before the chasm.

For three hundred years afterward the canyon was all but forgotten by white men. Then, in 1857, Lieutenant Joseph C. Ives went up from the lower course of the river, was stopped by the sheer walls, and finally reached the chasm by pack train. After wandering over some of the platforms he returned to Washington to write his report. "Ours has been the first and will probably be the last party of whites to visit this profitless country of the Hopi Indians," he wrote. "It seems intended by nature that the Colorado River, along the greater portion of its lonely way, shall be forever unvisited and undisturbed."

It remained for John Wesley Powell, a one-armed veteran of the Civil War, to explore and chart the river's course through the canyon. In May 1869 he started down the Green River in Wyoming along with nine men in four small wooden rowboats. The ten ran the boiling rapids and emerged three months later at the end of the Grand Canyon, dispelling forever rumors of a dreaded "lost course" underground.

On subsequent expeditions Powell brought William H. Holmes to the Grand Canyon to portray the chasm in drawings of intricate accuracy. Later Thomas Moran painted its beauty for the National Gallery of Art.

Some of the canyon's mystery having been dispelled, a succession of miners and explorers visited it during the late nineteenth and early twentieth centuries. Relics of their efforts to conquer the abyss, such as wooden buildings and iron tools, can be seen on mesas and buttes. Moran's paintings of the canyon brought tourists as early the 1880s, and in 1890 William W. Bass established a tourist camp, cut a trail from rim to rim, and strung a cableway across the river.

In 1819 about 600,000 acres of the Grand Canyon were declared a national park. Since that date millions of Americans have visited a spectacle that President Theodore Roosevelt declared "every American should see."

For walkers, of all the names connected with the Grand Canyon, that of Dr. Harvey Butchart is the most renowned. A professor of mathematics, he has walked nearly 15,000 miles of canyon trails, mapping and studying its stones, waters, and wildlife.

Geology and earth history are the essence of the Grand Canyon trails, which descend from modern forests on the rim to the black Vishnu schist at the bottom. As you pass through layer after layer, you walk back through three billion years to the roots of old mountains that were eroded away three times before life on earth even began. The story of the earth as you go down the Trail reads like this: marine shells and corals; sand dunes with tracks of primitive reptiles or amphibians; insect wings and primitive cone-bearing plants and ferns; flood-plain deposits with plants and the tracks of creeping land animals; shells and corals; fish scales; beach deposits with shells, seaweeds and crablike animals; old ripple marks, salt mounds, and sun cracks; limy plants which are the first trace of life; the once molten bedrock.

The biotic zone of the Grand Canyon is largely desert. One hundred feet below the rim, the junipers thin out and the Grand Canyon biota begins. Cacti, yucca, manzanita, and grasses are scattered over the blazing rocks, together with white thistle and an occasional delphinium. Ninety or so animal species dwell in the canyon, including mountain lions, bighorn sheep, burros, lizards, and in wet streambeds and along the riverside, toads, frogs, and fish.

The Bright Angel Trail, which runs from the north to the south rim, over a distance of approximately twenty-four miles, is the footpath for walkers. A few go from the north to the south rim in one day, two days is more sensible; but even a week is hardly long enough to appreciate this marvel.

The Trail begins among Western yellow pines and Engelmann spruces. On the north rim lives the rare Kaibab squirrel, a black tree squirrel with tasseled ears and a white tail that is found only on the approximately 30-by-70-mile area of the Kaibab Plateau in Arizona. Automobile traffic, disease, and fire prevention once brought the squirrel close to extinction but protection has now increased its numbers.

The easiest walk to the river and back is from the south rim and can be done in a day. Leaving the Tovar Hotel, the Trail switchbacks down two hundred feet through gnarled pinyons and junipers, past white limestone cliffs 225 million years old. At the bottom of the band the canyon's entire gamut of color—red, tan, purple, and gray—assaults the walker's eyes. The Trail winds down past a wall of gray, buff, and red sandstone. The colors change as the Trail drops approximately 900 feet through the Supai formation of red and gray sandstone and shale to the top of the Red Wall, a gray limestone stained red by iron ore. Below lies the mauve limestone and the greenish Bright Angel shale.

The Trail steepens and plunges to the Tonto Platform, the top of the 500-million-year-old Tapeats Sandstone layer, a brown band 225 feet deep. Under the Tapeats is Hakatai, a red-purple shale, and below this a black Vishnu schist, the ancient layer of the mountain roots that form the Inner Gorge of the Colorado River and is three billion years old. As the last eroded plain sank into the sea, it was covered first by a heavy layer of sand from ancient beaches and then, as rivers were gradually born, by layers of mud. Finally beaches of shells were formed, and these together with the sand and mud were changed into stone by pressure and heat. Fifty million years ago, powerful earth movements lifted the mile-deep layers of rock up out of the sea in the shape of a huge dome. Through this the Colorado River carved its way as it flowed to the sea.

Just before the Tonto Platform is an oasis, Indian Springs, with camp sites, enormous cottonwoods, hummingbirds, flowers and the cool refreshment of spilling water.

The trek to the bottom is short, steep, and hot, but walkers find relief by standing fully clothed under waterfalls that tumble down from Indian Springs. After a few minutes their clothing dries in the heat.

Then the roar of the river prevails, a muddy churning flow as cold as the air above it is hot. The average temperature of the Colorado River is about 52°F. A campsite is in view of the Phantom Ranch Suspension Bridge, which crosses the river to the tourist rest house by that name and to the fourteen-mile trail to the north rim.

Another well-known Grand Canyon route is the Tonto Trail, a three-month walk made famous by Colin Fletcher in his book, *The Man Who Walked Through Time.* He followed an old Indian footpath along the Tonto Platform from one end of the park to the other. The trail he took begins at Hualpai Hilltop on the far end of the West Rim Drive along the western edge of Grand Canyon

National Park. Nine miles down, past white limestone cliffs, sandstone, and shale, past cacti and crackling clumps of yucca, nestles the Havasupai Indian village. The escarpment on which it sits is a mammoth foundation for the buttes that tower above it. The Havasupai people (their name meaning "people of the blue-green waters") now live in wood and sheet-metal houses but cook outside just as their ancestors did. Gardens grow squash and vegetables, and they ride spirited horses under the enormous cottonwood trees that line the main street. Only horse and foot trails lead out of the village.

The Tonto Trail leaves the village and winds toward Mt. Sinyala, an immense natural Parthenon of limestone, rising a thousand feet above the Trail where it casts forbidding shadows at dawn and dusk and gleams white in the hot, brilliant sun of noon.

The Trail wends around Great Thumb Mesa to widely spaced trickles of water that seep out of smaller canyons. At these oases hummingbirds whir up from among the red monkeyflowers and the orange Indian paintbrushes. Yuccas spring from the thin soil, and from high rims burros and bighorn sheep look curiously down on the walkers below. Farther along, the cliffs of Fossil Bay seem to hang unsupported in space, then the trail rounds a bend, and the Colorado River flashes into view, moving like a line of thick brown paint within a vast frame of its own making.

Aztec Amphitheater, a colorful horseshoe of rock, brings the walker to Bass Camp and a footpath to the river, where the remains of the one-time cableway are to be seen. Here the rapids can just barely be heard, a faint roar in the distance; but the plants tell us the water is there. Prickly pears appear, then reeds and willows, and finally rushes and sedges, the water-loving plants of the river's edge. Looking up, the viewer beholds the massive stairs, tiers of stone that grow dimmer and more distant.

Walkers stand here saying nothing.

Back on the Tonto Platform, where the sparse rain collects in pockets, yellow agave flowers bloom not only petals, but seemingly also bees and butterflies. Quail hide in the shade and the pink canyon rattler, boldly unafraid of man, comes out on the rocks to sun itself.

The Tonto Trail intercepts the Bright Angel Trail across the river from the Phantom Ranch hotel. Most walkers from the north rim spend the night here before returning to the surface. Others cross the cable bridge, a spider-web in the gloom, and climb out the south rim.

Back on the Tonto Trail, after a walk of many hot miles, a narrow footpath emerges leading to an abandoned mining site on the top of Horseshoe Mesa. Rusty machinery, weathered timbers, and tumbled stone buildings occupy this empty stage, sole remaining actors in a futile drama. Beyond the mesa, the Tonto Platform tilts to bring the walker down onto Beaver Sand Bar, not far from the Little Colorado. Here the beavers, who so rarely see people that they are totally fearless, cut willows and work on their lodges side by side with the human visitors.

In this green spot Colin Fletcher tallied the wildlife—white-footed deer mouse, mountain lion, coyote, canyon rattler, toads, catfish, trout, several kinds of dragonflies, and a sandfly. He also counted the age of the spot, two billion years.

Beyond Beaver Sand Bar, Fletcher blazed a new trail to the Little Colorado River, following a precipitous ledge of red shale. In doing so, he became the first white man to walk from one end of the park to the other.

A mile up the Little Colorado stands the Sipapu, a huge mound created by a subterranean spring out of which the Hopi people believe their ancestors to have emerged.

Over boulders and sand, past blowing dunes, manzanita, and cacti, the Trail comes to the prehistoric cliff dwellings of the Grand Canyon. Built high on the sheer wall, they face the river and the vast chasm.

A few miles farther on, the Nakoweap Trail begins to climb the 6000 feet to the surface, where the quiet Tonto Trail ends among noisy campgrounds and traffic.

Bibliography and Maps

BEAL, DAVE. *Grand Canyon: The Story Behind the Scenery*. Grand Canyon, Arizona: Grand Canyon Natural History Society, 1969.

FLETCHER, COLIN. *The Man Who Walked Through Time*. New York: Knopf, 1967.

GOLDMAN, E. A. "The Kaibab or White-Tailed Squirrel," *Journal of Mammalogy*, Vol. 9, pp. 127–129 (1928).

KRUTCH, JOSEPH WOOD. *Grand Canyon, Today and All Its Yesterdays.* New York: William Morrow and Sons, 1958.

U.S. GEOLOGICAL SURVEY. A map of Grand Canyon National Park and vicinity is available from this source in Denver, Colorado 80225, or Washington, D.C. 20242.

Historical Trails

10

The Santa Fe Trail stretches from the city of Santa Fe, New Mexico, through corners of Colorado and Oklahoma and across the prairies of Kansas to Independence, Missouri. Today this old throughway is a drive-and-walk trail, much of it under macadam. Nevertheless there remain traces of the old ruts and camps, forts and markets and the scenes of massacres for walkers to discover.

Whiteman's history of the Trail goes back to the Spanish colonists. In 1539 a Spaniard, Fray Marcos de Niza, left Mexico City to explore Zuñi territory to the north and returned to tell Don Antonio de Mendoza, the Spanish Governor of Northern Mexico (now New Mexico) of "a great plain of grass and a city paved with gold." The Spanish colonists were obsessed with a dream of golden cities and the following morning Governor Mendoza summoned an adventurer named Estebianco, and dispatched him immediately north with an expedition to find and conquer the city the governor called "Quivira," from the military expression *qui vive*, "on the alert."

After months of wandering the hot Southwest, Estebianco had found only the simple adobe villages of the Zuñi along the lower Rio Grande. To save his Governor embarrassment by admitting the expensive expedition had failed, he sent back the message "Greatest thing in the world," and never returned.

His words did arrive, however; and upon hearing them, the explorer Francisco Vásquez de Coronado with an army of men

* For information about biotic communities along this trail see pages 276–277, 284–286.

153

dressed in velvet and silk, astride horses sheathed in shining armor, started north.

Several hundred anguished miles later, after braving drought, heat, and thorns, Coronado found the same simple people in the same unpretentious houses. Determinedly he searched on, discovering the Great Plains, the Continental Divide, the Grand Canyon, and the Colorado River, but not Quivira.

Even after Coronado's failure and death, stories of the golden city persisted. Other men rode into the desert and prairies in search of the mystical land. One was Juan de Onate, who set out in 1598 with 4000 men, 83 wagons, and several thousand head of cattle. A man with a flair, he finally, after a year's search, rode into an Indian village and named it Quivira. Today this city is called Wichita, Kansas.

Accurate descriptions of the mud houses of Quivira on the Arkansas River dampened Spain's interest in finding cities of gold with prospects of instant wealth, and support for expeditions was no longer forthcoming. As a result of uprisings, battles and disputes among civil and religious officials, Spain in 1821 finally lost control of Mexico. That same year William Becknell, an American merchant, made the Santa Fe Trail a long avenue of trade between the U.S. and New Mexico. Englishmen, Frenchmen, Spaniards, and Indians created a new business and the new Southwestern culture. Eventually merchants from New York and Philadelphia with cloth and hardware to sell, met New Mexicans headed east with their own goods to sell to the United States. Revolts over taxation by the Indians and New Mexicans led to conflicts along the Trail and eventually, on May 10, 1841, the U.S. declared war on Mexico. At the close of the year the Santa Fe Trail was a major cultural way.

Of the 800 miles of the Trail, 500 are on the Great Plains, the flat tabletop that tips gently upward from 1500 feet at Independence, Missouri to 4500 at the eastern edge of Colorado. There one branch of the Trail enters the mountains, climbing to 8000 feet at Raton Pass, its highest point.

The Great Plains are geologically one of the newest lands in North America. They arose from the sea as sandstone and shale. Volcanoes erupted on their western edge, and over a period of ten million years they precipitated out water from the clouds moving in from the Pacific which dumped rain on their western slopes. The eastern side, the edge of the Great Plains, was in the rain-shadow, a moistureless condition. Grasses and drought-resistant plants took over the flats, living, dying, and decaying to form the deep sod, forty feet deep in places, that is now the world's most productive soil for wheat and corn.

From east to west the Santa Fe Trail passes through four biotic areas: Midland Broadleaf Forest, the Tall- and Short-Grass Prairies, Southwest Coniferous Woodland, pinyon–juniper, and desert.

Originally the Trail wound through hundreds of miles of blue-stem, Indian buffalo, and grama grasses that plunged and pranced in the wind. Today these native grasses grow only around culverts, fences, and railroads; elsewhere they have been replaced by clover, wheat, corn, and rye.

In the mountains junipers appear at 5000 feet, ponderosa pines at 7000, and Douglas firs in the high passes at 9000 feet. The mountain flowers are primarily the purple cranesbill and scarlet penstemon. Giving the river banks in the mountains a cool green cover are narrowleaf cottonwood and oak. Cliffs and sandy slides are spotted with grasses, sage and juniper.

The Trail is flat and easy to walk with the exception of the Mountain Pass. However, few people have walked it since the coming of the automobile, for the heat and dust make it difficult.

Going west, the Santa Fe Trail leaves Independence, Missouri on *Interstate 70* and after a short distance becomes *U. S. Highway 56,* most of the way to Santa Fe.

At Gardner, Kansas, some fifty miles along, hickories, elms, and walnut trees of the Midland Broadleaf Forest give way to the prairie grasslands on the undulating terrain.

At Council Grove, Kansas, some hundred miles from Independence, on the Neosho River is an oak tree whose remains are still visible, where the U. S. government commissioners signed a treaty with the Osage Indians to permit the flow of commerce on the Santa Fe Trail without violence. The treaty was immortalized in 1857 when Kit Carson nailed to the tree a piece of buffalo hide on which he had burned the words "Council Grove." In the town of Council Grove, the Last Chance Store, built in 1857, still stands

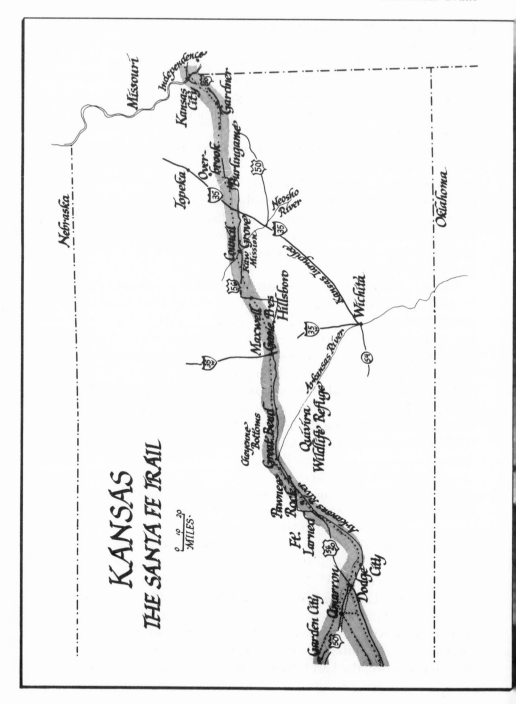

KANSAS
THE SANTA FE TRAIL

today as a reminder of the pioneers who purchased sowbelly, beans, and hardware before heading out onto the Great Plains.

Leaving the store, the Trail heads off into vast openness where even today towns are few and far between. Occasionally villages appear on the distant horizon, toy-like, with steeples reaching above rooftops and grain elevators. "And all along the long, flat road to these towns grow wild flowers," wrote Twig George after a walk-and-drive trip. "The flowers keep you going."

The Maxwell State Game Refuge offers the first long walking on the prairie. Trails cross lands grazed by buffalo, elk, and deer, and beside springs where mink and muskrat swim and water plants flourish.

Between McPherson and Ellinwood, the name Quivira appears frequently on roadside signs and billboards, marking the area scoured by Onate in his search for the golden city.

Relics of expeditions are exhibited in a museum on this stretch of *Highway 56*. South of the Trail lies the Quivira National Waterfowl Refuge, where gulls, sandpipers, egrets, ducks, geese, and herons may be seen.

Ellinwood, on the Trail, is today as in the past, a green oasis by the Arkansas River. Cottonwoods and box elders shade the resting places of early settlers and of migrating robins and boat-tailed grackles. During the 1800s in what is now the town's St. Zarah State Park, a fort was built of local sandstone to protect the highway travelers from the Indians. The fort, open to today's traveler, contains exhibits of Santa Fe memorabilia.

At Great Bend, named for the hairpin curve of the Arkansas River as it plies between shale and a band of conglomerate rocks, oil—that modern version of the pot of gold—has been discovered. The town bristles with refineries and supply houses but still offers a few traces of the old Santa Fe days. One is a spur trail running north to the Cheyenne Bottoms, a marshy depression in the prairie where the Cheyenne Indians hunted deer and geese and where the pioneers stocked up on game. It is now a wildlife refuge, covering 15,000 acres.

Ten miles down *U. S. 56* stands Pawnee Rock, a sandstone cliff that came to be feared by pioneers, as a spot where travelers were ambushed by Indians. Today it looms against the sky, a reminder of past horrors. It was at the top of this rock that Kit Carson at the age of 17, while standing guard, is supposed to have shot one of his own mules, mistaking it for an Indian. Many walkers stop here and climb to the top, to see the vast view of the prairie.

Old danger spots on the Trail are marked by the presence of forts. The most famous is Ford Larned on the steep bank of the Arkansas River bend where travelers stopped for water and, at various times, were attacked by the Cheyenne, Arapaho, Apache, Iowa, and Comanche Indians. By 1864 the Indian raids had become so frequent that no caravan left the base without a military escort. Today nine of the original stone buildings still stand at Fort Larned. Five are museums displaying military and pioneer artifacts, and the four others are still used by the Army. Surrounded by huge box elders and cottonwoods, the buildings look westward onto the rolling prairie landscape. In a pasture in front of the fort are the first visible ruts left by wagons following the old Santa Fe Trail.

Going westward along the Arkansas, the Trail arrives at Dodge City, the railroad town where cowboys of the late 1880s drove their cattle to be sold and shipped. This was a town of bars, brothels, and fighting, of thieves and gamblers, where many cowboys literally died "with their boots on" and were buried in Boot Hill Cemetery just off the Santa Fe Trail. Among those whose quickness on the draw made Dodge City famous were Wyatt Earp, "Wild Bill" Hickock, and Calamity Jane, whose names can be seen all over the town.

After a few miles the Trail reaches Cimarron, a rest spot where each wagon master had to decide whether to take the Cimarron Cutoff, a short route plagued by drought and Indians, or the longer, but less dangerous Mountain Pass route through Colorado. The Pass route, which is now *U. S. Highway 50*, begins in the heartland of the plains. Grain fields where meadowlarks sing on fenceposts and clouds form on the horizon stretch for hundreds of miles. Along the roadside grows the compass plant, so named because its broad, vertical, oak-like leaves are always aligned north and south.

Here also grow sage, miles of black-eyed Susans, and prairie coneflowers. The plains bee balm, easily identified by the stem passing through the center of each flower cluster, shares the fallow land with acres of the white prickly poppies. Daisy fleabanes bloom like a mist cloud along the Trail and everywhere butterflies

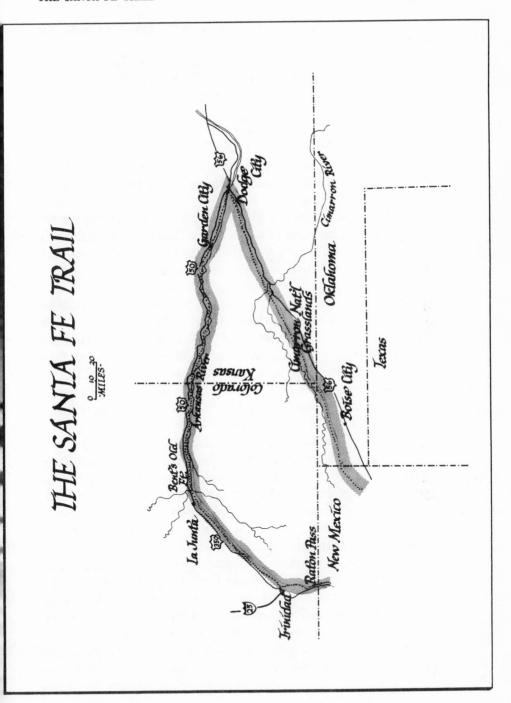

flit. Horned larks call and bobolinks and sparrows sing along the roadside.

The gradual upward tilt of the Great Plains as the Trail enters Colorado brings with it a change to a landscape where mountain-sides are dotted with pinyon pine and juniper. In canyons of sand-stone and conglomerate rocks, jays scream, crows call, and lizards skitter away from the walker's feet.

Lying east of Junta is Bent's Old Fort, a trading post built by William Bent and his brother in 1820. Although Bent burned down the fort to keep Indians from destroying it, a replica has been re-cently built.

Not far out of town, the Santa Fe walking trail follows the old wagon ruts that lie between the Santa Fe Railroad and *State High-way 183* into a coniferous forest where curve-billed thrashers sing, crested flycatchers dart overhead and woodpeckers pound dead trees.

The foot trail leads on to Trinidad, past the Victorian-Gothic mansion of a pioneer merchant, Frank Bloom, then climbs to Raton Pass, the highest point on the Trail. At this elevation Douglas fir and Western pine shelter Western horned owls, bob-cats, and mule deer. The air in this border town between Colorado and New Mexico is fresh and cool, and walkers often linger here for days, looking across at the Sangre de Cristo Mountains that appear to float, cool as crystal, above the parched desert.

Descending the mountain, the Trail passes through the Sug-arite Canyon Wilderness Park, ten thousand acres of pinyon and cedar, of bears and coyotes and of abandoned mines where for-tunes were won and lost. A favorite pastime of walkers here is to hunt for the old Santa Fe ruts in the forest. They are numerous and scattered widely since each wagon master picked his own individual route through the pass.

U. S. Highway 64 leads into Taos, a ski town where curios, Indian jewelry, and fashionable clothes are sold, and there are the tourist traps usually found in such places. A sense of the past re-mains in the original Taos, to the east of the modern town, where Pueblo Indians live as they have for centuries. Leading from Taos to the foot of the mountain slope are many miles of excellent trail, through the Cimarron Canyon Wildlife Area and the Carson National Forest, wild country that attracts kayackers, fishermen, campers, and photographers. Here the Mountain Pass route snakes down *State Highway 121 and 181* into Waltrous to join the Cimarron Cutoff.

The once-dangerous cutoff which shortened the route to Santa Fe by a hundred miles, is now *U. S. Highway 56*. Once called the "prairie ocean," it is a flat platter of violent weather—wild thunderstorms in summer, blizzards in winter—and at the time of the caravans had little or no water. The nightmare of every driver was of becoming lost or breaking down on this blazing waterless plain. Even today the thought of getting a flat tire along this section of *U. S. 56* is a worry to local drivers.

In the old days the only relief from thirst to be hoped for was in occasional rain pools in the otherwise bone-dry bed of Cimarron River. Appearing briefly after a rain, these pools suddenly come alive with frogs, dragonflies, and birds that vanish when the water dries up. For early travelers the rain could be a curse as well as a life-saver, since it turned the soil into a red mud that stuck to the axles and wheels and often bogged down a caravan.

The Cimarron Cutoff is marked by volcanic intrusions that loom on the horizon. One of these, Middle Spring Point of Rocks, juts above the Cimarron National Grasslands, where bison and sheep graze and eagles spiral above the volcanic cone. At Middle Spring Point of Rocks another landmark comes into view, the bright green of Upper Springs in the panhandle of Oklahoma.

Farther on down the road the Cold Springs are now enclosed in a stone house from which the water spills into pools outside, giving relief from the heat. Rimmed with willows and flowers, it is visited by herons, egrets, and gulls. A trail leads to a rock bluff above the pool, where scores of names have been carved by travelers, some dating back to 1840.

As the Cutoff Route climbs to the high desert and threads out of Oklahoma into New Mexico, two volcanic rocks, Rabbit Ears and Round Mound, are the next fixes on the skyline. Beyond these can be seen New Mexico's massive Point of Rocks.

West of it a historic side trail leads into a canyon where spring water descends in cascades and pools, surrounded by pinyon and juniper. The wagon ruts near this onetime campsite are so deep that the Soil Conservation Service has built earthen dams across them to prevent the hillside from eroding.

Another trail winds to the spot where in October 1849 the White family, along with other travelers were killed by Apaches. Here huge rocks lie on the parched land and mesquite grows in tight clumps.

At Canadian Crossing, a famous pioneer ford, the Cimarron Cutoff crosses the Canadian River. Joseph Brown wrote of the place in 1850, "The ford is rocky and shallow and easy to find. If missed, however, the traveler would not be able to cross in many miles." The crossing can be found today by taking a dirt road off U. S. 56 down the west side of the Canadian River. The wagon ruts lie where the river and road meet; the river can be crossed on the stones used by the wagoneers. Beyond the river are the most impressive ruts of the Trail. They go south–southeast toward Wagon Mound, the next fix on the horizon, and are cracked and dry, but after several miles they offer a view of the Sangre de Cristo Mountains, rising cool and blue in the distance.

At Wagon Mound which actually has the shape of a shoe pointed west but was named by a long-gone trader who saw it as "a wagon, bearing southwest with its yokes of oxen lumbering over the horizon," is a footpath up the Mound that affords a view of the blues, purples, and mauves of the New Mexico landscape.

The Cimarron Cutoff joins *State Highway 85* at La Junta and enters Las Vegas, a Spanish name meaning "well-watered meadows." This was the last resting and watering place before the sprint to Santa Fe. A quiet town today, Las Vegas was once a market center for Mexican ranchers, farmers with eggs, cheese, and milk, and for makers of pottery, jewelry, and rugs, who came to the open plaza to talk, dance, and sell their goods.

Out of Las Vegas the Trail crosses the Pecos River and comes into San Miguel, a sleepy village where the adobe buildings and dirt streets, the small farms on the outskirts, and the plaza at its center have barely changed since the 1800s. Even the woodpeckers come into town and drill the trees as if there were no one around.

Because the Sangre de Cristo Mountains were impassable, the old Trail snaked at their foot, then squeezed through Glorieta Pass, a narrow gap between the southern spur of the mountains and the red rock of the mesas. The town of Glorieta is practically a

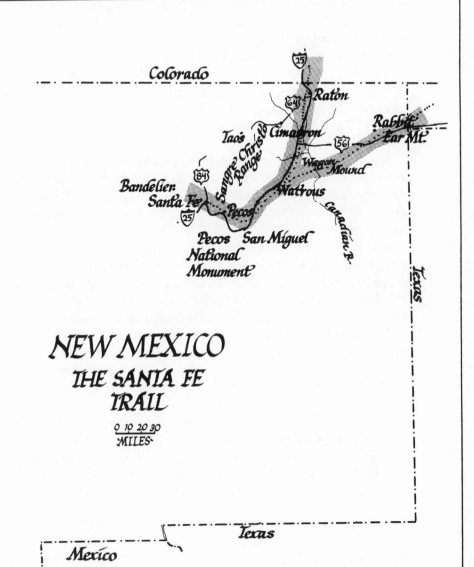

ghost town with a small store, a gift shop, restaurant, and small printing establishment, the Rio Grande Press. Downtown the streets are empty and quiet.

In the Santa Fe National Forest beyond Glorieta, a trail leads to the Pecos Pueblo, the largest in New Mexico at the time of the Spanish conquest. The village declined during the eighteenth century, when smallpox and Indian wars ravaged its population and by 1782 it had been abandoned. Today it is a spot to walk and meditate in.

Near by lies the Pecos Wilderness with more than 300 miles of beautiful mountain trails that wind through a forest of ponderosa pine and juniper where pine siskins flit. Chaparral and wild currant grow on dry exposures and the rare Mearns' gilded woodpecker shrieks from the mesquite.

The last hot miles into Santa Fe become a festival of scraggly-crested roadrunners that peer out of the grasses and dart from chaparral to clumps of yucca. To the consternation of drivers, they also run from one side of the highway to the other, and a few earn their name by running down the road alongside moving cars.

The reddish sculptured rocks on the Trail from Las Vegas to Santa Fe are sandstone, limestone shale, and anhydrite, carved into fantastic shapes by wind and water. They are marked by faults that have sliced open orange, yellow, red, white, and brown layers like those of a huge layer cake.

Santa Fe, a low-roofed city on a flat blue mesa, has kept much of the beauty and charm it had as the onetime center of Southwestern culture. In the plaza in front of the governor's palace, tradesmen still bargain and call out their wares; children run and play in streets lined with adobe houses.

Bibliography and Maps

AMERICAN ASSOCIATION OF PETROLEUM GEOLOGISTS. Geological Highway Maps, Mid-continent and Southern Rocky Mountain Regions, 1966. Available from the Association, P.O. Box 979, Tulsa, Oklahoma 76101. (Note: Road maps are available from the State Highway Departments of Colorado, Kansas, and New Mexico.)

BALDWIN, BREWSTER, and FRANK E. KOTTLOWSKI. *Santa Fe, Scenic Trips to the Geologic Past #1*. Socorro, New Mexico: State Bureau of Mines and Resources, 1968.

BROCKMAN, FRANK C. *Trees of North America: A Guide to Field Identification*. New York: Golden Press, 1968.

DRUMM, STELLA M., ed. *Down the Santa Fe Trail and into New Mexico: Diary of Susan Shelby Magoffin 1846–1847*. New Haven: Yale University Press, 1962.

DUFFUS, R. L. *The Santa Fe Trail*. Albuquerque: University of New Mexico Press, 1972.

LAMAR, HOWARD ROBERTS. *The Far Southwest 1846–1912: A Territorial History*. New York: W. W. Norton Company, Inc., 1970.

PEARCE, T. M., ed. *New Mexico Place Names: A Geographical Dictionary*. Albuquerque: University of New Mexico Press, 1965.

U.S. DEPARTMENT OF THE INTERIOR, BUREAU OF OUTDOOR RECREATION. *The Santa Fe Trail: A National Scenic Trail Study*. Washington, March 17, 1975.

WATTS, MAY THEILGAARD, and TOM WATTS. *Desert Tree Finder*. Berkeley: Nature Study Guide Publishers, 1974.

WATTS, TOM. *Rocky Mountain Tree Finder*. Berkeley: Nature Study Guide Publishers, 1972.

11

The Lewis and Clark Trail extends from Wood River, Illinois to the Pacific coast of Oregon, following both the outbound and the inbound routes of Meriwether Lewis and William Clark as they explored the Louisiana Purchase for President Thomas Jefferson in 1804–6.

The Trail begins as a water route, a river-bottom trek across the Great Plains on the banks of the Missouri between Nebraska and Iowa, northward through the Dakotas and westward into Montana. From the western edge of Montana to the Clearwater in Idaho, the way is mountainous. It then slopes westward along the Snake River in Washington to the Columbia River that dissects Washington and Oregon.

Although Lewis and Clark floated the rivers, they also walked the shores to gather geological and biological specimens for Jefferson, and it is these research trails that the present day pathway follows. Because sections of the river route have been channelized or inundated by large reservoirs and covered by cities, walking the Trail continuously is not possible or pleasant, and most walkers drive part of the way. At the time of this writing, 1000 miles of marked trail, 147 campsites and over 1500 parks and expedition sites were available, and another twenty-one campgrounds had been proposed by the Bureau of Outdoor Recreation.

Geologically the Trail goes from the sedimentary rocks underlying the Great Plains to the igneous and metamorphic rocks in

* For information about biotic communities along this trail see pages 262–263, 274, 284–287.

166

the Rocky Mountains. Volcanic lava covers the route along the Columbia River.

The Trail lies in the Midland Broadleaf Forest in Illinois, winds through the Tall- and Short-Grass Prairies to the Desert Shrubland at the foot of the Rocky Mountains. In Idaho, Oregon, and Washington it plunges through the Western Mixed and North-western Coniferous forests to enter the Rain Forest of the Pacific Coast.

Along the route of the expedition of 1804, the names of the persons who made up President Jefferson's Corps of Discovery live on in the names of towns, lakes, rivers, restaurants, hotels, roadside parks, and commercial products. To walk the Lewis and Clark Trail is to walk an adventure. Sites of discoveries and meeting places with Indians or wild animals are marked along the way and, although hydroelectric plants and cities are part of the modern Trail, they serve only to intensify the primitive beauty that still exists in many places.

The Trail begins at Wood River, Illinois, on the shores of the Mississippi. Here on March 14, 1804, the early morning mist lifted to reveal a 55-foot keelboat, two pirogues, a Newfoundland dog, seventeen soldiers, and eleven enlistees led by co-captains Meriwether Lewis and William Clark. The mouth of the Missouri River was their immediate destination; beginning there, they were to explore the unknown region known as the Louisiana Purchase.

The beauty of the landscape at that time can be glimpsed at West Alton Recreation Access, where *Interstate 270* joins *U. S. Highway 67*. At this spot elms and walnut trees have been planted where some 3000 buffalo once roamed the hills, and huge herds of deer, elk, and antelope grazed the grassy plains. Fishermen here still catch many of the same species that were noted by the Corps of Discovery more than 150 years ago: pike, bass, trout, rockfish, perch, flatfish, and silverfish.

Off *Interstate 70* and *U. S. Highway 61*, the Trail follows *State Highway 94* along the Missouri River to the August Busch Wildlife Area, where the birds and plants can be seen. Farther on, west of Defiance, are the home, shrine, and burial site of Daniel Boone. Lewis and Clark passed Boone's home during his seventieth year but do not mention him in their journals. Perhaps he was off on a hunting expedition; or perhaps the men were preoccupied with

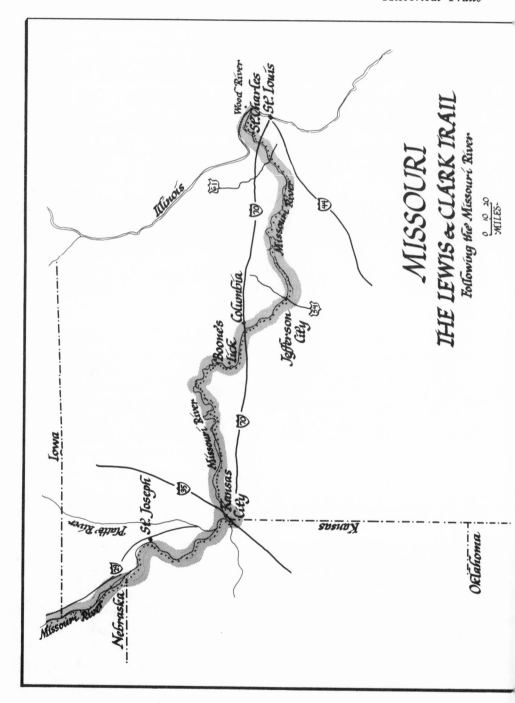

MISSOURI
THE LEWIS & CLARK TRAIL
Following the Missouri River

0 10 20
MILES

the river, for at that time the current was rough through this section, and the men had to swim and push the boats upstream.

Farther west, not far from Gore, off *State Highway 94*, the expedition was cursed with an epidemic of "boils and intestinal upheavals," and paused in what is now the Daniel Boone State Forest. Occasionally an Indian would approach, then vanish among the elms and thick willows, where today foxes call from the grasses and brown bats dart overhead.

Along the river from Wood Hole to Boone Forest the party watched fascinated as great white birds flew in clouds overhead. These were the now endangered whooping cranes, which at this writing number less than a hundred wild birds.

The next foot trails lie in the forest of Boonslick Frontier, off *Interstate 70* and to the south of Columbia. In this area Lewis gave the crew instructions on how to keep a diary, as he insisted that everyone must do, so that if an accident befell the party at least one record would survive for the eyes of President Jefferson.

As a general rule, Clark navigated the boat and drew maps while Lewis wandered the shores collecting plants, animals, and minerals and noting down everything as he had been instructed by President Jefferson:

Note the soil and the face of the country, its growth and vegetable production, the animals, mineral productions, volcanic appearances. Note the climate as characterized by the thermometer, by the proportion of rainy, cloudy, and clear days, by lightning, hail, snow, ice, winds. Note plants, flowers, times of appearance of particular birds, reptiles or insects. Note the names of the nations and their numbers, their customs and character, commercial possibilities, ordinary occupations of the tribes, and diseases, food, clothing, perculiarities of their laws.

North of *Interstate 70*, off *State Highway 87*, the trails of Boonslick State Park offer pleasant trails through oak, walnut, and elm groves where catbirds come to campsites to call and beg for handouts.

The Trail through Kansas City is confined to the historic sites and parks of the area. At Winthrop, off *Interstate 29* and *State Highway 45*, in what is now the Lewis and Clark State Park, is the spot where the expedition, on June 26, 1804, reached a bend in the Missouri where their direction changed from predominantly

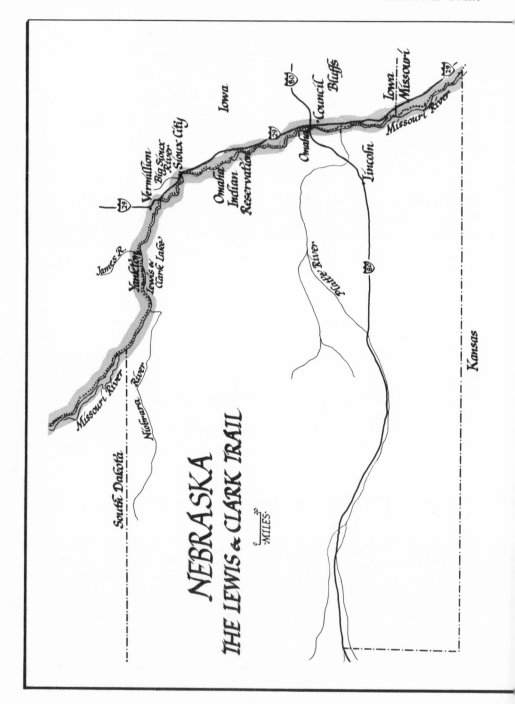

NEBRASKA
THE LEWIS & CLARK TRAIL

west to north. While pausing to check maps and compasses, Lewis recorded flocks of brant, the short-necked, black-chested geese whose descendants can still be found here today in spring and fall. Their swift, short flight and long, rolling honk distinguish them from Canada geese.

At St. Joseph, Kansas, off *U. S. Highway 36*, good foot trails lie along the west side of the river. Mink and muskrats live in the wetlands, and around Wyandotte County Lake and Brown County State Lake, a variety of ducks and shorebirds can be seen. The ambitious walker can cut across country to two Kansas Indian Villages. One is prehistoric, the other much like the villages Lewis and Clark found in the area in 1804. On exhibit in the latter are pottery, arrowheads, and dyed porcupine quills, used to decorate moccasins and clothing before the white man brought beads to the Indians.

Since the expedition walked both sides of the Missouri as it flowed between Iowa and Nebraska, a walker can try either side or both. On the Iowa riverbank *Interstate 29* leads to Waubonsie State Park and Pony Creek Park, south of Council Bluffs. On the Nebraska side of the river, off *U. S. Highway 73 and 75*, a pleasant trail connects the Leary Indian village and Plattsmouth Waterfowl Management area. Ducks, geese, swans, cranes, herons, and multitudes of red-winged blackbirds enliven the water and the shore, where in 1804 the captains halted their explorations to make friends with the resident Oto, Omaha, and Missouri Indian tribes.

At Omaha, Nebraska, and Council Bluffs, Iowa are the sites where Lewis and Clark met in council with the Omaha Indians, who though much feared turned out to be friendly and warned them of the "terrible" Sioux tribe ahead.

U. S. Highway 73 in Nebraska and *Interstate 29* in Iowa follow the trails of the expedition up the sides of the river here.

At Ponca State Park in Nebraska, on *State Highway 12*, is a trail that leads to the cliffs where Lewis almost died. In fulfilling Jefferson's requests to note minerals, Lewis had learned to identify them by smell and taste. On the cliffs he tested a pyrite with a chemical, released fumes of arsenic, and collapsed. He was rushed back to the keelboat where he took a dose of Benjamin Rush's salts, a miracle drug of the day that was used for every ailment. It cured Lewis "straight off," wrote Clark.

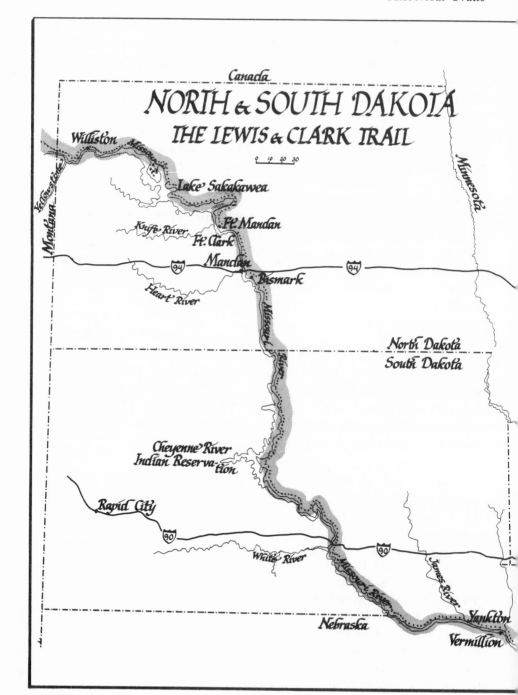

Poling through shallows, paddling the wild waters, the corps arrived at Vermillion, South Dakota, off *Interstate 29*. At what is now a campsite west of the town they faced the terrifying Spirit Mound. Tales of this spot that had reached Washington, D. C. in 1800 described a community of human devils about eighteen inches high, with huge heads and an endless supply of sharp arrows. The small darting devils were said to have killed all who came to the mound, so that the spot was judiciously avoided by Omaha, Sioux, and Oto Indians.

On the overcast morning of August 25 Lewis and Clark set out to investigate the mysterious report. The structure of the mound was so regular that it appeared to be man-made, but Clark observed that the stones and weathering were similar to other natural hummocks along the river, and concluded that the Spirit Mound was "nature's work."

As they approached, the winds blew across the timberless plains as they do today, forcing many insects up from the mound, and millions of small birds of various species including the purple martin, fed on them. Clark decided that the clouds of birds were reason enough for the Indians to believe this to be the residence of spirits. From the park the view is wide and extensive, although no one is certain any more which of several hummocks was the original devils' home.

Beyond the mound the Lewis and Clark Trail comes into prairie-lands where tall bluestem mixes with the short buffalo grass. Pairs of prairie horned larks fly over the fields and grasses.

Here a runner brought word that the Teton Sioux, a tribe reputedly so ferocious that Lewis had been warned to avoid them before leaving Washington, were near. With caution and apprehension, on a clear morning in late August the Corps of Discovery poled over the border of Sioux territory, beyond which no trader had gone for years, and entered the land of the Teton Sioux, the tribe whose name in sign language was a forefinger swiftly pulled across the jugular vein.

The expedition met the Sioux at what is now Yankton, South Dakota, on *State Highway 50*. The violent meeting for which the captains had trained the crew did not occur. The first village was so placid that the expedition was "almost disappointed." The

Sioux accepted gifts, nodded at Lewis's Great White Father speech, of which they understood not one word, and drank all the Great White Father's "milk" (whiskey). Clark noted that they were stout, bold-looking people (the young men handsome), decorated with paint, porcupine quills, feathers, leggings, and moccasins.

During the afternoon celebrations a baby was born. One of the crewmen wrapped him in an American flag and proclaimed him to be a U. S. citizen. The boy grew up to become a chief who was, not too surprisingly, pro–U. S. government all his life. Today along the Trail around the Lewis and Clark Lake, west of Yankton where the great Sioux lived, are numerous campgrounds.

South of Wagner are the site of the Yankton Treaty and the Fort Randall Historical Restoration. Many Lewis and Clark landmarks are buried under the water beyond Fort Randall Dam, but a few of the natural sandstone formations that Lewis thought were "ancient fortifications" remain to be seen. On the river banks fox and coyote pounce on rodents; sage grouse spread their tails, puff their throats, and dance; and occasionally one of the endangered sharp-tailed grouse will fly up from the grass.

Prairie dog colonies can be found between Pickstown and Chamberlain, a wild walking area. Here the Corps of Discovery had their first encounter with such a colony. Excited by the little "barking squirrels" that guard their holes by sitting erect, the crew came ashore to catch one for President Jefferson. They spent an entire day pouring buckets of water down the holes to float out the residents, and succeeded in getting one before dark. At dawn the "barker" was given "alive and barking" to a trader, to be delivered to President Jefferson—whose reaction has not been recorded.

At this junction of the White River and the Missouri, off *Interstate 90* near Chamberlain, is Crow Creek Indian Reservation. The water life along the river is rich: antelope, deer, beaver, coyotes, teal, pintails, mallards, and geese, are everywhere in spring and fall.

On the stretch leading to Pierre, Lewis shot ducks and Scammon, his Newfoundland dog, dove into the water and brought them back—the first and perhaps last Newfoundland bird dog.

Although the Missouri is dammed again at Pierre, and the old Lewis and Clark Trail is lost, the new Trail around Oahe Lake passes through open country to Indian villages that re-create the 1800s. The villages lie off *U. S. Highway 83*, which connects north and south *Interstates 90* and *94*. The grave of Sitting Bull lies just off *U. S. Highway 12*, on the Standing Rock Indian Reservation.

At the mouth of Bad River, just south of Fort Pierre and *State Highway 34* and *U. S. Highway 83*, Lewis and Clark, more or less complacent about the Indians now, steered confidently into the village of the Teton Sioux. After giving a speech and handing out gifts, Clark was annoyed to discover that the Teton Sioux chiefs were not satisfied with medals, beads, and certificates, but wanted whiskey, tobacco, and "everything the Expedition carried." In the belief that diplomacy would help, Clark invited the chiefs aboard the keelboat. Unfortunately the interpreters were out hunting and not a word was understood by either group. Each of the chiefs was given a quarter-cup of whiskey, and Clark with two riflemen escorted them back to shore. As they were departing the shore a young chief drew his bow and threatened Clark, who drew his sword. Out on the river, the alert crew trained the cannon on the Sioux chiefs; the braves aimed their arrows.

For a long moment Clark and the Sioux played with disaster; then Clark coolly ordered his men to lower their guns and sent them back to the boat for reinforcements. He now faced the arrows of the Teton Sioux alone. When reinforcements arrived, Clark calmly pivoted, turned his back, and walked to the rowboat. A murmur of admiration for such bravery swept through the Sioux; then the chiefs quickly counseled and asked to renegotiate. Clark agreed reluctantly to meet on what he dubbed Bad Humored Island to emphasize his feelings. He had so impressed the Teton Sioux, however, that peace was established almost immediately and the Corps of Discovery moved on.

The Arikaras, the next Indian tribe on the Missouri, were quite another story. Intelligent and friendly, they were architects of large, comfortable lodges with willow wattle siding, straw and mud roofs. The Arikara women particularly admired York, Clark's black servant, for none had ever seen or heard of a black person before. Squaws pursued him, children tried to rub off his color, and the record states that York, for his part, "thoroughly enjoyed the attention."

This country can be walked off *U. S. Highway 83*, where trails and campsites edge the dammed Missouri.

Just north of present-day Bismarck, at the mouth of the Heart River, the walker comes to the spot where the expedition paused while Lewis stuffed a Western badger and prepared pressed plants for President Jefferson. Almost every day he identified a new plant species, eventually adding 200 to the world list of known plants. One was the artichoke, which after being shipped east by Lewis and Clark found its way to Italy, where it was cultivated and developed. Its origin in North America had been forgotten until several years ago, when a botanist discovered the wild progenitor growing along the Missouri.

While Lewis collected plants, the Mandan Indians came down the bluffs to watch. Their friendly manner and good spirits decided the two captains to spend the winter with them. The winds were blowing across the prairie, the ducks and geese were migrating south, and in the mornings Clark's rheumatism was bothering him. Today the winter camp of 1804, Fort Mandan, still stands, north of Bismarck off *U. S. Highway 83* and *Alternate 200*.

That winter the temperatures dropped to 45 below zero. It was "so cold," wrote Lewis, "that the whiskey froze after being left outside only 15 minutes." At night the frozen river clapped like a rifle shot, and the crew crowded round the fire to write and read and to talk to the Indians. On these nights at the Bismarck Camp, Lewis and Clark learned how tremendous their assignment was. The Mandan Chief, Big White, who had traveled the west, drew on the mud floor of his house the mountains and rivers ahead, including one mighty waterfall. As Clark carefully copied his work on paper he realized that the Missouri did not reach the Pacific. It was another river, what we know as the Columbia, equally long and just as powerful, that flowed to the sea.

On a December evening a Frenchman, Toussaint Charbonneau, came to Fort Mandan and obtained the job, which he kept until the end of the trip, of Indian interpreter for Lewis and Clark. With him was his Shoshone Indian wife, Sacajawea, who had been kidnapped by the Minitarees and sold to Charbonneau as a slave. She was now nine months pregnant and soon went into labor. Dreading the pain of giving birth, she asked Lewis to pulverize some snake rattles in his mechanical grinder. Sacajawea dissolved the potion in water, drank, and within ten minutes gave birth to a boy with ease and no complications, much to Lewis's amazement.

When the ice broke up and the birds returned, Sacajawea begged Lewis to take her on the expedition in the hope of finding her people. She could speak three Indian tongues, and knew much about the Shoshone land. Lewis consented and on April 17, 1805 the Corps of Discovery left Fort Mandan with Sacajawea holding her baby at her breast.

Today off U. S. Highway 83 the memory of the famous mother haunts the trail around Lake Sakakawea, named for her and pronounced Sacajawea. At Riverdale the North Country Trail (see chapter 8) joins the Lewis and Clark, crosses Garrison Dam, and starts west to the Pacific Ocean.

The lake is the result of damming and in no way resembles the state of the river in 1805. "Waves, whirling water, and hard riffles" made up the scene then.

A trace of the lost whirling waterway can be seen from the trails off U. S. Highway 83 between Wolf Creek to Snake Creek in the Hille Game Management area. Ducks, geese, deer, swallows, muskrats and raccoons re-create the wilderness atmosphere of that toilsome spring, as do the bluestem grasses on both sides of the Missouri to Williston, North Dakota. Above the flat land an occasional golden eagle still soars.

Where the Yellowstone River meets the Missouri west of Williston, the corps saw their first Ursus horribilis or grizzly bear. Dozens were feeding on the abundant yampa in the open prairies. Lewis feared these "great monsters" and almost lost his life to one just beyond what is now the Montana–North Dakota border, off State Highway 58. He had shot a buffalo and was watching it die, without reloading his gun, when a grizzly lumbered up to him. On the open, level plain, with not a tree to climb, the bear charged Lewis, who ran about 80 yards before realizing he could not outrun the bear. Leaping into the water and moving to where he could stand but where the bear would have to swim, he stood ready to fight. Suddenly the grizzly wheeled and retreated as fast as he had given chase.

The Trail crosses into Montana on the north shore of the Missouri River. Off U. S. Highway 2 at Poplar, the Lewis and Clark Memorial Park offers a look at this one-time habitat of griz-

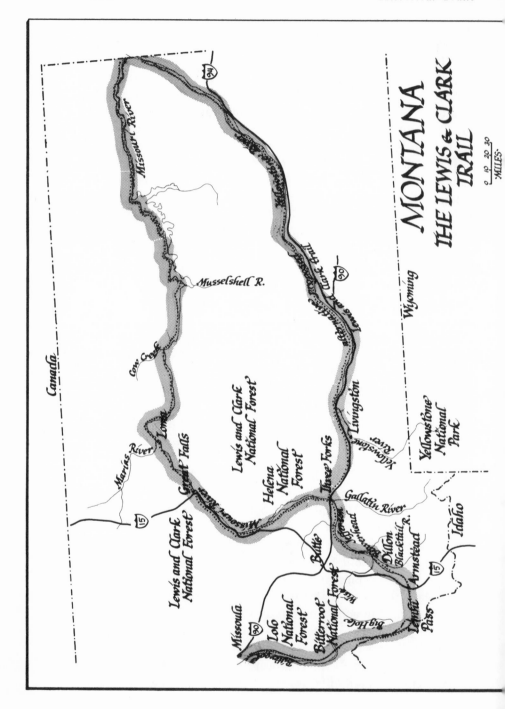

zly and wolf and at some of the plants Lewis and Clark discovered: its Western spring beauty, the wild turnip, and the salmonberry, whose fruit is pleasant but rather acid. The biotic area here is the Short-Grass Prairie, the home of the antelope and the prairie falcon.

On down *Highway 2* and off *U. S. Highway 191*, south of Glasgow, bighorn sheep roam the Charles M. Russell National Wildlife Refuge. The description of these handsome animals, with their curled horns and white rumps, carefully set down by Lewis for his President, is still quoted in some mammal books today.

On May 21 the corps came to the Musselshell River, which can be reached on *State Highway 200*. The strange terrain led Lewis to believe that here he might find the ancient monsters, the dinosaurs whose bones had aroused Jefferson's wonder. Lewis found only pine and cedar and short prairie grasses. Otherwise the soil produced little vegetation except the prickly pear.

Between *U. S. Highway 191* and *U. S. Highway 87* the region along the Trail is now dotted with excellent campsites.

For the expedition the river became more treacherous and narrow and on May 16 Lewis, exploring up Cow Creek off *U. S. Highway 191*, climbed to the top of a butte and beheld the distant Rocky Mountains, snow-covered and jagged. "These points of the Rocky Mountains," he wrote in his journal, "were covered with snow and the sun shone on it in such a manner as to give me the most plain and satisfactory view. I felt a secret pleasure in finding myself so near the head of the heretofore conceived, boundless Missouri." Lewis also knew the mountains meant hardship and this, he wrote, "in some manner countered my joy."

A few miles farther, the Corps faced a life-and-death decision. In what is now Loma, Montana, at *U. S. Highway 87*, the Missouri splits into two forks. Chief Big White had not told Lewis which one to take, the one that was clear or the other, which was muddy like the Missouri. The crew urged the captains to take the muddy one. Caution prevailed, however, and each of the captains checked out a branch. Lewis took the muddy one soon discovering that its course led northward and was not the major source of the Missouri. He named the river the Marias and returned to Loma. Clark, having reached snow-covered mountains, was convinced his was the route to be followed, and rejoined Lewis to confer. As usual the two were in agreement. Since the water was so swift and the way so narrow, they dug holes and cached all the heavy equipment for their return.

The expedition set out in good spirits and on June 11 heard the "agreeable sound of a fall of water." A white spray rose on the river amid a tremendous roar. These were the falls Big White had described at what is now Great Falls, Montana, on *Interstate 15*. Lewis rejoiced for he knew they had taken the right fork.

The way around the falls proved to be more than eighteen miles and took twenty-four days of hauling, shoving, and pulling the boats over rough terrain and through miles of moccasin-piercing cacti. The expedition was forced to move the heavy boats on primitive wheels made from trunks of cottonwood trees, arriving back on the Missouri limping and almost exhausted.

A "portage of agony," Lewis called the route around the falls. Its hazards can be appreciated to some degree at Portage, Montana, off *U. S. Highway 87*. A trail and campsites are available at Giant Springs along *U. S. Highway 87 South*. Here Sacajawea recognized her homeland, much to the joy of the captains, who watched the skyline for signs of her people in the hope of being guided across the Rocky Mountains. The Shoshones were around, but hiding from what they took for Indian enemies rather than white men.

From Great Falls the Lewis and Clark Trail goes through the Gates of the Mountain Wilderness off *Interstate 15*, north of Helena, to Three Forks, the land where for weeks the expedition hunted for the Shoshone Indians in the dense pine and fir forest.

On August 10, hungry and tired, Lewis, Sacajawea, and a few of the crew carved out the present-day Lewis and Clark Trail to Three Forks, traveling between cliffs where rattlesnakes coiled and across crackling sagebrush land where antelope ran. Their search took them up the Jefferson River, along the present *State Highway 41*, across *Interstate 15* to today's Deerlodge National Forest and the Beaverhead River. They found no Shoshones. Pushing westward the path they took winds around what is now Clark Canyon Dam, south of Dillon, off *U. S. Highway 91*. There they lost the trail. Solid forest took over. Perplexed, Lewis sent Sacajawea and the crew to explore the course of another river and set out by himself into the hills.

Crossing the sagebrush, he saw an Indian approach on horse-

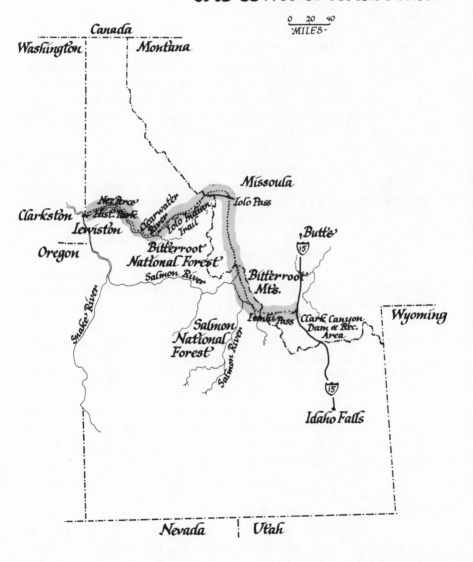

IDAHO
THE LEWIS & CLARK TRAIL

0   20   40
· MILES ·

back. Lewis held up his hands to signal friendship and ran eagerly
toward the brave, uncovering his red hair so that he would be identified as a white man.

Upon their meeting, Lewis held out a gift, which the Shoshone
snatched and then backed off before the captain could pull up his
sleeves and show his white arms. *"Tabbabone,"* Lewis called out.
The Indian started, cracked his whip, and galloped off. Unfortunately Lewis had said the word for "stranger" instead of *"taiva-
vone,"* for white man. To the Shoshone "stranger" meant enemy.
Two months had passed since the expedition entered the Shoshones'
land; that night Lewis wrote of his great mortification and disappointment in being unable to communicate with the brave.

The corps reassembled the next day and started up what is now
a narrow road that runs west out of Clark Canyon, Montana to
Tendoy, Idaho. High in Lemhi Pass Lewis bent down and stared at
the water. It flowed west, not east; they were camped on the Continental Divide. Any trickle they followed west would eventually
bring them to the Pacific Ocean.

At dawn they started down the steep pass on a well-trod dim
trail. Halfway down it Sacajawea recognized where she was. She
and Lewis quickened their pace and came upon an old woman with
a young squaw. Lewis approached them gently, gave them gifts, and
painted their own cheeks vermillion, the peace symbol of the Shoshones. Nodding and smiling the woman led the expedition to a
group of warriors who were gathered about two miles away. With
warm gestures of friendship, Captain Lewis first showed his white
arms, then presented them with an American flag. Sacajawea was
asked to interpret English to a chief whom she recognized as her
brother. They embraced with tears of joy, and her brother and the
other Shoshone chieftains agreed to supply the expedition with
horses and lead them over the mountains to the big rivers that
flowed west. Today the trail they took up and then down Lemhi
Pass to Tendoy, *State Highway 28*, is a good brisk walk.

With knowledgeable guides, the corps set out again. Sacajawea
decided to stay with the expedition until it reached the Pacific,
then return to her people on the way home.

Paralleling what is now *U. S. Highway 93*, they took the Bitterroot River toward present-day Missoula. The route is now dotted
with campgrounds and fishing sites, and the walking is rough. The

Trail past cottonwoods and yellow pine, and through shallow eddies where ducks float and herons stalk and dance, is best followed here in a kayak or a canoe.

Just south of Missoula, at Lolo Fork on the Bitterroot, the Shoshone chiefs pointed the way up the pass. Beyond lay mountains, canyons, and such wild water that they would go no farther. The Corps bade the Indians goodbye and, with Sacajawea guiding, plodded on.

Along this section, *U. S. Highway 12*, supplies ran out and the men scrounged for berries, crayfish, and lily bulbs. Unable to kill the elusive forest animals, they were forced to eat horsemeat and roots. Today this canyon is verdant with ranches, forests, hot springs, and cold trout streams and the walker finds it difficult to believe that the men could not survive here in 1804.

Highway 12, labeled "The Lewis and Clark Trail," traces the dispirited footsteps of the crew for 228 miles from the south end of Missoula through Lolo Pass to Lewiston, Idaho. Although it was discouraging for the crew, the Trail passes through miles of superlative forests, along clear streams, to the confluence of the Snake and Clearwater rivers in Idaho.

Once over Lolo Pass, the Corps came down-mountain into the land of the Nez Percé, level country rich with plants, game, and salmon, in what is now Clearwater National Forest. Here the Indian women showed the expedition how to survive on roots, make bread, and gig the salmon. Lewis and the crew found the Nez Percé the most intelligent and friendly of all the Indian nations they had encountered. The Nez Percé helped them build boats, and then launched them into the currents of the Clearwater. Crossing Idaho on this river they met the Snake River at present-day Clarkston, Washington where, at Sacajawea's insistence, two Nez Percé guides, Twisted Hair and Tetoharsky, maneuvered the expedition through the wild rapids and cascades to the Columbia River. Just outside Lewiston, Idaho, on *Highway 12*, the Nez Percé National Historic Park commemorates this Indian nation.

Not far beyond the Idaho–Washington border the expedition rode out of the canyons and forests into bluebunch and wheatgrass prairies. Buffalo, elk, and antelope roamed the banks of the swift and treacherous river. Today the lower Snake has been harnessed by four dams and is crossed by *State Highways 127* and *261*.

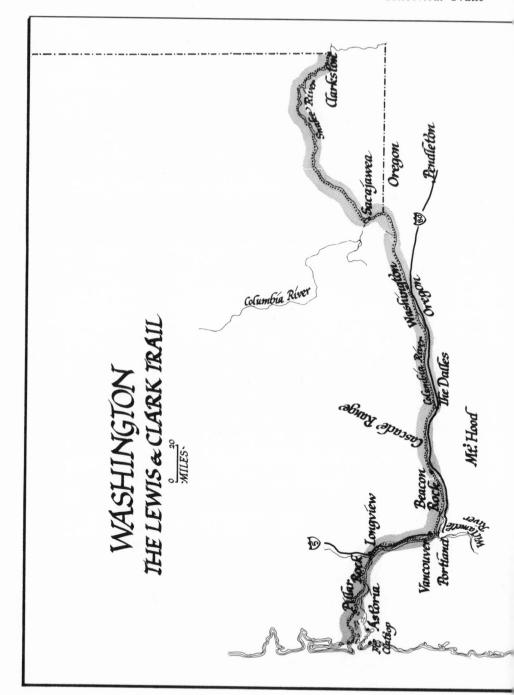

WASHINGTON
THE LEWIS & CLARK TRAIL

Ranches lines its bank. Foot trails at Lyons Ferry and in Sacajawea State Park bring the walker to the roiling confluence of the Snake and Columbia at Pasco, Washington.

The expedition reached this long-sought objective on October 16, 1805. Here on the sage and wheatgrass plains, among the bison and antelope, they celebrated with the Yakima Indians, relatives of the Nez Percé. At daybreak they bid their new friends farewell and pushed out onto the currents of the mighty Columbia.

Interstate 80N parallels on land the expedition's tumultuous ride down the Columbia on the Oregon side, as *State Highway 14* does on the Washington side of the river. For almost two hundred miles the Corps traveled through the high desert land of the golden eagle and prairie dog, the eagle's favorite prey. Mt. Hood appeared against the sky at almost every bend as the river rushed the Corps to the Dalles, a forbidding waterfall and the beginning of the coastal forest. Of that amazing falls, now dammed, Lewis wrote: "At this place the water of this great river is compressed into a channel between two rocks not exceeding 45 yards wide . . . the whole of the current of this great river must at all stages pass thro' this narrow channel."

After conferring with the Indians, a portage around the Dalles was selected, leading through Indian villages where braves were spearing salmon, and squaws were smoking them in riverbank lodges. Beyond the Dalles lay cascades that are now covered by Bonneville Dam, and once more Lewis looked for a land route around this water that plunged and leaped forty feet into the air. No easy route could be found, and the boats had to be roped down the roaring falls. At the bottom the crew was met by herds of sea otter, the first sign that the ocean was not far ahead. They pressed on to the site of present-day Portland, where fog and rain obliterated the river for weeks and where they were kept awake at night by logs, from four to seven feet in diameter, riding up on the shore on the tide.

Not until late November did the members of the expedition finally see salt water, and their cheers were loud and long. They were on the bay, however, not the ocean, for Jefferson had told them they would find the Hudson Bay Company here. None of the trappers of the company appeared, however, and the expedition pushed on to the north side of the bay, off present-day *State High-*

way 4 and 401, to make camp with the Chinook Indians. Here, in November, they saw the long-sought Pacific Ocean for the first time and settled down to wait, President Jefferson having instructed Clark "to hail any vessel in the name of the President and come home by ship" if they desired.

Since they were still not on the ocean shore, they broke camp a few weeks later and paddled across the bay to Fort Clatsop (*U. S. Highway 101 and 26*). A national monument today marks this last campsite of the Corps of Discovery, named for their hosts, the resident Clatsop Indians.

After waiting and watching for a ship for almost three months, in March 1806, no ship having appeared, they started back east. Lewis was longing to explore the Yellowstone River, and Sacajawea was eager to go home.

The return trip up the Yellowstone River can be walked by following *Interstates* 90 and 94, *U. S. Highway 10,* and Wyoming *State Highway 16* between Three Forks and Sidney, Montana.

Lewis, Clark, and the Corps arrived in Washington, D. C. in the spring of 1807 to a heroes' welcome. All the members of the expedition but one man who died of appendicitis in Missouri completed this extraordinary search for knowledge.

Interstate Highways Giving Access to the Lewis and Clark Trail

Illinois:
   Interstate 270

Missouri:
   Interstate 70
   Interstate 35
   Interstate 29

Nebraska:
   Interstate 29
   Interstate 80

South Dakota:
   Interstate 90

North Dakota:
   Interstate 94

Montana:
   Interstate 15
   Interstate 94
   Interstate 90

Idaho:
   Interstate 15
   Interstate 80N

Oregon:
    Interstate 80N

Washington:
    Interstate 205
    Interstate 5

Bibliography and Maps

BAKELESS, JOHN. *Lewis and Clark: Partners in Discovery.* New York: William Morrow and Company, 1947.

CHIDSEY, DONALD. *Lewis and Clark: The Great Adventure.* New York: Crown Publishers, Inc., 1970.

DEVOTO, BERNARD, ed. *The Journals of Lewis and Clark.* Boston: Houghton Mifflin Company, 1953.

GILBERT, BIL. *The Trailblazers.* New York: Time–Life Books, 1973.

PALMER, RALPH S. *The Mammal Guide.* Garden City, N.Y.: Doubleday and Company, Inc., 1954.

PETERSON, ROGER TORY. *A Field Guide to the Birds.* Boston: Houghton Mifflin, 1968.

U.S. DEPARTMENT OF THE INTERIOR, BUREAU OF OUTDOOR RECREATION. A brochure on the Lewis and Clark Trail, containing a small map of the entire route, is available from the Bureau's Denver office, P.O. Box 25387, Denver, Colorado 80225. (Note: State road maps are sufficient for following the route taken by Lewis and Clark along the Missouri, Yellowstone, Bitterroot, Clearwater, Snake, and Columbia rivers.)

12

THE NATCHEZ TRACE *

░░░░░░░░░░░░░░░░░░░░░░░░░░░░░░░░░░░░

F rom Natchez, on the Mississippi River, northeastward across
Mississippi and Alabama, up through Tennessee to Nashville, jags the forbidding Natchez Trace. A 450-mile-long
footpath that passes through forests hung with swatches of Spanish moss, through black swamps and canebrakes, the former Indian
trail became, in the late 1700s, a footpath for river boatmen who
floated down the Mississippi River, left their hand-powered boats at
Natchez, and walked back up to the Ohio River. Today the way is a
macadam parkway for drive-and-walkers, bikers, equestrians, and
hikers. The Trace (from a French word meaning "footpath") is
easy to traverse. From approximately 250 feet above sea level at
Natchez, the trail rises to just 1000 feet at Nashville. Most of the
way is paved, but side excursions in the old Trace wind into the
original forests.

Snaking through the rolling plains in Tennessee, the Trace
slithers in and out of the Eastern interior highlands, crosses the
Tennessee River in Alabama, and goes into Tennessee, a land that
is primarily underlaid by limestone, the beds of ancient Appalachian seas. Three biotic communities cloak the route: Southeastern
Pine, Midland Broadleaf, and the Southern River-Bottom forests
of cypress, tupelo, and sweetgum.

Patches of sun, voices of primitive birds, and dark, dripping caves
create an atmosphere that is as moody as the trail's own history.

"I have ridden and walked many trails," said bike and walker
Bill Craighead of Ft. Worth, Texas, "though none with the mood

---

* For information about biotic communities along this trail see pages 271–274.

188

as sad and melancholy as the Natchez Trace. Perhaps it is caused
by the tall loblolly pines, the dark live oaks festooned with moss or
the bald cypress and tupelo standing knee deep in ink-black water
keeping the Trace in perennial shade. But I don't think so. I think
it is the nefarious history of the Trace that has lingered on."

Originally hammered into the soil by the feet of prehistoric
tribes and by the Natchez Indians after A.D. 1200, the Trace came
to the attention of Europeans in 1541, when De Soto followed it
into an Indian village to spend part of the winter with a tribe of
Chickasaw Indians. While there he sent back to Spain a description of the giant forests along the trail, of alligators, caves, Indian
fields, and giant woodpeckers.

More than a hundred and fifty years later, an adventurous French
trader whose name is unknown to us set up business at French Lick,
now Nashville, and encouraged his friends the La Loire brothers to
establish a trading post in Natchez, the Indian village at the end
of the footpath on the Mississippi.

Within five years the post became a prosperous and luxuriant
French colony. Pecan, pawpaw, sweetbay, magnolia, catalpa, persimmon, locust, wild plum, and tulip-trees graced the streets of
Natchez. Colonists settled their houses among oaks and buckeye
trees. The wild cherry and the cabbage palm grew in their gardens
and climbed over fences, the trumpet vine, whose flowers brought
hosts of iridescent hummingbirds to the fort on the bluff. As the
colony expanded, resentment arose among the Natchez and in 1729
they attacked and destroyed the French town. This massacre was
the opening incident of the French and Indian wars, which lasted
for thirty years and virtually wiped out the tribe.

At the end of that struggle, the young and adventurous Daniel
Boone, taking only an axe and a gun, left his home in English-held
Carolina and set out for Nashville. Clearing brush, felling trees, he
blazed the Wilderness Trail across Kentucky, leaving his name on
tree and rock in the manner of trail-blazers of his day. As he pro-
gressed he cut down huge chestnuts to make "raccoon bridges"
across creeks and cleared campgrounds on "good sites" with water
and views.

After a year of this, he joined his Wilderness Trail to the Natchez
Trace at Nashville, thus linking the populous east with the frontier.

The Wilderness Trail is now almost entirely paved, but wild

parts are still to be found by the persistent around *Interstate 65* out of Nashville to Bowling Green, *U. S. Highway 62* and *U. S. Highway 150* to Danville and *U. S. Highway 150* to London. From London the Daniel Boone Parkway extends to Bonnyman, where it ends and where the walker with map and compass can begin to bushwhack from town to town, inquiring along the way for the old Wilderness Road to Knoxville, Tennessee. The way is still alive with legends told in the hills, and if these are completely accurate, whatever direction the walker takes is beautiful and not much changed. Black bears still hunt for beechnuts and huckleberries, and the mountain maple flourishes as it did when Boone slashed his way to the Natchez Trace.

Before the end of the century, both roads were heavily used by settlers, traders, government officials, gamblers, singers, craftsmen, ministers, and dancers, all heading for the river towns where they hoped to make a living. Primarily, however, the Trace was traveled northward by boatmen who brought wares down the Mississippi to Natchez but could not go back upstream. The men sold their flatboats for house lumber, and rode horses or walked past canebrakes (native bamboo savannahs) and swamps, and through briars and thickets to Nashville, where they took the Ohio River to the Mississippi. Along the way some of history's most heinous thieves and murderers lay in ambush. Although these men are not heralded by the parkway their presence haunts the umbra.

The first outlaws to terrify walkers along the Trace were two homicidal maniacs, Micajah, "Big Harpe," and Wiley, "Little Harpe." Sons of a Tory who had been driven into hiding after the Revolution, the two young men, according to a newspaper report, had a "dried and lifeless look and the stare of animals." They committed their first robbery on the Wilderness Trail in 1797. Their victim was a poor minister whom they robbed of a few dollars. Upon reaching home he gave a vivid description of the pair: "Their actions were erratic and half-controlled, and two dirty and ragged women were with them. The filthy men, however, throbbed with a strange fury; when they accosted me, they yelled, 'We are the Harpes.' " This was the only crime the Harpes committed that did not end in murder.

The horrors of their countless slayings became campfire talk on the Trace, and led within a year to an effort by government officials to round up all land and river pirates. The result of this was to drive the outlaws together at a hideout at Cave-in Rock on the Mississippi. The Harpes' stay with the other outlaws was not long. One night, after a boat had been robbed and most of its passengers murdered, the bandits were huddled around a fire. Looking up, they saw a horse flying over the cliff above them, eyes bulging and legs flailing. Tied to its back was a naked rider who stared down at the rocks before he and horse struck with a "terrible splash of blood." In a few moments the Harpes strode down the hill, laughing at the ingenuity of their latest murder. The deed was too much even for these hardened outlaws, and they drove the brothers into the forest.

After three more years of violence, the husband of one of the Harpes' victims found "Big Harpe," wounded him, cut off his head while he was still alive, and nailed it to a tree. It hung near Red Bank at the crossing of Robertson's Lick, en route to Chattanooga on *U. S. Highway 27.* Before Harpe died he told his vengeful executor that he regretted only one murder. "When I got mad at my kid," he said, "I grabbed him by the heels and slugged him against a tree." Following the death of his brother, "Little Harpe" ran off into the canebrakes.

About this time keelboats that could be sailed and pulled upstream began arriving at Natchez. Keelboat crews were a hard group who fought among themselves and who, lacking a river opponent, tackled the townsmen of Natchez. Despite such brawls the town boomed, making fortunes off the keelboat crewmen with booze, women, and other wares.

On the scene came Samuel Mason. He arrived in town with a paper stating that he was "a brave soldier in the Revolution and a Justice of the Peace in Kentucky," and set up business. Before the year was out, after killing the outlaw who had just married his daughter on their wedding day, he had vanished into the swamps along the Trace, where he turned highwayman. The atrocities he committed made front-page headlines as far away as Louisville, Kentucky. Travelers reported being followed by an "eerie presence" for hours and hours before being assaulted in the jungle-like shadows of the Natchez Trace.

After two years of plundering the rich boatmen and merchants on the Trace, Mason returned to Natchez in disguise and staged a respectable comeback. One evening at a party, however, he was identified, accused of murder, and carried off to trial. Convicted, he received thirty-nine lashes as punishment. Insane with rage, he returned to the cypress and black-oak-covered Trace to rob and murder again. This time, as an added twist, he dismembered the bodies of his victims and scattered them on the road. After several such murders a posse rode out and caught him only to see him escape again. He set up camp this time in a canebrake about forty miles north of Natchez. Here, with a companion who called himself Setton, he killed and cut up many more travelers. One day Setton led one of the few of Mason's victims who had survived to their hideout. The victim turned on Mason and killed him, whereupon he and Setton returned to Natchez with the dead outlaw's head preserved in a ball of clay. They were showing it off in the courthouse when a stranger who had just entered, recognizing "Setton," shouted: "That's Little Harpe." The outlaw jumped through the window and escaped but was captured and killed on the Trace in Greenville, twenty miles north of Natchez. His head was mounted on a pole as his brother's had been and displayed on the Trace.

By this time the U. S. Postal Service was using the Natchez Trace, and gained permission from the few remaining Chickasaw and Choctaw Indians to improve and straighten it. The effort to rid the trail of outlaws was hardly noticeable.

Onto the Trace came John A. Murrel, who outdid even the Harpes. He lured slaves off plantations, then beat and sold them. During the 1820s and '30s he also organized a group of miserable slaves who were, on a certain day, instructed to rebel and kill their masters, whereupon he and his gang in their turn would kill the Blacks and loot the plantations. Fortunately the rebellion never came off.

After 1812, when the steamboat *New Orleans* docked at Natchez, boatmen and merchants were able to go back upstream. Travel along the Trace dropped off, and most of the land pirates moved to the river. Ten years later, by the Treaty of the Dancing Rabbit Creek, the Choctaw Indians ceded all lands east of the Mississippi to the United States and the tribe moved to Oklahoma. A few months later, after a bitter debate and great pressure, the Chickasaws signed a similar agreement and followed the Choctaws into oblivion. Their ancestral villages along the Trace, which for centuries had bound the two nations together, were gradually overgrown by trees and ferns. The abandoned road was used briefly again when General Grant marched his army from Port Gibson to Raymond, slashing back the briars and felling the trees along the way. A year later, what was left of the Confederate General Hood's army retreated over the Trace to Tupelo, Mississippi; when the last man had passed, the road was forgotten again. Pileated woodpeckers and the now almost certainly extinct ivorybill ranged among the black oaks and hickories, and blue-eyed grass, the flower of hard-used trails, flourished in sunny spots. In time the wagon ruts were taken over by sassafras and greenbrier, and for the next forty years the Trace belonged to nature.

In 1909 the Mississippi Daughters of the American Revolution, in a flurry of southern patriotism, marked the overgrown trail with stone posts. For another twenty years these small monuments and a few ruts were all that remained of the wilderness trail from Natchez to Nashville.

With the onset of the Depression and the coming of the New Deal, Congressman Jeff Busby of Mississippi joined forces with the DAR and obtained federal funds to pave the old Trace and bring it into Jackson, the capital of Mississippi.

The haunting beauty of the forests penetrated by the modern road, the relics of Indian history, and the sites of dark doings along the old Trace, brought so many walkers and bikers to the road that in 1938 Congress established the Natchez Parkway. Today about 100 miles of the macadam remain to be completed, but it is to be hoped they never will be. The Bureau of Outdoor Recreation is now reclaiming the old wagon ruts for a foot path.

Biologically few areas in the United States are as striking as the country around the moody Natchez Trace. Redbud, dogwood, azalea, and rhododendron flowers spangle the roadside in spring. Wild roses and red honeysuckle color it in summer. The limbs of baldcypress and live oak are draped with curtains of moss, and form dark aerial corridors for the abundant red, gray, and flying squirrels. Armadillos grunt in the dimness and rattle the leaves of the forest floor. The dampness absorbs the sounds of voice and footstep, and walkers move in hushed silence.

The geological base of the Trace also contributes to its atmosphere. It is almost entirely of limestone, the remnant of ancient seabeds which have been eroded into caves in many places. In any

MISSISSIPPI
NATCHEZ TRACE

0 10 20 30
·MILES·

Tennessee

Corinth   72

45   Buzzard
                Roost

Tupelo   Tupelo
Nat'l Battlefield
                Davis
                Lake

Mississippi River   Old Trace
                              88

                         15

Arkansas
Louisiana

                         55

              Canton
                    Cypress Swamp
61   Jackson   Ridge Road

20   Alabama

              Rocky Springs

Port Gibson
Canebrake   Red Lick
Emerald   Washington
Mound   Natchez
                553

Natchez Trace Nat'l Parkway

Tennessee River

one of these the walker can imagine the Harpes, Mason, and Murrel hiding out.

Today the Natchez Trace Parkway begins at Washington, Mississippi, six miles northeast of Natchez on *U. S. Highway 61*. Another six miles up the road, in the quiet countryside where American redstarts and brown thrashers flit through the treetops, stands Emerald Mound. The shield-shaped earthen structure is one of the many ceremonial mounds built by the prehistoric ancestors of the Natchez Indians. Emerald Mound covers nearly eight acres, and once supported temples and elaborate civic processions. Ceremonial dances were performed here, as well as solemn religious rituals.

Highly advanced farmers, these Indians produced enough beans, corn, and pumpkins to feed a large population of craftsmen, artists, and public workers. Eventually these Mississippi Valley Indians went out on the Trace to trade pottery, fishhooks, and arrowheads for shells from the Gulf Indians and copper from the people who lived around the Great Lakes.

A rest area at *State Highway 553* and Coles Creek is a showplace of wild geraniums and blue dayflowers, as well as a nesting area of the Carolina wren. Here the mood of the Trace is light, and the wild things are friendly. For the next twenty miles the walker takes the old Trace into the shadowy forest, and the biker and auto driver stay on *State Highway 553* to Russum.

Just out of Russum, another stretch of the original Trace leads into a tupelo forest green with club moss and ferns. In its shadow mockingbirds imitate everything from wrens to bike brakes, and Kentucky and Parula warblers flash through the forest crown like a whirling light show. On the soundscape is heard the dull drum of the red-headed woodpecker, the stunning carpenter of the pine and red cedar.

On up the Trace stands Mangum Mound, where copper ornaments, probably trade goods from the north, have been found in hilltop graves. In contrast to this quiet spot, a few miles farther along is Rocky Springs Park, a lively campground with modern trinkets and plastic trade goods. Kids laugh, bikes glitter in the sun, and here the Trace is noisy and gay.

A nature trail at this historic site passes the area where Murrel revealed his plans for a slave uprising to a young man named Virgil Stewart, who had joined him on a trip up the Trace. The walker can follow their footsteps up the Trace to Jackson. No mention is made of the outlaws at the trailside rests, for the Mississippi DAR is eager to forget them. Labels on the trees identify only the slender tupelo, famous for the fine honey its blossoms provide, the royal ferns that arise like great hands from the wet earth, and other plants of the forest.

A few miles beyond Jackson is Cypress Swamp, where pitcher plants and sundews (both insectivorous plants) grow in abundance, and where many a long-ago traveler was waylaid and clobbered. Great blue herons and snowy egrets now hunt among the reeds where the Harpe brothers hunted their victims, and kingfishers dive for fish as their ancestors did when the Murrel gang killed slaves who became too rebellious to keep. Patches of Virginia spiderwort color the once bloody trailside blue. At Beaver Dam, a few miles along, a family of beavers maneuver logs and mend leaks in their dams.

Hurricane Creek, another ten miles up the way, wends through an oak–pine forest where great swatches of crimson clover grow. Bluebirds nest in the fenceposts along the way, and the white-breasted nuthatch scolds from the chinquapin tree, that small relative of the vanished American chestnut. Several miles farther along, another stretch of the old Trace parallels the modern parkway and walkers follow deep ruts through a dense, dark forest.

The terrain and vegetation change as the Trace arrives at the hilly country near Davis Lake. Ridges, valleys, and bright outcrops of limestone mark the countryside, and the vegetation is more like that of the north. Maples and hickory replace tupelo and cypress. At Davis Lake the Forest Service provides camping, swimming, and trails to explore.

Some ten miles farther along, on the edge of an oak and pine forest, the walker encounters an abundance of the famous royal purple phlox, a native of Texas. Seeds of this handsome flower were sent to England by Thomas Drummond in the early 1800s and were planted in Kew Gardens, where they thrive today and whence they returned to America. When British seed catalogues featured them in the late 1800s, many Mississippians ordered and planted them. The phlox escaped gardens and now festoons the Natchez Trace Parkway.

Near Lake Davis is the Tupelo National Battlefield, where the

Confederate General Stephen D. Lee attacked the Union forces, and farther on up the road is the site of the last Chickasaw village. A memorial nature trail displays the plants the Indians cultivated: corn, squash, and potatoes.

At the northeast edge of the city of Tupelo, automobile travelers and bikers leave the unfinished Parkway and take *U. S. Highway 45, State Highways 30* and *25*, and *U. S. Highway 72* to Buzzard Roost, where the Trace Parkway picks up again. The walker, however, can go overland to Bear Creek Mound and Cave Springs on the Old Trace.

At Buzzard Roost, the Chickasaw Chief Levi Colbert ran ferries across the Tennessee River. Since Colbert's ferry was on the south bank of Bear Creek, travelers coming from the north had trouble shouting loudly enough to make him hear; often they had to wait for days in the outlaw-infested forest. When the U. S. Army moved troops down the Trace, Colbert became the wealthiest man in the Chickasaw nation by charging a dollar a head for the crossing.

' Across the Tennessee River at Rock Springs, the Colbert Creek Trail leads through stands of wild iris and live oak to a clear, flowing spring edged with arrowhead and wild hydrangea.

On up the parkway at Sweetwater Branch, a short trail displays some of the abundant wild plants, including waterdock, pokeweed, and sumac.

Five miles farther along is Old Trace Loop Drive, a two-and-a-half mile road that follows an Indian path on the limestone ridge. The Natchez Indians, aware of the value of the valley soils for farming, built their trails on the poor soils of the ridges.

A series of old iron mines along the Buffalo River, the first such mines in the South, extends along the ridge to Meriwether Lewis Park where the parkway ends. Here Meriwether Lewis, of the Lewis and Clark Expedition of 1804–6, died mysteriously while traveling the Natchez Trace.

The final Natchez Trace stone, laid by the DAR, lies at Pasque on *State Highway 100* in the outskirts of Nashville. The monument sits where the Mississippi boatmen, after surviving the hazards of the Natchez Trace, took the Cumberland and Ohio rivers west to the Mississippi. Northward from the stone, tradesmen and government officials took off along Daniel Boone's Wilderness Trail to Washington, D. C.

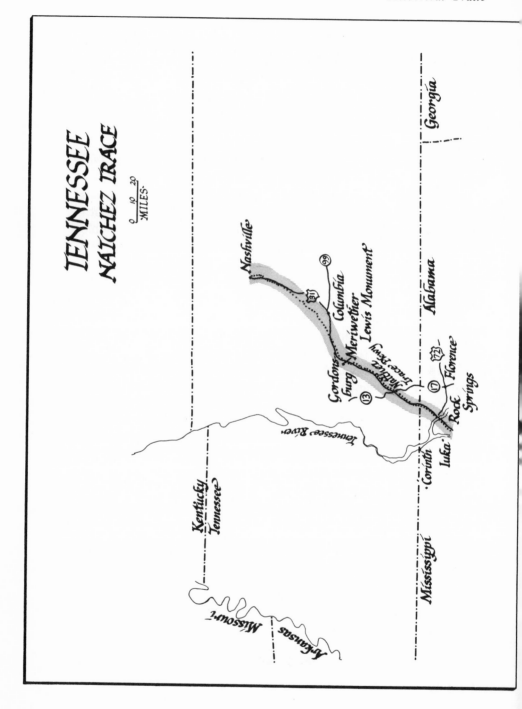

The trees, birds, and wildflowers around the last marker are those that existed when the ancestors of the Natchez Indians bent the grasses with their moccasins to form the Natchez Trace.

Bibliography

BROCKMAN, FRANK C. *Trees of North America: A Guide to Field Identification.* New York: Golden Press, 1968.

COATES, ROBERT M. *The Outlaw Years: The History of the Land Pirates of the Natchez Trace.* New York: Literary Guild, 1930.

DILLON, RICHARD. *Meriwether Lewis, A Biography.* New York: Coward–McCann, 1965.

"Natchez Trace, Indian Trail to Parkway, The," *The Alabama Review,* September 1962.

"Natchez Trace in Alabama, The," *The Alabama Review,* January 1954.

Natchez Trace Parkway, The. Leaflet; free. Available at visitors' centers and along the parkway.

Natchez Trace Parkway Survey. Senate Document No. 148, 76th Congress, Washington: Government Printing Office, 1941.

PHELPS, DAWSON A. "The Tragic Death of Meriwether Lewis," *William and Mary Quarterly,* July 1956 (3rd ser., Vol. XIII).

ROBBINS, CHANDLER, BERTEL BRUUN, and HERBERT S. ZIM. *Birds of North America: A Guide to Field Identification.* New York: Golden Press, 1966.

U.S. DEPARTMENT OF THE INTERIOR, NATIONAL PARK SERVICE. A map and information on the Natchez Trace National Parkway is available from the Park Service's Tupelo Visitor Center, R. R. 1, NT–143, Tupelo, Mississippi 38801.

13

THE CHISHOLM CATTLE TRAIL *

The Chisholm Cattle Trail, now largely buried under highways and towns, once ran through grasslands between the sandstone escarpments of Texas northward into the Tall-Grass Prairie of Oklahoma and Kansas. A vast natural meadow road for bison, after the Civil War the Cattle Trail became the greatest domestic animal migration route in the world. For twenty years it was pounded by the hooves of more than fourteen million steers being driven by cowboys to the railroads in Abilene, Newton, and Wichita, Kansas. Today the dust has settled, and grasslands have been fenced and given over to cotton, ranges, cities, and highways. Nevertheless, small sections of the Chisholm Trail are now parks and pathways that preserve the grasses and the rip-roaring cowboy history.

The Chisholm Trail is flat and easy to walk except for the heat in summer and the constant wind. Most people drive and explore the Trail, some ride it on horseback, and a few walk the long, open miles.

The geology is that of the plains, the newest land in North America, which until very recently (approximately 10,000 years ago) was part of the Gulf of Mexico.

The Trail penetrates 1500 miles of mesquite, Southeastern oak savannah, and Tall-Grass Prairie. River bottomlands of cottonwood, rushes, and reeds stitch the grasslands with threads of dark green. From the air the Chisholm Trail looks like a river of grass flowing between shores of post and backjack oak and elm.

* For information about biotic communities along this trail see pages 276–277, 284.

200

This natural pasture was a favorite hunting area of the Cherokee Indians. Grazing their horses as they went, crossing the duck- and crane-filled rivers, for generations they moved at a leisurely pace through this grassy country, harvesting bison, antelope, and elk.

Into the Indian hunting land at the turn of the nineteenth century came young Jesse Chisholm, half Cherokee, half Scotsman. He got his love for this grassland from the Cherokees, and frequently traveled through it on visits to his Indian brothers and the white settlers. After the Civil War he established a trading post near Wichita, loaded his wagon with goods, and set out to trade along the way. In the course of his business he steered hundreds of cowboys and drovers up the green route, rescued several white men from the Indians, and taught the cowboys how to stop grass fires and where to find plants to eat. Chisholm died in 1868, poisoned by bear grease he had boiled in a brass kettle. Well loved by Indian and cowboy, he is immortalized by a marker erected over his grave that reads: "JESSE CHISHOLM. Born 1805. Died 1868. No one left his home hungry." The stone sits in Blaine County, Oklahoma, thirty miles northwest of El Reno, off *U. S. Highway 270* on the north fork of the Canadian River. He died without ever knowing that the great Trail was to bear his name.

The Chisholm Trail began in Brownsville, Texas, on the Mexican border, where drovers bought and rustled cattle or rounded up wild herds and set out on one of the great adventures in American history—the cattle drive. Hundred of young men left upper-class homes to join the trek through this wild land. Their adventures included encounters with Indians, saloon keepers, sheriffs, gamblers, women, and stampeding animals. The noise and hullabaloo of the drives were surpassed only by the destruction they inflicted on native plants and wildlife along the 1500 miles of the Chisholm Trail.

The land is less altered on the southern stretch of the Trail than the northern one and the walker can enjoy the primitive country north of Brownsville along *U. S. Highway 77*. The niches and dips are freckled with mesquite and jammed with tumbleweed. The horned toad skips over the parched, stony land, and the spotted skunk digs for grubs in the mesquite biome that is its native habitat.

Beyond San Antonio the Trail, now *Interstate 35* and *U. S. Highway 81*, goes between the East and West Cross Timbers, forested

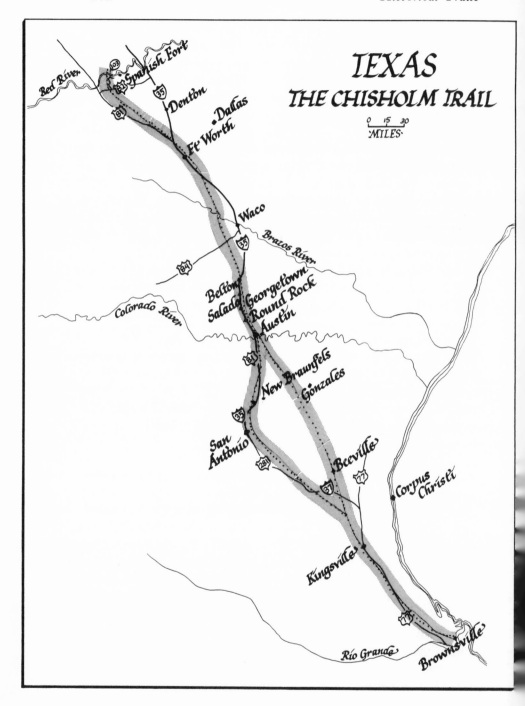

TEXAS
THE CHISHOLM TRAIL

0   15   30
·MILES·

areas that cross the northeastern part of the state. Along side roads and at the edges of ranches and ditches, scattered clumps of high prairie cordgrass, bluestem, and Indian grass grow tall. Once these graceful plants rippled from horizon to horizon.

At what is now Austin the drovers found an easy crossing of the Colorado River, after which they spread out into the pastureway, between rolling cotton fields to the east and the Balcones Escarpment and the Edwards Plateau to the west. Today the walker can find the crossing on bridges in downtown Austin.

Going north, side trips off *Interstate 35* pass through carpets of Texas squaw weed and acres of red and yellow blanketflower or gaillardia, a flame on the praire from April to June.

Round Rock, named after the huge rock in Bushy Creek, is a town for walking. The quiet streets are lined with many buildings dating to cattle-drive days, including the St. Charles Hotel (1850), the favorite hangout of cattlemen who were confident enough of their cowboys to leave them in charge of the herd for a night. Rustling and the stampeding of the cattle were their major worries. A twig snapping, a boom of thunder, even a raised voice, could start a herd running. One animal would run, then another, then ten, and finally the entire herd would be running, heads back, eyes bugging with fear. A stampede was a disaster that could be stopped only if a cowboy got ahead of the herd's leaders and turned them until the entire herd was running in a circle. Gradually, then, the circle would tighten until the animals slowed down and came to a stop.

Along the Blue River one night in 1872, a herd stampeded during a storm and the cowboys spent the entire night trying to turn them. "In the morning," a trail rider named Teddy Blue Abbott wrote home, "we found one of our men beside his horse. The horse's rib was scraped bare of hide and all the rest of horse and man was mashed into the ground as flat as a pancake."

The Chisholm Trail cuts through Georgetown, in cotton country, and comes into Salado, where the Stagecoach Inn brags of visits from Robert E. Lee, Ulysses S. Grant, and Jesse James. Pioneer houses date back to trail days, and the Central Texas Area Museum specializes in Chisholm Trail history.

The next stop is Belton, the home of the Sanctificationists, a group of pioneer women who deserted their husbands' beds after a minister told them sex was a sin. Belton was also famous for a sheriff who repeatedly extorted fees from Chisholm Trail cowboys going past the town. One day in 1870, so the story goes, a young man could not pay up and the sheriff accepted a steer. The boy roped the animal to a tree, cut the rope almost through before leaving, and rode on. By the time he reached the Leon River, now Belton Lake Reservoir, the steer had broken free and caught up with him.

At Belton Lake the Trail goes west on *State Highway 317* to Mother Neff State Park. This was a favorite campsite for the drovers. The grasses were tall and luxuriant and the Cross Timberland where Indians lurked behind trees was far away. The major fear at Mother Neff was of stampedes. To prevent them the cowboys sat up all night singing to their herds, and to keep awake they boiled coffee grounds for hours to make "six-shooter," a brew so strong it "propped their eyes open."

West of Waco the old Chisholm Trail crossed the deep and often raging Brazos River, where the drovers were forced to float their wagons and swim their cattle. Lake Whitney, Cleburne, and Acton state parks have fine walking trails in this river land, now altered by the dams and reservoirs.

Commerce Street in downtown Fort Worth was once a campground where cattle and men gathered before crossing the Trinity River. In the area of City Hall and the Court House, saloon doors swung open and music blared. Here the drovers outfitted themselves with saddles, six-shooters, ropes, and food for the rest of the trip. The Trinity River today, as it flows through Fort Worth and out across the plains, except for an excellent bike and walk trail along quiet, tree-lined banks, is much as it was in the late 1800s.

Veering northwest, the Chisholm Trail follows the Wise–Denton county line, paralleling *U. S. Highway 81*, into what was once a lush prairie with rivers easy to ford. The land, farmed and developed today, harbored prairie-dog colonies, coyotes, and acres of wildflowers from the county line to the famous Red River, on the border between Texas and Oklahoma.

Just below the mouth of Fleetwood Branch, east of *U. S. 81N* on *State Highway 103*, the Texas Rangers set up the Red River Station, now Spanish Fort. In the Trail days government inspectors checked the brands on the cattle at this station. Men found in possession of unbranded steers were subject to a heavy fine. Often

they were simply tossed into a wagon, ridden out of town, and released in the middle of Indian territory. Some never made the walk back to the station.

Since crossing the Red River, with its quicksands and rushing waters, was hazardous, the cattle were fattened for several days to make them more buoyant. Ready to move, the cowboys would strip to their shorts and, running as fast as they could, drive the cattle swiftly through the brush and into the water. Those who survived the crossing thanked their lucky stars and moved on.

In Oklahoma, *U. S. Highway* 81 closely follows the old Chisholm Trail past a stretch of blackjack oaks known as Blue Grove. To the west the land is open, rolling prairie. The common birds here are meadow and horned larks, field sparrows, and bobolinks, and the horizon stretches twenty miles before and behind. Clouds, sun, and stars take over and the sky overwhelms the prairie.

A dirt road leading east from Addington runs across the prairie to Monument Hill, a flat-topped mesa on which are piled red sandstone boulders, heaped there by cowboys who then scratched their initials on them. The old Duncan Store, a famous rendezvous for cowboys, is east of Duncan, now an oil town. Beyond it, the Trail winds north on *U. S. 81* through Marlow (named after two brothers who lived in a dugout on the banks of Wildhorse Creek) and on to Chisholm Lake.

In Rush Springs, once a popular cowboy camping ground, is a municipal park where the spring still bubbles out of the earth with cool sounds. East of Chickasha, the crossing of the Washita River once was a problem for the drovers. The grass was so lush that the cowhands had to whoop and holler, ride and circle, often for hours, to get the cattle to stop grazing and move across the river.

State Highway 92 out of Chickasha follows every turn of the old Chisholm Trail through Amber and Tuttle to the Canadian River, where the route divided. The northwest branch ran to El Reno along today's *U. S. Highway 81* to Dover, and a less-used branch led through present-day Yukon.

On the north bank of the North Canadian River, Jesse Chisholm built his home at Council Grove in Blaine County. Indians and cowboys rode miles to trade and talk to him and to learn the whereabouts of the grazing grasses, bluestem and grama, the bison, antelope, and deer. They spiked their diet of beans with tasty prairie chicken, venison, and antelope tongue, and named one creek Turkey Skeleton for the leftovers of that bird. Beyond Dover the land is almost totally flat, and in Chisholm Trail days it supported more prairie dogs than New York City has people. Not a tree grew in this land of "diggers," and the cowboys struggled to get their animals around their holes and burrows.

Hennessey, also on *U. S. Highway 81*, is named for the cross-country freight-hauler Pat Hennessey, who was killed and had his wagons burned by Indians, and whose grave lies a block off the highway. This is a walk town with interesting old streets.

U. S. Highway 81 follows the Chisholm Trail to Enid, where it strikes off to Kremlin, a Russian community of singular beauty. On up *U. S. 81*, the crossing of the Salt Fork of the Arkansas River at Pond Creek is a landmark where the Chisholm route intersected an Indian warpath called Black Dog Trail, named after an Osage chief on whose territory the drovers trespassed. According to the religious beliefs of the Osage, scalps must accompany the braves to their Happy Hunting Ground, and a blond scalp better than a black one. Consequently, blond cowboys were terrified of losing theirs at this crossing. Many outfitters went so far as to hire Negro cowboys to avert disaster; others rushed across Black Dog Trail at night and took shelter at Stewell's Stockade, a mile south of Jefferson.

Beyond Pond Creek the Chisholm Trail veers northeast through land once inhabited by the vanishing prairie dog. Here Buffalo competed with longhorns for grama grass—and lost. East of Medford the Trail leaves Oklahoma, crosses into Kansas, and arrives at what in 1800 was the end of Indian Territory.

In Kansas the Trail spears eastward across the open prairie through acres of sunflowers to Abilene, the first terminus of the Trail. As the rails were laid southward to meet the cattle herds and cowboys, Newton became the second terminus and Wichita the third. Within a month of the arrival of the railhead in this village of Indian huts, the primeval serenity was transformed into a howling collection of saloons, stores, houses, and hotels. Today's Wichita is not ribald, and the Trail along the Arkansas is quiet. At Cow Town is a restoration of the buildings that were hammered together when, in mid-August, some 2000 cowboys celebrated the end of their long, hot trip up the Chisholm Trail.

State Highway 15 follows the old Trail on to Abilene, the original terminus of the long haul, where hotels, cattle depots, barns, pens, and loading chutes awaited the outfits. From here cattle cars rolled north to Chicago's stockyards, to supply a new U. S. industry—the stockyards.

By 1880 barbed-wire fences and armed farmers defending their property ended the cattle drives. The railroads took over from the drovers, and the old Chisholm Trail was lost under asphalt, industry, and townscape.

Bibliography and Maps

Chronicles of Oklahoma, Vol. 14, No. 1: *The Two Cattle Trails.* Tulsa, Oklahoma, 1941.

COSTELLO, DAVID F. *The Prairie World: Plants and Animals of the Grassland Sea.* New York: Thomas Y. Crowell Company, 1969.

IRWIN, HOWARD S. *Roadside Flowers of Texas.* Austin: University of Texas Press, 1960.

PHILLIPS PETROLEUM COMPANY. *Pasture and Range Plants.* Bartlesville, Oklahoma, 1963.

U.S. FOREST SERVICE. An excellent map of the Cross Timbers National Grasslands is available from the Forest Service's Southern regional office, 1720 Peachtree Road, N.W., Atlanta, Georgia 30309. Note: The Mobil travel map of Texas covers the Chisholm Cattle Trail in that state.

WHITEHOUSE, EULA. *Texas Flowers in Natural Colors.* Dallas: Dallas County Audubon Society, 1936.

14

T H E   O R E G O N   T R A I L *

[1][1][1][1][1][1][1][1][1][1][1][1][1][1][1][1][1][1][1][1][1][1][1][1][1]

The 9935-mile Oregon Trail, across which 400,000 emigrants trekked from Independence, Missouri to the Willamette Valley in Oregon, is a trail of historical monuments, prairie lands, hills and mountains: a drive-read-and-walk path.

From Missouri this historic U. S. trail crosses Kansas, Nebraska, Wyoming, and Idaho, following the route of Western settlers along the Blue, Kansas, Little Blue, North Platte, Sweetwater, Pacific Creek, Big Sandy, Black, Bear, Snake, and Columbia rivers.

On today's Oregon Trail, of which about 900 miles are suitable for the nature walker, the weather—winds, raging storms, heat, and mountain floods—is about all that remains of the wilderness that the emigrants encountered in the 1840s and '50s. Gone are the assaulting Indians, the stampeding bison and marauding grizzlies, gone are the plagues and diseases. Along the route only monuments to these hazards recall the hugeness of the struggle to reach the "rich and peaceful Willamette Valley; a valley more fertile than anywhere else on Earth; rain, warmth in winter, comfortable in summer; Indians share the land with white man, a place for all"— according to an 1840 poster.

No continuous trail blaze marks the Oregon Trail, for it is broken by cities, dams, and industrial complexes. From Kansas across Nebraska, for instance, walkers can find portions of it, thanks to a series of granite markers placed by the Nebraska Historical Society. Parks and recreation areas, wagon ruts and mountain roads are also walkable. The majority of Oregon Trail fans, however, drive to his-

* For information about biotic communities along this trail see pages 264–265, 268–269, 274, 284, 285–287.

torical sites to enjoy picnicking and historical restorations and exhibits. A few seek old battlegrounds and collect buttons, broken glass, arrowheads, and bits of pottery from the soil.

The geology of the route is the geology of two-thirds of the nation. After the limestone of the Missouri Valley, the Trail crosses the sedimentary rocks of the Great Plains, the igneous and metamorphic rocks of the Rocky Mountains, the volcanic layers in Oregon, and finally the sand and limestone of the Pacific coastal plain.

The Oregon Trail begins in the biotic area of Eastern Broadleaf Forest, penetrates the Grasslands, where tall-, short-, and bunch grass grow, and rolls out across the Desert Shrublands to the Western Mixed, Coniferous, Pine and Western Subalpine biomes. It terminates in the Northwestern Coniferous Forest, having taken in just about every biotic community in the Northwest.

The longest of the historical overland routes, the Oregon Trail was first explored by fur traders and explorers. Lewis and Clark (see Lewis and Clark Trail, page 166) mapped and recorded the Western section of the Trail, but Benjamin Bonneville is credited with taking the first wagons through South Pass in the 1830s, unblocking what prior to this had been the major obstacle in a road to the West. John C. Frémont, a decade later, surveyed a large portion of the Trail for the U. S. Army.

The overland emigration began in 1841, when a few families set off for Oregon. They were followed in 1843 by a larger company, numbering a thousand. Leaving Independence, Missouri, they rode northwest to Fort Kearney, Nebraska, then traveled up the Platte River to Fort Laramie, Wyoming. They reached the Sweetwater Branch and crossed through the Indian-held South Pass in the Rockies to Fort Bridger, Wyoming. Plodding on to Fort Hall, in the Snake River area, they crossed to Boise, Idaho, the Grande Ronde Valley, Blue Mountains, and Walla Walla, Washington. Here they took the shores of the Columbia River to Oregon City in the Willamette Valley.

All along the route, the rigors of their journey are recorded on tombs and monuments. Another story is not told, however: although the Trail was a new beginning for many white men, for the Indians it was the beginning of the end. The total cost has not been tallied, and some debts still remain unpaid to the Pawnee, Dakota,

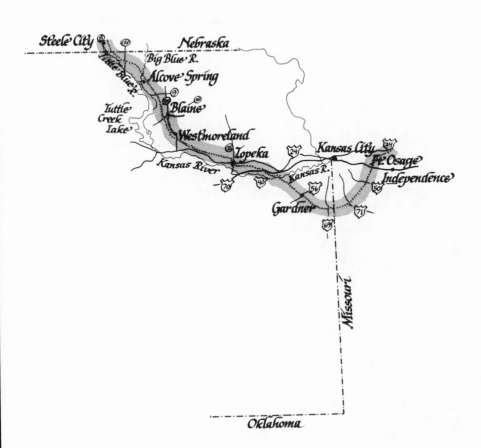

MISSOURI & KANSAS
THE OREGON TRAIL

0   10   20
·MILES·

Cheyenne, Crow, Shoshone, Arapaho, Sioux, Ute, and Blackfeet Indians. The Oregon Trail opened the country for some people but closed it to others.

Although the wild land around Independence, Missouri, the starting point of the Oregon Trail, has been urbanized, many magnificent walnut trees such as were admired by the emigrants still grow in the parks today. Most walkers begin at Independence Court House and the Albert G. Boone Store, which dates back to 1842, when the emigrants clustered at Independence Landing.

The Trail changes from sidewalk and cityscape to a woodsy footpath west of *U. S. Highway 69* in Johnson County, Kansas. Here ten miles of oak, hickory, and walnut shade the Trail.

At Gardner, along *U. S. Highway 56*, is the junction of the Oregon and Santa Fe trails, now covered with macadam and cement but marked by a monument. A foot trail is picked up again at Clinton Reservoir between *U. S. Highways 75* and *70* north of Topeka. Some ten miles on is the Pottowatomie Mission, off *U. S. Highway 75*. Here sunflowers and meadowlarks can be enjoyed as well as the historic artifacts. The area was originally a mission for the Christianization of the Pottowatomie Indians, then became a U. S. government agency. In May 1849 it was the scene of tragedy, when Asiatic cholera struck a large outfit of Oregon Trail emigrants camped along the Kansas River. Within a week fifty of them were dead.

To the east of *State Highway 99*, between Vermillion Creek and the Black Vermillion River, stretch twenty-five miles of prairieland. Sideoats and hairy grama grasses bend over the Trail, and pheasants and white-tailed deer cross old wagon ruts.

U. S. Highway 77 leads to the next footpath, at Alcove Spring. About a hundred paces off the highway, the spring spills over a rocky ledge where its name was cut by George McKinstry in 1846. In his diary he wrote: "Here is a most beautiful spring and fall of water 12 feet. Mr. Bryant of our party named it 'Alcove Spring' . . . I this day cut the name of the spring in the rock at the top of the falls."

Beyond *State Highway 15E* the Oregon Trail follows the Little Blue River out of Kansas into Nebraska. Two sites along the road preserve Trail history, the Junction of the Ways and the Hollenburg Ranch, built in 1857 by Gerat H. Hollenburg, who made his

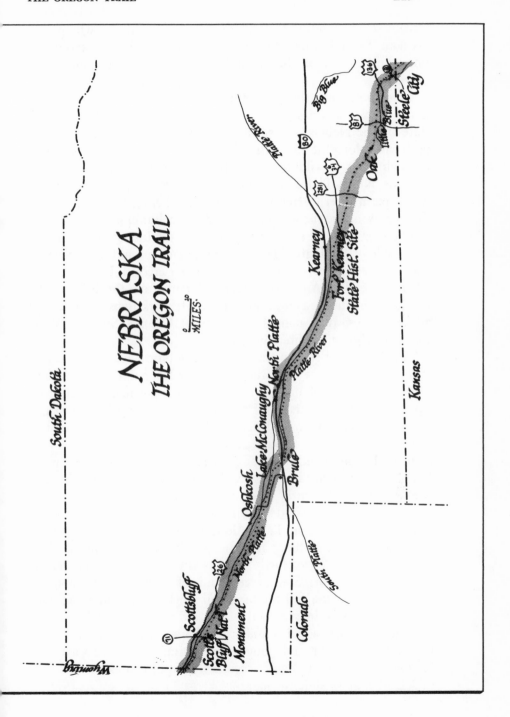

fortune selling goods to the Oregon–California travelers who passed his door. Several years later the ranch became a Pony Express station, the only one on the entire Trail that has not been altered or moved.

Three miles over the Nebraska border, beyond *State Highway 8*, is the first of a series of Oregon Trail markers placed across the state by the Nebraska Historical Society. Ten miles of wild footpath wind along the Little Blue River, under large cottonwoods and through fields of wildflowers. At the confluence of the Little Blue and the North Platte the Trail passes through private property, where permission to trek must be obtained from the owners. Box elders grow above the winged pigweed and columbine.

The next historic site is Fort Kearney, off *Interstate 80* on the south side of the Platte. The fort and parade ground have been restored in recent years, and a visitors' center erected. Established in 1848 by the U. S. Army to protect emigrants from the Indians, the fort once included a large hospital tent, workshops, and several adobe stables. It is named in honor of Colonel Stephen Watt Kearney, who built it literally by hand.

The Trail lies between the fort and the North Platte River, and is now sown to corn and wheat. By paralleling *Interstate 80* and *U. S. Highway 26* along the river's edge, it is possible to walk from Fort Kearney to Scotts Bluff at the western edge of Nebraska, a distance of more than 100 miles. The Trail passes Pony Express stations and wanders through antelope, white-tailed deer, and lark country. In spring and summer giant bur reeds, cattails, water plantains, and arrowhead decorate the bottomlands. Weasels dart through the underbrush, otter and killdeer run over the muddy river flats, and in May and September clouds of sandhill cranes drop down upon the Oregon Trail. Along the highway grow gunweeds, hawksbeard, blue lettuce, and the ponderous musk thistle. The golden-flowered Platte thistle attracts the walker with its strange un-thistle-like color. Sneezeweed and black-eyed Susan abound along the *Interstate*, and the beautiful hawksbeard shines like gold coins all across Nebraska. Out of the old prairie-dog holes in the ground peer occasional families of wide-eyed burrowing owls. Coyotes call at night, and along the water trail ocean-loving avocets, long-billed curlews, and gulls, seemingly out of context in this vast tableland of grass, stalk the flats.

Beyond Gothenburg, which lies almost in the center of the state, is a Pony Express station surrounded by hosts of blue salvia and heal-all, where prairie horned larks nest in spring.

Out of North Platte, on *U. S. Highway 83*, are several historical sites: Fort McPherson National Cemetery and, west of the city, the Buffalo Bill Ranch and the Wild West Arena. Several miles farther on, foot trails follow the old Oregon Trail beside a chain of State-administered lakes where sandhill cranes abound during migration, and where great blue herons and white-fronted Canada geese may be seen. Eagles and hawks soar the thermal winds high above these silver lakes.

The Trail follows the South Platte River to Diamond Springs, then California Hill, and then heads north to Windlass Hill, an eroded mound down which the ruts of the old trail lie almost three feet deep. Windlass Hill was once the most feared spot in Nebraska; many wagons rolled out of control here, coming to grief in the buffalo grass and stones at its foot. No other walk in Nebraska so vividly brings back the struggle of the emigrants as this stretch of the Trail.

The Trail follows *U. S. Highway 26* to Scotts Bluff. The terrain along the way is less changed by agriculture and development than eastern Nebraska; much of it is precisely as the emigrants saw it, with its grasses, wildflowers, and ground-nesting birds. Called the Sandhill Prairie, this biome is an ancient sandy area mysteriously dumped on the Great Plains by prehistoric winds or water, no one knows which. Courthouse and Jail Rocks, huge geological blocks, loom out of the sand like earthen tombs, and the land is bright with shell-leaf, penstemon and clusters of yellow nippleweed.

Miles ahead appears the famous profile of Chimney Rock, a magical attraction for travelers past and present. About fourteen miles west of Bridgeport a gravel road crosses *Interstate 80* and intercepts the footpath to Chimney Rock. The base of the extrusion is sandstone; the shaft is of brule, an ancient clay; and the spire, which is too dangerous to climb, is an interlayering of volcanic ash and clay. So fragile is this chimney that the emigrants thought it would last only a few years, and many sketched it in their diaries so that it might be remembered. However, except for the fading of the names the emigrants carved on the soft rock, it is just as the early travelers saw it.

Carving names was a joyful pastime of the emigrants, and most indulged in the game when they reached Chimney Rock. Wrote James W. Evans in 1850: "I carved my name and the name of my wife. There were several Ladies and Gentlemen on Chimney Rock with me; and after I had completed my name I looked to my left and there stood a young lady who had cut foot and hand holds in the soft rock, busily engaged in inscribing her name about two feet higher than my own!" Unfortunately her name has been worn away, and no one knows who she was.

Off *U. S. Highway 26, State Highway 71* leads to one of the most renowned spots on the Oregon Trail, Scotts Bluff, today a 300-acre tract with museum, interpretive center, and a good stretch of Trail to walk. The name of the bluff goes back to 1832, when an Oregon-bound party one evening came upon the bleached bones and grinning skull of a human being. Certain signs and features identified him as the lost fur trapper, Highram Daniel Scott. He was lying sixty long miles from the place where his fur-company companions abandoned him. During a severe illness, Scott had not been able to ride his horse with the company and the leader had decided to leave him behind in the charge of two men, who were ordered to take him in a bullhide boat down the North Platte to an appointed rendezvous among the "strange spires of sandstone." When the two men arrived with Scott at the prairie bluffs, the company was not there. A dead campfire indicated that they had gone on without waiting. Forsaking Scott, the two men had taken off at a run to catch up with their companions. Scott crept as far as the bluffs and died. "Poor Scott," wrote Warren Ferris, one of an 1832 party, "the wild and picturesque bluffs stand in the neighborhood of his lonely grave." And so the wind-sculptured sandstone of what many diary-keeping emigrants called the most beautiful spot they had ever seen, has since borne his name.

At Scotts Bluff judging by the wild things, the West begins. The Western ponderosa pine mixes with the bur oaks. The mountain plover, poorwill, Western night hawk, Say's phoebe, magpie, Bullock's oriole, McCown's longspur, and rock wren, all Western species, appear for the first time. Western lupine grows beside beargrass, and overhead the Western golden eagle rides the contorted winds that twist off the bluffs. The Townsend's solitaire, a bird of

the Sierra and Cascades, shares this picturesque land with the antelope of plains and flat lands.

Scotts Bluff inspired diarists to poetic phrases. Wrote Alonzo
Delano in 1849: "It seems as if a wand of a magician had passed
over a city and like that in the Arabian Nights, had converted all
living things to stone."

Oregon Trail ruts are visible around the strange buttes, especially
near the old Robidoux Trading Post. Along the banks of the North
Platte to the Nebraska–Wyoming border, ruts lie on the south side
of the North Platte where the hills and distant mountains covered
with buffalo grass speak of a new biome, the Short-Grass Prairie.

Ten miles east of Fort Laramie, near Lingle, a monument commemorates the Grattan Massacre of August 17, 1854. Between
1840 and 1890 the Mormons were among those going west. They
generally stayed on the north bank of the North Platte to avoid
persecution by the other emigrants; but on that August day a train
of Mormons crossed to the south bank. One of the men was struggling with a lame cow at the end of the column when she suddenly
spooked and ran into a nearby Sioux village. Terrified of the Indians,
who were actually friendly, the man left the cow and went to Fort
Laramie, where he reported the incident. The young lieutenant in
charge of the fort on that particular day, overreacting, took along
twenty-nine men, a cannon, and an interpreter as he rode out to
reclaim the cow, which by now had been butchered and eaten. The
officer, unable to find the person who killed the cow, fired the
cannon at the home of a suspect. A Sioux was wounded; his brothers
rushed in and killed the lieutenant and five other men. The surviving soldiers then fled but were overtaken and killed. By the time the
story of the cow and shooting reached the Eastern newspapers, the
lieutenant had become a hero killed in the line of duty while pro-
tecting emigrants and their property. Rage and hatred flared, and
the U. S. government dispatched soldiers into battle, thus beginning the Western Indian wars that lasted until the century was
nearly over.

Across the river is the Fort Laramie National Historic Site,
reached by an old steel bridge built by the U. S. Army in 1875 to
span the Laramie River. A deep, fast torrent, it was named for a
French trapper, Jacques Laramee, who camped there in 1818.

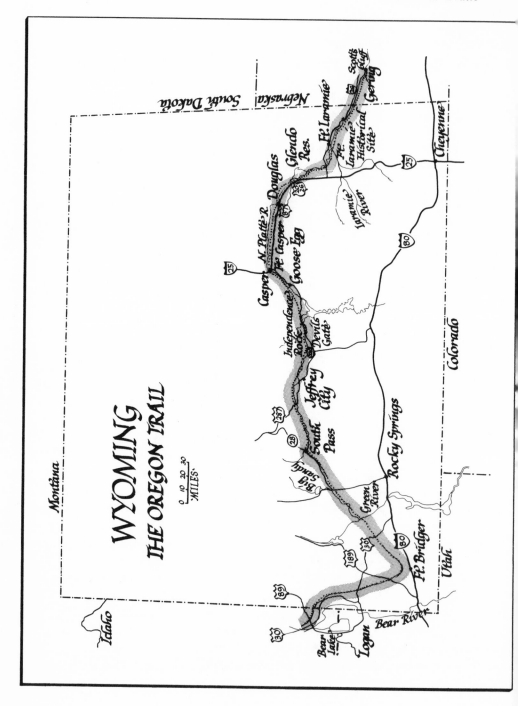

WYOMING
THE OREGON TRAIL

0 10 20 30
MILES·

Montana

Idaho

South Dakota

Nebraska

Scott's Bluff
Gering
Ft. Laramie
Ft. Laramie Historical Site
Laramie River
Cheyenne
25
80
Colorado
Glendo Res.
Douglas
26
87
N. Platte R.
Casper
Ft. Caspar
Goose Egg
25
Independence Rock
Devil's Gate
Jeffrey City
287
South Pass
28
Big Sandy
Green River
Rocky Springs
189
30
80
Ft. Bridger
Utah
89
30
Bear Lake
Logan
Bear River

The Trail follows the south side of the North Platte into Casper, Wyoming. On the highest areas along the way, Western yellow pine and Douglas fir mark the beginning of the Western Coniferous Forest. The lowlands are in the Short-Grass Prairie biome, where antelope mingle with occasional prairie dogs and numerous ground squirrels. Sixteen historical monuments stand between Fort Laramie and Casper; one is the James Bridger Ferry Monument, established in honor of the hunter, trapper, and scout who helped map the Oregon Trail for the U. S. government. The site of the ferry landing that Bridger set up in 1854, after a lifetime of adventure, is now a grassy area where the lark sparrow sings.

The Trail passes huge oil refineries on the way into Casper, where it is lost among streets and buildings. It reappears again at West 13th Street in front of Old Fort Casper, built in 1858, burned nine years later, and restored in 1960.

Out of Casper the Oregon Trail continues along the south bank of the North Platte as *State Highway* 220. It passes through the town of Goose Egg and goes on to a superb view of the Red Buttes, rising above the sagebrush with dramatic suddenness. The Buttes have been immortalized by William Jackson, the famous Western artist, in his many sensitive paintings.

The wind blows dry here, and the sagebrush is dense and cruel. "The most barren land I've ever seen," one emigrant, B. C. Clark, wrote in his diary. "I found eight oxen lying in a heap by the roadside, relics of 17 wagons and the carcasses of 27 scattered dead oxen."

A gentle slope down the river bank, just before *State Highway* 220 crosses the bridge over the North Platte, leads to the original ford of the Oregon Trail. Those who wade across the river can follow deep ruts up the bank and over the hot, barren land to Steamboat Rock. Waterless and stony, the way crackles with sounds of grasshoppers. Crickets sing in clumps of wheatgrass, mice harvest its seeds, and the landscape of the waterless northern desert meets the horizon in all directions. Rising over the gray-green sagebrush stands Independence Rock, the natural monument just short of the halfway point. The rock was a skyline mecca to the emigrants who were traveling away from the North Platte, for it meant water and grass after days of barrenness. Independence Rock is an imposing dome of igneous rock, flecked with white spar and mica, and a "register in the desert" for some forty or fifty thousand pioneers. The stone is durable and their names are easily readable today.

The rock, which can be climbed on the west side, stands above the Sweetwater River and looks down on the deep and foreboding cleft known as Devil's Gate. The route to it is a line of graves that emphasize the treacherousness of this stretch of the Oregon Trail. The cleft is thirty feet across at the bottom, 300 feet wide at the top. Through it the emigrants floated, pushed, and hauled wagons, horses, cattle, and supplies. Many slipped, fell, and were trampled to death. Those who succeeded in getting through looked ahead to Split Rock, an igneous peak with a distinctive notch. Beyond Devil's Gate, *U. S. Highway* 287 follows the Oregon Trail; but the walker need not take it, since the original ruts are scattered a mile to each side of the highway. The emigrants fanned out here after passing through Devil's Gate, seeking the grasses on the shoulders of the Sweetwater. From Jeffrey City to South Pass, *State Highway 287*, lined with willows and drought-loving greasewood, offers fourteen miles of desert beauty.

U. S. Highway 287 joins *State Highway 135* at Ice Sleuth, a gift from the earth to the hot travelers of the Oregon Trail.

One emigrant, Grandville Stewart, wrote: "Somewhere in this vicinity is a grassy swamp where we dug down about 18 inches and came to a bed of solid clear ice. We dug up enough to put into water-kegs and enjoyed the luxury of ice water all that hot day while we traveled through the infamous South Pass of the Rocky Mountains." The last ice was collected in 1847. Today some may still be found in the spring, but only in surface sheets, not solid chunks, for the peat beds that once held the ice all year have been severely altered by roads and settlement.

Beyond the Sweetwater Bridge, the Trail lies on the south bank of the river all the way to the South Pass. This is perhaps the most remote and untouched segment of the Oregon Trail in Wyoming. Wagon ruts are visible for many miles through the open country, and the mountains in the distance beckon the walker toward the Continental Divide at South Pass, the border of the old Oregon Territory.

Beginning at South Pass (7550 feet) are fifty-three miles of open trail, dirt roads, and public land. Here lie monuments to Narcissa Whitman and Elizabeth Spaulding, the first white women to go through the pass. No names are carved here and no abandoned campsites exist, for few lingered in this waterless saddle. They spurred their oxen and hastily rattled on to Pacific Springs, now a bog, where they watched the water flow not east but west, toward the Pacific. Here also they would look back, happy to be through South Pass.

The first white man to enter the pass was Robert Stuart on October 22, 1812. After him no white man was permitted through it for another twenty years, for the country was inhabited by Crow Indians, who protected their territory with guns and arrows. In 1832, however, Captain Bonneville and his party were able to talk their way through on their mission to Christianize the Indians. To-day the pass is little changed, still a hostile, dry land inhabited by kit foxes and mule deer. Prairie falcons wing through, pursuing mice and ground squirrels. At night the voice of the coyote echoes around the rocks, and for a brief period in spring bright flowers bloom wildly, lighting up South Pass with a flash of color. Then they fade and live the rest of the year as seeds.

From South Pass to the Idaho border the emigrants fanned out in all directions, along Lander's Road, Sublet Cutoff, Slate Creek Cutoff, Ham's Fork Cutoff, and Blacks Fork Cutoff. *Highways 187, 189, and 89* intersect these trails, which are now being marked for walkers by the Bureau of Outdoor Recreation. In this forested land the mountain man Jim Bridger met the Mormon leader Brigham Young, a man whom Bridger detested to such an extent that he joined the United States troops in Utah to fight in the "Mormon War" of 1857. Notwithstanding his dislike of the Mormon leader, Bridger told him in this forest how to get to Great Salt Lake, which Bridger himself had discovered in 1824. Although walkers can take the cutoffs through the forest, drive-and-walkers follow *Interstate 80* into Fort Bridger.

Fort Bridger was a disappointment to the emigrants, who expected a more impressive army installation in this famed Indian country. "The fort is a shabby concern," wrote an emigrant, Joel Palmer, on July 25, 1842, "built of poles and dobbed with mud." In fact, three mud cabins sat within the fort and there were fifty Indian teepees outside.

Looming off in the distance are the handsome snow-topped Wasatch Mountains, rising like saw blades on the Idaho skyline.

From Fort Bridger to the Idaho border, old ruts can be found among the aspen and birches along the Bear River. The way is pastoral to stunning Bear Lake in Idaho, which is like a huge blue diamond set into the forests. From the bridge at the confluence of the Thomas Fork and the Bear, the ruts of the Oregon Trail are clearly visible across this scenic valley. Sagebrush, grass, and relatively undisturbed shrubland lie to either side of the Trail. The rock formations of basalt are strikingly handsome.

From Big Hill on the Bear to Soda Springs, the walker tramps for miles in wheel ruts as he passes through what was once caribou country and is now called Caribou National Forest, in memory of those big northern deer which did not survive the settling of this country.

Where the Oregon Trail intersects *U. S. Highway 30* at Soda Springs, the water that bubbles up under a jutting rock is warm and flavored with limestone, sulphur, and bicarbonate of soda. The spring is mentioned in almost every emigrant diary, as it was in that of Joel Sharp, who wrote: "By sweetening the water of those springs it made very fine drinks."

A half mile farther down the road is Steamboat Springs, so called because it once emitted puffs of steam and a sound not unlike the chug of a steamboat. Though the once famous spring was inundated when the Bear was dammed, it goes on bubbling and can be seen sending up spurts of carbon dioxide on a calm day. Other springs can still be found under the cedar and pine trees on the banks of the Bear. In 1849 one emigrant counted more than a hundred springs boiling up from the submerged lava beds.

Out of Soda Springs the Oregon Trail goes northwest cutting across the high desert to the village of Chesterfield, a pioneer town whose brick schoolhouse, dozen or two log dwellings, false-front store, and independent people make this a favorite town for walkers.

Out of Chesterfield, the Oregon Trail is covered by the waters of Portneuf Dam as far as Fort Hall Indian Reservation. Here the route leads on to the Snake River. The basalt-rimmed edge of the river takes the Oregon Trail across Idaho through barren country with a mix of sagebrush, juniper, and high-desert wildflowers. Along canyons cut by the river, hawks, owls, and eagles nest in rock crannies, from which they fly out over the open desert and hunt for rodents.

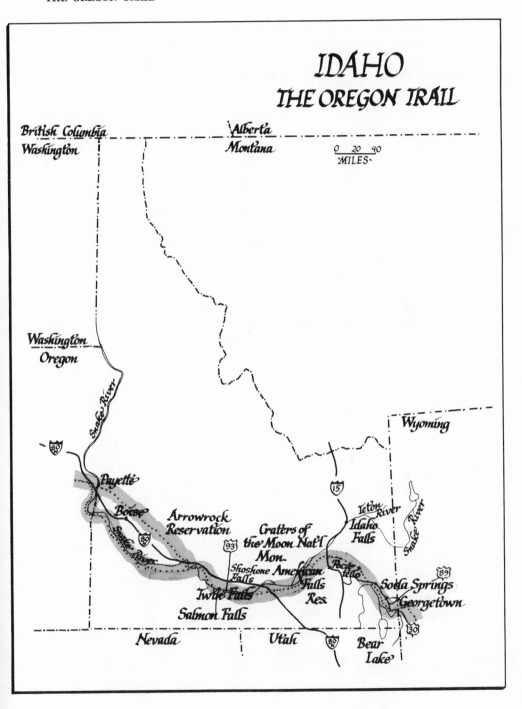

IDAHO
THE OREGON TRAIL

West of Pocatello the American Falls Reservoir covers the old trail for four miles; then *State Highway 37* leads to Massacre Rocks, where Indians on August 10, 1862 attacked a wagon train. The day after the massacre, John C. Hillman wrote to a friend in St. Louis:

On Saturday about 5 P.M. I was riding ahead of the train a mile or so in search of grass and a camping place at which we might remain over Sunday. On looking up the road ahead of me I saw a horseman coming toward me in a hasty manner.

This was a rare thing to see any person coming eastward and especially in so hasty a manner. On his approaching me I discovered that he was a man belonging to our wagon and who left us on the previous day to overtake a friend of his who he had learned was in a train two days ahead of us. The first thing he said to me was "My God, John, the Indians have massacred a train and robbed them of all they had and they are only a short distance from us." I went back to inform my train, expecting an attack at any moment.

In an hour's driving we came to the place where the horrible scene took place. I found quite a quantity of blood and fragments of such things that emigrants usually carry with them and it was evident that the Indians had done their hellish deed in a hasty manner and left.

Because of darkness, Hillman's wagon was obliged to camp on the very spot. No further attacks occurred, and the group pushed on to the next campsite, where Hillman found three dead men, several wounded, and one dying woman. His account continues:

Some thirty men from the ox trains (attacked the previous day) started out in pursuit of the Indians. After traveling some seven miles they suddenly came upon them and a fight immediately commenced. At the first fire, three quarters of the white men ran, the red men pursued, and after a running fight of some three miles the Indians ceased their pursuit.

As word of the marauding Indians spread from ox train to ox train, all the parties joined Hillman's group, forming an army of two hundred wagons and seven hundred men, women, and children.

"This morning," the letter concludes, "we all started together after burying the dead and came thirteen miles to Raft River where we are all camped for the day and where I am writing this. Here the road forks, one for Oregon and Washington and the other for California." Hillman added in a postscript: "The Indians I have alluded to were Snakes and it is thought were in large force."

The walk to the ford at Raft River, where the letter was written, passes another "register rock" dating back to 1849, where the names are mostly illegible. Ruts made on the road to California, Washington, and Oregon are still visible and can be followed for nine miles over lava rock through sagebrush and greasewood. The way to Twin Falls on the Snake River is dusty and hot in summer.

In the 1840s the falls boomed and sent white spray rising up into the torrid desert air. Emigrants loitered in the coolness and many camped here for days. The north falls are now only a trickle of water, and the south ones are completely dry. A reclamation and water power program for irrigation has stilled this once raging cascade, and the land that was once sage and greasewood is green with wheat and alfalfa.

Beyond Twin Falls the Oregon Trail splits, one branch crosses the Snake River and generally becomes *U. S. Highway 80N*, past Boise to Fayette. The crossing of the Snake was made at Three Island Crossing, a freak in the geology of the canyon where an opening appears in the steep walls. This spot was one of the most hazardous on the entire trip, and emigrants wrote about it in vivid language.

Samuel Hancock wrote in 1845:

. . . we arrived at the crossing of the Snake and two men of the company forded it for the purpose of hunting on the other side. One was scalped and the other never returned.

We now make preparations for crossing the river which is very rapid and deep and perhaps 200 yards wide. . . . The crossing was effected by propping up the wagon beds above the reach of the water and having three men on horseback beside the team of the first wagon to which all the others were chained, each to the preceding one, and with a man on horseback to keep the team straight. We reached the opposite bank safely though some of the smaller cattle were forced to swim.

The crossing remained a death trap and an unavoidable test of ingenuity until 1871, when the Glen Ferry opened at Three Islands.

The second route keeps to the south side of the Snake all the way to Payette. William H. Winter wrote of it in 1843: "This is perhaps the most rugged, deserted and dreary country between the Western borders of the U. S. A. and the shores of the Pacific. It is nothing less than a wild, rocky, barren wilderness of wrecked and ruined Nature and a vast field of volcanic desolation."

Today most walkers prefer this route because of that same "barren wilderness." *State Highway 78* parallels the Trail from Indian Cove past Jackass Butte. Plants are acres apart, flat buttes lie like huge blocks, and twenty-one miles of ruts can be followed across the Salt Desert. Tortured clumps of grass, thistle, and thorn grow intermittently. When the winds arise, around ten o'clock in the morning, the golden eagles take to the updrafts and ride high over this hot land with its rodents, coyotes, and grassland songbirds.

West of Givens Hotsprings, thirty dusty miles lead into Fort Boise and the green valley of the Boise River, speckled with ducks, geese, and reeds. Nothing remains of old Fort Boise, not even the marker that was once erected on the Snake River near the confluence of the Boise and the Snake Rivers: roads and developments have devoured it.

From the Idaho border *Interstate 80N* parallels the Trail northwest across Oregon to the Columbia River. The walking route is a country road out of Brogan to Keeney Pass, through open rangeland where roadside coneflowers and lupines bloom. Over the sagebrush landscape, juniper-covered hills bristle like hedgehogs.

At the little hamlet of Weatherby, the Trail leaves Burnt River Canyon and enters a quiet region far from the sound of the highway. Peaceful streams, farms, and old buildings line the way to Baker.

Beyond Baker, *U. S. Highway 30* follows the Oregon Trail to North Powder and for five miles north of it. Ahead rises La Grande Ronde, the largest mound in the Blue Mountains. The Oregon Trail winds up this dome to the southeastern summit, at 2727 feet, and one of the most glorious views on the entire Trail. All around is a circle of white jagged mountains that rise above the green valley floor. Cottonwoods mark the river's course and afternoon clouds decorate the vaulting sky. Many emigrants would have stopped here for weeks but for the fact that low supplies forced them to push on to the settlements ahead.

Lost to history is the Alicel, Elgin, and Tollgate Route which led

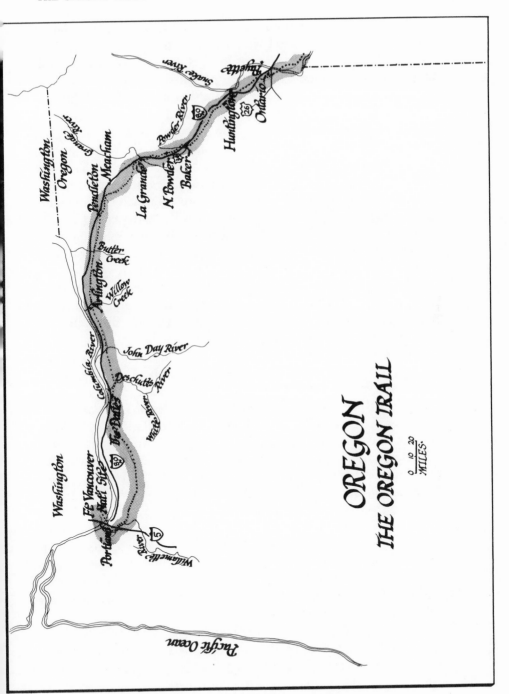

to the home of a well-loved man, Presbyterian missionary, Marcus Whitman, who is credited with inspiring the emigration to Oregon. In 1847 a group of Cayuse Indians, believing that their children who died of measles had been poisoned, murdered Whitman, his wife, and twelve other persons and burned all the buildings at the Walla Walla Mission. The deed turned emigrants away from this route, and time and neglect soon obscured the way.

A new trail was cut through the Grande Ronde Valley, up the steep and narrow Ladd Canyon. Today this is rangeland, hills are capped with forests, and meadows offer miles of good footpath. The walker can enjoy the great forests through which the emigrants passed on their way to the next stop, Umatilla (today called Pendleton). Here the Trail strikes out across the Blue Mountain Summit over Dead Man's Pass, and along the Umatilla River until eventually it arrives on the benchland of the Columbia River.

The junction of the Columbia and Umatilla was a point of inspiration and rededication for travelers of the Oregon Trail. Here they celebrated because a mere two weeks of travel to the dreamed-of Willamette Valley lay ahead.

The Trail can be walked at Echo West and Boardman, between *State Highway 207 and 206*, as well as in the Deschutes River State Park, near Biggs, where the Trail now is *State Highway 206*.

Barlow Road takes the walker through miles of Douglas fir and hemlock to *U. S. Highway 197* and west to Barlow Pass. After Barlow Pass the Trail was and still is all downhill, but it was not necessarily a pleasure for the emigrants. Laurel Hill was the worst descent for the wagons. Chickens, pots, blankets, and tools flew out on the rocky descent and wagons often careened into the forest with all a family's possessions.

Laurel Hill comes into *U. S. Highway 26*, a new road that leads into Oregon City. The walker who takes to its edge and looks down over the Willamette Valley can sense the elation the settlers must have felt as they beheld their new home. "The valley is more verdant than I could have ever believed," wrote a diarist as his wagon creaked down this road.

In Oregon City, among office and apartment buildings, surrounded by cement and traffic, the Oregon Trail comes to an end. It is commemorated by a monument where Oregon Trail walkers gather to ponder the past and future of America.

Highways Crossed by the Oregon Trail

Missouri:
  Interstate 70
  U. S. Highway 24
  U. S. Highway 50
  U. S. Highway 71

Kansas:
  U. S. Highway 69
  U. S. Highway 169
  U. S. Highway 56 (junction
    of the Oregon and Santa Fe
    trails)
  Gardner
  State Highway 10
  U. S. Highway 59
  U. S. Highway 40
  Big Springs
  Interstate 70
  Topeka
  U. S. Highway 75 (cross the
    Kansas River)
  U. S. Highway 24
  State Highway 99
  U. S. Highway 17
  Westmoreland
  State Highway 16
  Blaine
  State Highway 9
  Alcove Springs
  U. S. Highway 77
  State Highway 15E

Nebraska:
  State Highway 8
  U. S. Highway 136
  Little Blue
  U. S. Highway 81

Oak (delightful city park)
U. S. Highway 281
U. S. Highway 34 and 6
Ft. Kearney State Park
Interstate 80
Brule
South Platte
U. S. Highway 26
Oshkosh
State Highway 27
State Highway 92
State Highway 71
Scottsbluff National
  Monument

Wyoming:
  U. S. Highway 26
  U. S. Highway 85
  Interstate 80
  Torrington
  North Platte River
  Ft. Laramie Historical Site
  Interstate 25
  Douglas
  Highways 87, 20, and 26
  Casper
  State Highway 220
  Goose Egg
  Devil's Gate
  Independence Rock
  Jeffry City
  State Highway 287
  State Highway 135
  State Highway 28
  South Pass
  Big Sandy
  Green River

U. S. Highway 30 and
   Interstate 80
Fort Bridger
U. S. Highways 189, 187, 89
U. S. Highway 30

Idaho:
   U. S. Highway 89
   Bear River Valley
   Georgetown
   Soda Springs
   Chesterfield
   Interstate 15
   Interstate 80N
   Pocatello
   State Highway 78
   Ft. Hall
   U. S. Highway 30N
   State Highway 37
   Twin Falls
   Shoshone Falls

U. S. Highway 93
The Trail Splits
Payette
Rejoins
Interstate 80N
State Highway 78

Oregon:
   Ontario
   State Highway 201
   U. S. Highway 30
   Huntington
   State Highway 207, 206
   U. S. Highway 26
   Baker
   Meacham
   Arlington
   The Dalles
   Portland
   Fort Vancouver Historical
     Site

Bibliography and Maps

BROCKMAN, FRANK C. *Trees of North America: A Guide to Field Identification.* New York. Golden Press, 1968.

COSTELLO, DAVID F. *The Prairie World: Plants and Animals of the Grassland Sea.* New York: Thomas Y. Crowell Company, 1969.

CRAIGHEAD, J. J.; F. C. CRAIGHEAD; and RAY J. DAVIS. *A Field Guide to Rocky Mountain Wildflowers.* Boston: Houghton Mifflin Company, 1963.

FRANZWA, GREGORY. *The Oregon Trail Revisited.* St. Louis: Patrice Press, 1972.

MATTES, MERRILL J. *The Great Platte River Road.* Lincoln: Nebraska State Historical Society, 1969.

MATTHIESSEN, PETER. *Wildlife in America.* New York: Viking Press, 1959.

MOODY, RALPH. *The Old Trails West.* Promontory Press, 1963.

PHILLIPS PETROLEUM COMPANY. *Pasture and Range Plants.* Bartlesville, Oklahoma, 1963.

PETERSON, ROGER TORY. *A Field Guide to Western Birds.* Boston: Houghton Mifflin Company, 2nd rev. ed. 1961.

ROBBINS, CHANDLER S., BERTEL BRUUN, and HERBERT S. ZIM. *Birds of North America: A Guide to Field Identification.* New York: Golden Press, 1966.

NATIONAL GEOGRAPHIC SOCIETY. *Water, Prey and Game Birds of North America.* Washington, D.C.

U.S. DEPARTMENT OF THE INTERIOR, BUREAU OF OUTDOOR RECREATION. *The Oregon Trail: A Potential Addition to the National Trails System.* Contains maps useful to walkers. 1000 Second Ave., Seattle, WA 98104.

General Bibliography

BERGLUND, BERNDT. *Wilderness Survival.* New York: Scribner, 1975.

BRIDGE, RAYMOND. *America's Backpacking Book.* New York: Scribner, 1973.

BUNNELLE, HASSE. *Food for Knapsackers.* San Francisco: Sierra Club Books (Totebooks Series), 1971.

CARRA, ANDREW J. *The Complete Guide to Hiking and Backpacking.* New York: Winchester Press, 1977.

COLWELL, ROBERT. *Introduction to Foottrails in America.* Harrisburg: Stackpole Books, 1972.

ELMAN, ROBERT. *Hikers' Bible.* Garden City, N.Y.: Doubleday, 1973.

FLETCHER, COLIN. *The New Complete Walker.* New York: Knopf, 1974.

KEPHART, HORACE. *Camping and Woodcraft.* New York: Macmillan, 1948.

POTOMAC APPALACHIAN CLUB. *Lightweight Equipment for Hiking.* Washington, D.C. 1977. A consumer's guide with sources.

RUDNER, RUTH. *Off and Walking.* A Hikers' Guide to American Places. New York: Holt, Rinehart, Winston, 1977.

SAIJO, ALBERT. *The Backpacker.* San Francisco: One Hundred One Productions, 1977.

VAN LEAR, DENISE, ed. *The Best About Back Packing.* San Francisco: Sierra Club Books (Totebooks Series), 1974.

WELCH, MARY S. *Family Wilderness Handbook.* New York: Ballantine, 1973.

PART THREE

Short Trails Near Cities

15

The National Trails System Act of 1968 authorized, in addition to the National Scenic Trails, the establishment of recreation trails on federal lands. These are shorter than the super trails; their prime reason for being is their accessibility to urban areas. As of January 1978 the Recreation Trails were:

Alaska

Pinnell Mountain Trail near Fairbanks. 24 miles. Foot trail. Fairbanks District Office, Bureau of Land Management, Department of the Interior.

The northernmost maintained hiking trail in the United States, located off the Steese Highway about 90 miles north of Fairbanks. Traverses alpine ridge tops with outstanding vistas of the Alaska Range, Brooks Range, and the Yukon River Valley. Beautiful wildflower displays, as well as views of the midnight sun, in the latter part of June. Unique plank construction permits hikers to cross marshy muskeg areas safely.

Arizona

Hunter Trail, Picacho Peak State Park. 2.3 miles. Foot trail. Arizona State Parks Board.

The trail starts near the park entrance, some 45 miles west of Tucson, and ascends to the summit of Picacho Peak. The peak is a fairly well preserved volcanic cone. Vegetation is sparse and is composed of cacti typical of the Sonoran Desert, plus some introduced species. The area supports small mammals and reptiles, wild burros, and coyotes. The peak provides a 360-degree panorama of surrounding lands, distant mountains, and sheer cliffs up to 1000 feet high. There are interpretive displays at the campground.

North Mountain Trail near Phoenix. 0.9 mile. Foot and horse trail. City of Phoenix Park and Recreation Department.

In North Mountain Park, 10 miles north of the center of Phoenix, this trail begins at the 1400-foot contour and terminates at an observation platform at the 2138-foot level, providing a panoramic view of the area. The trail passes interesting formations of sandstone, schist, and granite, and sparse growths of cactus, mesquite, ironwood, and greasewood.

South Mountain Park Trail, Phoenix. 14 miles. Foot, bike, and horse trail. City of Phoenix Parks and Recreation Department.

Through the center of South Mountain Park. The trail is on desert terrain, sparsely vegetated with brush and a wide variety of cacti and other plant life. Unusual geologic formations can be seen. This is the initial component of a proposed 110-mile loop trail for hiking and riding, originally conceived by the Arizona State Horsemen's Association. There is an extensive network of connecting trails.

Squaw Peak Trail, Phoenix. 1.2 miles. Foot and horse trail. City of Phoenix Parks and Recreation Department.

In Squaw Peak Park, the trail ascends Squaw Peak along a series of switchbacks through fissured ledges to the bare rock summit. There is a pronounced grade with several moderate-to-near-level portions. The environment is sparsely vegetated desert with a gravelly soil. Birds and small mammals are plentiful. An observation point below the summit provides a good trail terminus for those not wishing to climb the last steep segment.

Arkansas

Sugar Loaf Mountain Nature Trail, Greer Ferry Lake. 1 mile. Foot trail. U. S. Army Corps of Engineers.

Nature trail constructed on an island rising 560 feet above the man-made lake. There is a wide variety of vegetation ranging from lichens and mosses through many species of trees. The island houses a wildlife refuge. Interesting sandstone formations can be observed. Access is by concession-operated barge or via visitor's own boat. Built by the Corps of Engineers, this trail has been specially honored by the Chief of Engineers.

California

California Aqueduct Bikeway. 67 miles. Foot and bicycle trail. State Department of Water Resources.

This trail is on the levee of the northernmost portion of the aqueduct from Bethany Reservoir through portions of three counties to O'Neil Forebay, in the San Luis Creek State Recreation Area. Swimming is available at both ends, and there is fishing all along the route. Scenic hills to the west are particularly attractive in the wildflower season. Sanitation, drinking water, and picnic areas are provided. Ladders and float booms provide for escape in case of an accidental dip into the water.

East Bay Skyline Trail, San Francisco Area. 14 miles. Foot and horse trail. East Bay Regional Park District.

Along the eastern skyline of San Francisco Bay, between Redwood Regional Park and Anthony Chabot Park. The trail passes near 315-acre Lake Chabot. Much of the area is chaparral, grass, and mixed woodland. Higher elevations along the trail provide unusually fine views of the bay. Plans include an eventual extension, both north and south, up to a distance of 25 miles.

Gabrielino Trail, Angeles National Forest. 28 miles. Foot and horse trail. Forest Service, U. S. Department of Agriculture.

Entirely within the Angeles National Forest. This trail forms a huge semicircle from Chantry Flats, along several rivers, to the city of Pasadena. Hikers go through canyon bottoms and along ridge tops, the highest point being 4100 feet. Both deciduous and coniferous trees are to be found, along with chaparral country and the ruins of an old resort. A peaceful Indian tribe, who formerly lived

along the coast in summer and on the mountains in winter, gave
the trail its name.

Jedediah Smith Trail, Sacramento. 26 miles. Foot, bicycle, and
horse trail. County of Sacramento, Parks and Recreation Department.

From Discovery Park, at the confluence of the Sacramento and
American rivers, to Nimbus Dam at Lake Natoma, the entire trail
lies within the American River Parkway of metropolitan Sacramento and other heavily populated areas. The trail features routes
for bicyclists and equestrians that are separate throughout its
length. It will eventually become part of an interconnecting network stretching from the San Francisco Bay area to the vicinity
of Lake Tahoe.

King Range Trail, near Eureka. 20 miles. Foot, horse, and off-road
vehicle trail. Bureau of Land Management, U. S. Department of
the Interior.

Part of an extensive trail system planned for the King Range
National Conservation Area. Lies in very rugged land, characterized by steep slopes and dense underbrush. Provides access to the
mountains and the Pacific Ocean via connecting trails which are
quite steep. Return from the beach can be difficult. Tidal action
prevents beach travel to other points. Wildlife is rather abundant
and rattlesnakes are fairly common. Views of rugged scenery and
ocean front are plentiful.

Penitencia Creek Trail, San Jose. 5.5 miles. Foot and horse trail.
City of San Jose Park and Recreation Department.

Starting at Alum Rock Park's northwest entrance, this loop
trail follows Penitencia Creek, climbs the Mt. Hamilton subrange
and returns to its beginning point along the creek. The trail features California's inner coast range terrain, flora, and fauna; there
are trailside mineral water springs.

South Yuba Trail, near Nevada City. 6 miles. Foot and horse
trail. Bureau of Land Management, U. S. Department of the Interior.

Along the north side of the South Yuba River Canyon. The first mile and a half are a self-guided nature trail traversing a rugged canyon with trees, flowers, and spectacular views of the river and surrounding country. Historical remnants of Gold Rush days can be found. There is good hiking and hunting with an abundance of small game.

York Trail, East Oakland. 3.5 miles. Foot and horse trail. City of Oakland, Office of Parks and Recreation.

Takes an easterly course from Leona Park to Skyline Boulevard, passing through two canyons and along a spring-fed stream while climbing 900 feet. The lower canyon is densely vegetated with second-growth redwoods, ferns, and flowering shrubs. Brush- and grass-covered hills are found at higher elevations. Old mine workings and evidence of early logging add historical interest. There are excellent views of the San Francisco Bay area. Horse staging areas, a rest stop, springs, and a fire pit are available.

Colorado

Highline Canal Trail, Denver. 18 miles. Foot, bicycle, and horse trail. South Suburban Metropolitan Recreation and Park District, Denver.

Segment of the 80-mile Highline Canal winding through metropolitan Denver. Constructed along the tree-lined maintenance road on the bank of the canal, the trail provides visual relief and physical separation of the human communities within the urban area. A greenway, primarily of cottonwoods and native grasses; under lease from the Denver Water Board.

Highline Canal Trail, Aurora. 13 miles. Foot, bicycle, and horse trail. Aurora City Parks and Recreation Department.

This lies along another segment of the 80-mile Highline Canal which winds through metropolitan Denver. Constructed along the tree-lined maintenance road on the bank of the canal, it is also managed under a 25-year lease agreement with the Denver Water Board.

District of Columbia

Fort Circle Parks Trail, Washington, D. C. 19.5 miles. Foot and bicycle trail. National Park Service, Department of the Interior.

The trail now consists of several segments in and around a number of units of the National Capital Parks system. Portions have been constructed in Rock Creek Park, Fort Dupont Park, Anacostia Park, and elsewhere. When completed, some 23 miles of designated National Recreation Trail, in noncontinuous segments, will loosely join fourteen forts and batteries that protected the Capitol during the Civil War. In addition to those historic sites, from which it takes its name, the trail involves stream valleys, flood plains, pine woods, and upland forests as well as landscaped areas. Connections to other trails, walks, and roads lead to Mount Vernon, Arlington National Cemetery, Hains Point, the C & O Canal, and other sites of great beauty and historic significance in and near the capital city.

Georgia

Stone Mountain Trail, near Atlanta. 6.5 miles. Foot trail. Stone Mountain Memorial Association, Atlanta, Georgia.

Trail network within the Stone Mountain Memorial Park, a Confederate memorial, noted for its unusual monolithic granite outcropping. The trail is mostly level, winding around the base of the mountain in an area of oak–hickory climax forest with lovely wildflowers. Much of the trail was established and is maintained by local Boy Scouts by agreement with the Stone Mountain Memorial Park Association.

Illinois

The Illinois Prairie Path, Chicago area. 22.7 miles. Foot, bicycle, and horse trail. The Illinois Prairie Path, Inc., Chicago, Illinois.

This trail is located on a portion of an abandoned railroad right of way. In use as a hiking trail and by bicyclers and horsemen, as well as by urban residents whose homes often abut the trail. There are several street and rail crossings, as well as a variety of second-growth vegetation, including many shrub and tree species. Conceived and developed by the Illinois Prairie Path Association, a private, nonprofit group, this was the first trail formally submitted to the Secretary of the Interior for inclusion in the National Trails System.

Kentucky

Long Creek Trail, Golden Pond. .25 mile. Foot and wheelchair trail. Tennessee Valley Authority.

This quarter-mile demonstration trail, within the Land-Between-the-Lakes Conservation Education Center (a large woodland area near Lake Barkley) is designed to enable physically handicapped people to become acquainted with the outdoors. The wide flat trail follows a creek, is paved, and can easily be used by the blind with the aid of a companion, or by people on crutches or in wheelchairs. There are nine interpretive stations and a shelter for quiet appreciation of the songbirds and wildlife in the area. For anglers, there is a specially designed site where bass, crappie, bluegill, and catfish may be caught.

Maryland

Touch of Nature Trail, Patapsco State Park. .32 mile. Braille trail. Maryland Park Service.

This trail loops through an oak–hickory forest just a few miles west of Baltimore. Honeysuckle provides ground cover over the hilly terrain. A donation by the American Legion Auxiliary paid for construction of the trail on State land, and the Maryland State School for the Blind assisted in route layout and design, which includes Braille signs and a pavilion for listening to taped interpretive lectures.

Michigan

Belle Isle Bicycle Trail, near Detroit. .9-mile loop. Bicycle trail. City of Detroit Parks and Recreation Department.

An 8-foot-wide paved bicycle trail, entirely within Belle Isle Park, less than five miles from downtown Detroit. It is located in the 250-acre central wooded area of the island. Interesting wildlife and vegetation can be seen from the trail, including a herd of about 50 deer.

Mississippi

Shockaloe Trail, Bienville National Forest. 23 miles. Foot and horse trail. Forest Service, U. S. Department of Agriculture.

This loop trail, within 50 miles of Jackson and Meridian, Mississippi, is divided by all-weather gravel roads into nine sections for rides of various lengths. Nature areas and examples of land use management practices are included for visitor information and enjoyment. Includes two trail-head camps with comfort stations, developed in cooperation with the Pearl River Development District.

Missouri

Elephant Rocks Braille Trail, Elephant Rocks State Park. 1 mile. Braille, foot, and wheelchair trail. Missouri State Park Board.

This 5-foot-wide macadam path is located within Elephant Rocks State Park, which features massive granite outcroppings weathered and eroded to the color and configuration of carved elephants. Interpretative signs, both printed and in Braille, explain the natural and historic features of the park. A system of knotted ropes at trailside assists blind visitors in enjoying the trail.

Nebraska

Fontenelle Forest Trail, Omaha–Council Bluffs. 3.9 miles. Foot trail. Fontenelle Forest Association, a private nonprofit organization.

The trail begins at Fontenelle Forest Nature Center and traverses an attractive forested area affording a wide vista of the Missouri River and surrounding country. The first three-quarters of a mile are a self-guided nature trail. An extensive network of connecting foot trails provides access to the entire 1200-acre natural area of the Fontenelle Forest. Though privately owned, the trail is open to the public.

New Jersey

Palisades Long Path, Palisades Interstate Park. 11 miles. Foot trail. Palisades Interstate Park Commission.

Extends from the New Jersey side of the George Washington Bridge to the New York–New Jersey State line atop the Palisades cliffs, offering panoramic views of nearby New York City and the Hudson River valley. Hikers can observe bridges and river traffic, as well as dense vegetation and huge rock formations, and can look down on trees growing on riverbank and slope.

Palisades Shore Trail, Palisades Interstate Park. 11.25 miles. Palisades Interstate Park Commission.

Along the New Jersey shore of the Hudson River, the trail lies on extraordinary terrain at the foot of the Palisades, mostly at river's edge, affording hikers many views of the Palisades cliffs and New York City's skyline. Passes under the George Washington Bridge and among huge boulders and outcrops.

Fall colors are splendid along both Palisades trails.

New Mexico

Organ Mountain Trail, Las Cruces. 8.7 miles. Foot and horse trail. Bureau of Land Management, U. S. Department of the Interior.

Two segments leading from the Aquirre Spring Recreation Area into the desert–mountain environment of Organ Mountain in southern New Mexico. Designed to protect and interpret the natural environment which ranges from pinyon–juniper through ponderosa pine, then spruce, and finally barren rock at the higher elevations. A campground and horse stable are available. Part of the trail is over an easement granted to the Bureau of Land Management by New Mexico University. One hour's drive north of El Paso.

New York

Harriman Long Path, Harriman State Park. 16 miles. Foot trail. Palisades Interstate Park Commission.

Near the Hudson River, about 20 miles northwest of New York City. The trail winds along wooded ridge tops in 45,000 acres of uplands, dropping occasionally into valleys, and crosses a portion of the Appalachian National Scenic Trail.

North Carolina

Bob's Creek Trail, McDowell County. 8 miles. Foot trail. Bowaters Carolina Corporation.

Consists of an 8-mile-long loop and a 3.5-mile loop and leads to and through a 500-acre pocket wilderness area adjoining timber lands. The trail routes through hardwood forests and dense laurel thickets, passing many small waterfalls, rock formations, and shelters. Numerous species of woodland plants and wildflowers are present along the way.

Ohio

Harriet L. Keeler Woodland Trail, Brecksville Reservation, Cleveland Area. .5 mile. Braille, foot, and wheelchair trail. Cleveland Metropolitan Park District.

A 6-foot-wide asphalt nature trail which loops through a natural area featuring exotic trees. Nearly level, the trail can be used independently by the handicapped. A plastic-coated guidewire aids the blind and provides a convenient handhold for other handicapped persons. Braille markers dot the route.

Oregon

Tillamook Head Trail, Ecola State Park. 6 miles. Foot trail. Oregon Highway Division, State Parks and Recreation Branch.

Located between the towns of Seaside and Cannon Beach on the northern Oregon coast, the trail provides access to a spruce–hemlock-alder forest environment, with salmonberry and huckleberry understory, and to precipitous seaside lands. Wildlife include deer, elk, and smaller animals, plus numerous birds. Sea birds may be observed on offshore rocks. The park on Tillamook Head tends to have steep terrain and is precipitous on the west side. The trail's history involves the Lewis and Clark Expedition and coastal defense works during World War II.

Willamette River Trail (Eugene section), City of Eugene. .97 miles. Foot, bicycle, and wheelchair trail. City of Eugene Parks and Recreation Department.

This trail lies in Skinner Butte Park, whose high butte affords splendid views of distant scenery. It follows the riverbank closely in and around a variety of trees. There are several picnic sites, and a wide variety of activities and natural attributes are available in the park.

Pennsylvania

Fairmount Park Bike Path, Philadelphia. 8.5 miles. Foot and bicycle trail. City of Philadelphia, Fairmount Park Commission.

Located in one of the oldest and largest urban parks in the nation, this trail follows the banks of the Schuylkill River. Five and a half miles of connecting trails lead users throughout the park. Rich in history, Fairmount was the site of the national centennial of 1876. Numerous mansions, remaining from original country estates, have been preserved; one now serves as an American Youth Hostel. An internationally famous art museum graces one end of the trail. There is a non-tidal basin where rowing races are held by colorful rowing clubs and during the migration seasons waterfowl pause here. Bikers will find a great variety of flowers and flowering shrubs, as well as trees, in this well-maintained example of the nineteenth-century concept of a landscape park.

South Dakota

Bear Butte Trail, Bear Butte State Park. 3.5 miles. Foot trail. South Dakota Department of Game, Fish and Parks.

Just outside Sturgis, South Dakota, the trail starts near Indian ceremonial grounds and leads to the summit of Bear Butte, a registered National Natural Landmark. From there, the hiker has outstanding vistas of Bear Butte Lake and, in the distance, snow-capped peaks and the Black Hills National Forest. Unusual features include a natural prairie environment.

Sunday Gulch Trail, Custer State Park. 4 miles. Foot trail. South Dakota Department of Game, Fish and Parks.

Located at Sylvan Lake, near Rapid City, this loop trail along the lake shore provides access to nearby overlooks. Scenery is spectacular on this rugged, picturesque trail, with unusual rock formations, abundant wildlife, a crystal-clear lake, and beautiful vistas of a timbered mountain setting. The wildlife preserve of Custer State Park is surrounded by the Black Hills National Forest.

Trail of Spirits, Seiche Hollow State Park. .5 mile. Foot trail. South Dakota Department of Game, Fish and Parks.

A self-guiding trail near Aberdeen, this one provides access to a series of unique colored springs, rich in Indian lore, that make up a registered National Natural Landmark. Expansion of the existing trail network is expected.

Tennessee

Honey Creek Trail, Scott County. 5 miles. Foot trail. Bowaters Southern Paper Corporation.

This loop trail leads the hiker through a 109-acre pocket wilderness along the scenic gorges of two streams. At one point, an overlook is available, giving a view of the Big South Fork from a vantage point of 250 feet above the river. The trail passes a number of small waterfalls, cliff and boulder formations, and several natural "rock houses" formerly used by Indians for temporary shelter on hunting expeditions.

Honeysuckle Trail, T. O. Fuller State Park. .5 mile. Braille trail. Tennessee State Parks Department.

This half-mile loop, close to Memphis, is a self-guided nature trail designed for use by the blind as well as by sighted persons. A variety of ferns, shrubs, and trees provide the sound, smell, and feel of a mature hardwood forest. There are 14 Braille markers for tree and plant identification, and an 8-inch-wide gravel strip along one side of the trail as a guide for blind hikers' canes. The trail was built by the Memphis Queens Chapter of the National Campers and Hikers Association, with the assistance of Boy Scout Troop #335 and the Tennessee State Parks Department.

Laurel–Snow Trail, Dayton. 8 miles. Foot trail. Bowaters Southern Paper Corporation.

In the 710-acre Laurel–Snow Pocket Wilderness Area established specifically to preserve unusual scenic and natural values. There are outstanding waterfalls and overlooks in a wilderness environment. The area is managed for public use and enjoyment, although privately owned.

North Ridge Trail, Oak Ridge. 7.5 miles. Foot trail. City of Oak Ridge.

This trail runs along Black Oak Ridge, the northern boundary of the city of Oak Ridge, within a 564-acre greenbelt of hardwood forest. The trail is easily accessible from several points and offers a relaxing sense of isolation with glimpses of the Cumberland Mountains. It was developed by Tennessee Citizens for Wilderness Planning.

Virgin Falls Trail, White County. Approximately 8 miles. Foot trail. Bowaters Southern Paper Corporation.

The trail begins at a point approximately eight miles south of

DeRossett, and leads to a 317-acre pocket wilderness. There, it forms a loop which leads past several unusual natural and scenic areas. At Virgin Falls, which gives the trail its name, a stream emerges from a cave, runs 50 feet, plunges over a 110-foot cliff, and disappears into another cave. This fairly rugged trail takes between six and eight hours to hike completely.

Texas

Cargill Long Park Trail, Longview. 2.5 miles. Foot and bicycle trail. City of Longview Parks and Recreation Department.

Trail extends the length of a narrow linear park. It was built on an abandoned railroad right of way through a residential area and connects several neighborhoods. It is lighted for night use and is to be developed with diverse facilities for recreation activities. Most of the trail is heavily wooded and is tended by local garden clubs.

Greer Island Nature Trail, Fort Worth. 3 miles. Foot trail. City of Fort Worth Parks and Recreation Department.

A self-guided nature trail on a 32-acre island in Lake Worth (within the city of Fort Worth). Connected by causeway to the main shoreline. Heavily used by local schools and Scout troops as an outdoor nature laboratory. The environment is an extension of the Eastern deciduous forest in near-primitive condition, with a disturbed area providing an example of ecological succession. The plans for Greer Island Nature Trail were prepared by the National Audubon Society.

Washington

Lake Washington Bicycle Path, Seattle. 3.2 miles. Foot and bicycle trail. City of Seattle, Department of Parks and Recreation.

A segment of a longer trail along the west shore of Lake Washington. The trail lies in a landscaped linear park parallel to Lake Washington Boulevard and provides additional access to Seward Park. The environment consists of grass and trees along the lake shore. Users are afforded views of the distant Cascade Mountains, as well as recreational boating and sailboat races on the lake.

Lake Washington Ship Canal Waterside Trail, Seattle. .25 mile. Foot trail. U. S. Army Corps of Engineers.

Located in the city of Seattle, the trail lies beside the Montlake Cut, a canal connecting Lake Washington to Puget Sound (via the Hiram M. Chittenden locks). The area is heavily developed urban–industrial, but the immediate trail environment has been landscaped with flowering trees, evergreens, and a wide variety of shrubs and ground plantings. The Montlake Cut provides opportunities for leisurely walking, sightseeing, and fishing, with an observation deck and fishing pier. The walk connects with the University of Washington Arboretum Trail. The major attraction on the trail is a steady parade of vessels using the canal. Designed and developed with the assistance of the Seattle Garden Club in cooperation with the city of Seattle and the University of Washington.

Fred Cleator Interpretive Trail, Federation Forest State Park. 1.3 miles. Foot trail. Washington State Parks and Recreation Commission

Thirty-five miles from Tacoma and 45 miles from Seattle on old Nachez Trail, which crosses the Cascade Range. The trail is constructed so that wheelchairs may be used during the summer. Emphasis is given to interpreting major tree and shrub communities of the Northwest.

West Virginia

The Gentle Trail, Huntington. .4 miles. Braille and foot trail. The Huntington Galleries.

The trail is oriented toward nature education and recreation, with special emphasis on providing services to the blind and handicapped. The trail is a loop traversing an immature maple complex and a more mature oak–hickory complex. There is a fragrance garden at the end of the trail. There are many interpretive signs in both regular print and Braille.

Wisconsin

Elroy–Sparta Trail, between Elroy and Sparta. 30 miles. Foot, bicycle, and snowmobile trail. Wisconsin Department of Natural Resources, Bureau of Parks and Recreation.

A portion of the Wisconsin Bikeway. Constructed on an abandoned railroad right of way, the trail passes through three tunnels. Provides easy riding in a hilly, scenic area of Wisconsin. An unusual feature of the trail is that it is designated as a snowmobile trail during the winter, and all motorized travel is prohibited in summer. It is strongly supported by local communities along the trail.

Lake Park Bicycle Trail, Milwaukee area. 3.1 miles. Bicycle trail. Milwaukee County Parks Commission.

This loop trail swings around Lake Park in a residential area bordering Lake Michigan. It is easily accessible from downtown Milwaukee. The trail connects various recreation facilities within the park—including a golf course and a swimming beach. It has an 8-foot-wide paved surface in an urban landscaped park environment.

Warnimont Park Bicycle Trail, Milwaukee area. 1.5 miles. Bicycle trail. Milwaukee County Parks Commission.

This bicycle trail is readily accessible from the city of Cudahy at Sheridan Park. Although the environment is urban, the park through which the trail passes features a golf course, a trap range, and wooded areas, with the waters of Lake Michigan forming a continuous horizon to the east.

Ice Age Trail, Kettle Moraine State Forest. 25 miles. Foot and snowmobile trail. Wisconsin Department of Natural Resources, Bureau of Parks and Recreation.

Forty miles north of Milwaukee. Passes through forested areas of several types, both highland and swamp, and past kames, eskers, kettle holes, and moraine lakes in a State Forest noted for its special geological features. These resulted from the advance and retreat of continental glaciers during the Ice Age. There are five trailside shelters along the trail.

Sugar River State Trail. 23 miles. Foot, bicycle, and snowmobile trail. Wisconsin Department of Natural Resources, Bureau of Parks and Recreation.

Approximately one-half hour's drive from Madison, this trail is located on an abandoned railroad right of way. The trail environment is rural, lying in the gently rolling farmland that is the most scenic part of Green County. The Sugar River Valley abounds in wildlife. The railroad bed has been modified by adding a hard pack of limestone screenings, providing a smooth and solid base for the trail activities.

PART FOUR

Biotic Communities

Major Biotic Communities of the United States*

I. Tundra
  1. Western Alpine Tundra.
  2. Eastern Alpine Tundra.
II. Coniferous Forests
  3. Northeastern Coniferous Forest. Black, white, and red spruce, balsam fir.
  4. Northwestern Coniferous Forest. Pacific Douglas fir; red cedar, Western hemlock.
  5. Western Subalpine Coniferous Forest. Engelmann spruce; subalpine fir.
  6. Western Mixed Forest. Ponderosa and sugar pine; mixed conifers.
  7. Western Coniferous Forest. Ponderosa pine; Douglas fir.
  8. Western Pine Forest. Lodgepole pine.
  9. Eastern Pine Forest. Jack, red, and white pine.
  10. Southeastern Pine Forest. Loblolly, slash, and longleaf pine.
III. Temperate Deciduous Forests
  11. Northeastern Hardwood Forest. Birch; beech; maple; hemlock.
  12. Eastern Broadleaf Forest. Chestnut oak; tulip-tree.
  13. Midland Broadleaf Forest. Black oak; buckeye; hickory.
  14. Eastern Mixed Forest. White and scarlet oak; shortleaf pine.
  27. Southeastern Oak Savannah. Post and bur oak; tall grasses.
IV. Southern River Bottom Forest
  15. Cypress–Tupelo–Sweetgum Forest
V. Southwest Coniferous Woodland
  16. Pinyon–Juniper Woodland
VI. Southwest Woodland
  17. Chaparral. California live, black, and blue oak.
  18. Mesquite.
VII. Desert
  20. Needlegrass–Yucca.
      Desert River Bottom Grand Canyon

* (Numbers refer to maps of biotic communities)

VIII. Grasslands
    19. Tall-Grass Prairie. Indian and bluestem grass.
    21. Short-Grass Prairie. Buffalo and blue grama grass.
    22. Bunch-Grass Prairie. Bluebunch and wheatgrass.
  IX. Desert Shrublands
    23. Northern Desert. Sagebrush.
    24. Southern Desert. Creosote bush.
    25. Salt Desert. Greasewood.
   X. Subtropic Zone
    26. Pine Flatlands, Tropical Hardwood Hammock. Cypress heads; grasslands.

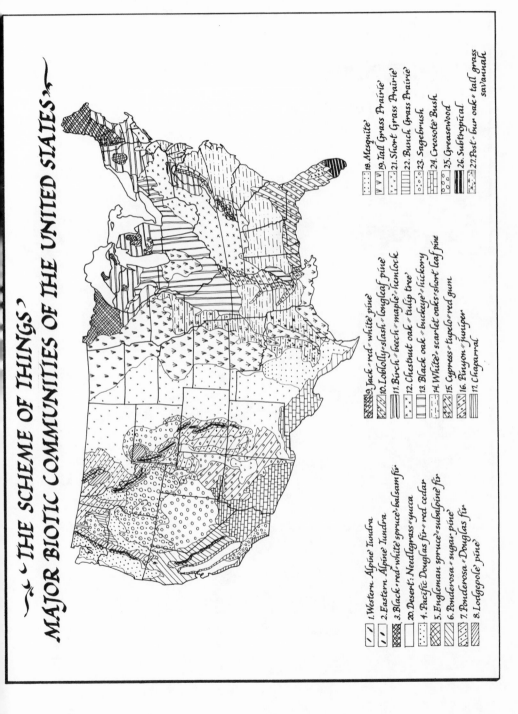

THE SCHEME OF THINGS
MAJOR BIOTIC COMMUNITIES OF THE UNITED STATES

1. Western Alpine Tundra
2. Eastern Alpine Tundra
3. Black-red-white spruce-balsam fir
20. Desert: Needlegrass-yucca
4. Pacific Douglas fir-red cedar
5. Engleman spruce-subalpine fir
6. Ponderosa-sugar pine
7. Ponderosa-Douglas fir
8. Lodgepole pine

9. Jack-red-white pine
10. Loblolly-slash-longleaf pine
11. Birch-beech-maple-hemlock
12. Chestnut oak-tulip tree
13. Black oak-buckeye-hickory
14. White-scarlet oaks-short leaf pine
15. Cypress-tupelo-red gum
16. Pinyon-juniper
17. Chaparral

18. Mesquite
19. Tall Grass Prairie
21. Short Grass Prairie
22. Bunch Grass Prairie
23. Sagebrush
24. Creosote Bush
25. Greasewood
26. Subtropical
27. Post-bur oak-tall grass savannah

I. TUNDRA
1. Western Alpine Tundra
Trails: Pacific Crest, Continental Divide

Mountain aster

Hoary Marmot

Rock ptarmigan

Glacier lily

Star-of-Parnassus   Mountain gentian

Willow ptarmigan   Rocky Mountain sheep

Rocky Mountain goat

Water Pipit   Pika

Dominant Plants and Animals of the Major Biotic Communities

Western Alpine Tundra: Dominant Plants and Animals.

PLANTS

Flowers: grass-of-Parnassus; mountain gentian; blue columbine; glacier lily; alpine sunflower; sky pilot; alpine buttercup; alpine forget-me-not; mountain aster.

Others: sedge; poa grass; dwarf willow; liverwort; moss; lichen.

MAMMALS

Rocky Mountain goat; Rocky Mountain sheep; pika; hoary marmot.

BREEDING BIRDS

Willow and rock ptarmigan (year around); water pipit; horned lark; rosy finch; white-crowned sparrow.

PATROLLING BIRDS

Common raven; golden eagle; gray and Steller's jay; Clark's nutcracker.

Eastern Alpine Tundra: Dominant Plants and Animals.

PLANTS

Flowers: Lapland rosebay; diapensia; alpine-azalea; Juneberry; skunk currant; dwarf raspberry; Mt. Washington avens.

Others: sedge; holy-grass; highland rush; Iceland lichen; Greenland sandwort; haircap moss; bearberry; willow; dwarf bilberry; mountain-heath; Labrador tea.

MAMMALS

Red-backed mouse.

BREEDING BIRDS

Slate-colored junco; white-throated sparrow.

PATROLLING BIRDS

Canada jay; various hawks and owls.

259

II. CONIFEROUS FORESTS
3. Northeastern: black, white, red spruce – balsam fir
Trails: North Country, Appalachian, Long Path, Long Trail

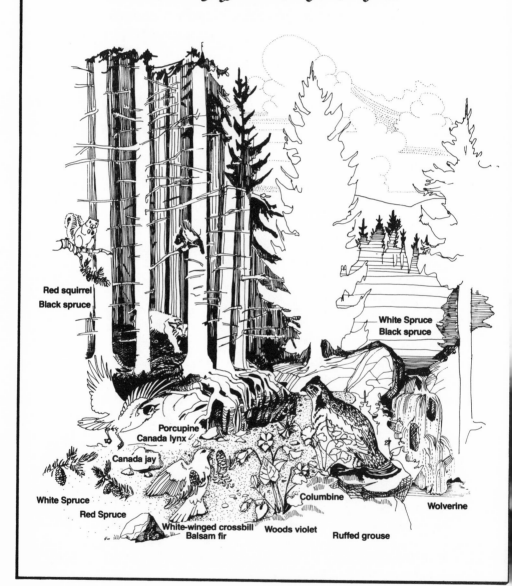

Red squirrel
Black spruce

White Spruce
Black spruce

Porcupine
Canada lynx

Canada jay

White Spruce
Red Spruce

White-winged crossbill
Balsam fir

Woods violet

Columbine

Ruffed grouse

Wolverine

Northeastern Coniferous Forest: Dominant Plants and Animals.

PLANTS

Trees: Red, black, and white spruce, balsam fir; white birch; mountain-ash.

Flowers: Three-toothed cinquefoil; mountain honeysuckle; oxalis; corn lily; beadlily; woodrush; columbine; wood violet; bunchberry; bluet; false lily-of-the-valley; goldthread.

MAMMALS

Moose; marten; wolverine; Canada lynx; Canada woodchuck; porcupine; red squirrel; Northern water shrew; pipistrelle bat; black bear; least weasel; bobcat; Northern flying squirrel; beaver; rock vole; jumping mouse; snowshoe hare.

BREEDING BIRDS

Spruce grouse; ruffed grouse; sharp-shinned, Cooper's, and broad-winged hawk, goshawk; peregrine falcon (vanishing); pigeon hawk; long-eared, barred, screech, and great horned owl; yellow-billed and black-billed cuckoo; Northern hairy, downy, Newfoundland downy, and Northern pileated woodpecker; yellow-bellied sapsucker, whip-poorwill; common nighthawk; chimney swift; ruby-throated hummingbird; crested, olive-sided, yelow-bellied, and least flycatcher; Canada jay; common raven; common crow; brown-headed cowbird; brown-capped chickadee; red-breasted nuthatch; winter wren; pine grosbeak; pine siskin; Harris', white-crowned, and fox sparrow; slate-colored junco; cedar waxwing; blackpoll, Cape May, black-throated green, magnolia, myrtle, bay-breasted, and Blackburnian warbler; brown creeper; golden- and ruby-crowned kinglet.

II. CONIFEROUS FORESTS

4. Northwestern: Pacific douglas fir - red cedar - western hemlock
Trails: Pacific Crest, Oregon, Lewis and Clark

Mountain bluebird

Red cedar

Western hemlock

Black-tailed deer

Roosevelt elk

Douglas fir

Lubine

Monkey flower

Incense cedar

Black bear

Oxalis   Cinquefoil

Sword fern

Calliope hummingbird

Northwestern Coniferous Forest: Dominant Plants and Animals.

PLANTS

Trees: Pacific Douglas fir; Western hemlock; incense cedar; Western red cedar; Alaska cedar; Pacific yew; grand fir.

Understory: sword fern; mosses; canyon live oak; golden chinquapin; Oregon myrtle; Pacific dogwood.

Flowers: rhododendron, azalea, Oregon grape; oxalis; salmonberry; monkeyflower; lupine; cinquefoil; columbine; trillium; Indian paintbrush; thimbleberry; huckleberry.

MAMMALS

Roosevelt elk; black-tailed deer; black bear; otter; raccoon; mink; Douglas squirrel (chickaree); fisher; marten; ring-tailed cat; black-tailed jackrabbit; snowshoe hare; bushy-tailed wood rat; Western red-backed mouse; Northern pocket gopher; beaver; Townsend's chipmunk; Western gray squirrel; Northern flying squirrel.

BREEDING BIRDS

Sharp-shinned and Cooper's hawk; Western goshawk; marsh, Western red-tailed, and sparrow hawk; peregrine falcon, golden and bald eagle; screech, short-eared, and saw-whet owl; black and Vaux's swift; common nighthawk; rufous hummingbird; belted kingfisher; ruffed and blue grouse; California quail; American coot; killdeer; common snipe; spotted sandpiper; glaucous-winged gull; red phalarope; winter wren; robin; Calliope hummingbird; varied, hermit, and Swainson's thrush; Western and mountain bluebird; Townsend's solitaire; golden- and ruby-crowned kinglet; cedar waxwing; Hutton's, solitary, and warbling vireo; orange-crowned, yellow, Audubon's, black-throated gray, Townsend's, and MacGillivray's warbler; pileated, hairy, and downy woodpecker; yellow-bellied sapsucker; Western and olive-sided flycatcher; horned lark; violet-green, bank, rough-winged, barn, and cliff swallow; gray and Steller's jay; common raven; common crow; Clark's nutcracker; chestnut-backed chickadee; red-breasted nuthatch; brown creeper; dipper; house wren; Wilson's warbler; Western tanager; black-headed and evening grosbeak; purple finch; gray-crowned rosy finch; pine siskin; red and white-winged crossbill; Oregon junco; white-crowned sparrow.

II. CONIFEROUS FORESTS

3. Western Subalpine:
Engleman spruce, subalpine fir
Trails: Pacific Crest, Continental Divide

Engleman spruce

Subalpine fir

Golden eagle

Blue columbine

Moss companion
Buttercup
Larkspur
Alpine chipmunk

Violet-green swallow

Western Subalpine Coniferous Forest: Dominant Plants and Animals.

PLANTS

Trees: Engelmann spruce; subalpine fir; mountain hemlock; Western white pine; whitebark pine; Western mountain-ash.

Flowers: buttercup; aster; shootingstar; glacier lily; blue columbine; larkspur; moss campion; harebell; yampa; umbrellaplant; anemone; pasqueflower; whitlow-grass; stonecrop; grass-of-Parnassus; purple saxifrage; serviceberry; mountain gentian; beargrass.

MAMMALS

Yellow-bellied marmot; grizzly and black bear; mountain goat; bighorn sheep; red-backed vole; alpine chipmunk (Sierras); long-eared chipmunk (Sierras); dusky shrew; water shrew; fisher; marten; otter; mountain lion; Canada lynx; beaver; deer mouse; bushy-tailed wood rat; snowshoe hare; pika.

BREEDING BIRDS

Rufous hummingbird; golden eagle; peregrine falcon; blue grouse; ruffed grouse; winter wren; varied, hermit, and Swainson's thrush; mountain bluebird; Townsend's solitaire; golden-crowned and ruby-crowned kinglet; cedar waxwing; orange-crowned, black-throated gray, Townsend's, and hermit warbler; pileated, hairy, and downy woodpecker; Western and olive-sided flycatcher; violet-green and rough-winged swallow; gray and Steller's jay; common raven; Clark's nutcracker; mountain and boreal chickadee; red-breasted nuthatch; dipper; Wilson's warbler; Western tanager; evening grosbeak; pine siskin; red and white-winged crossbill; Oregon junco; white-crowned and fox sparrow.

II. CONIFEROUS FORESTS
6. Western Mixed: ponderosa-sugar pine-white fir-dogwood
Trails: Pacific Crest

White fir

California wood fern

Incense cedar

Oxalis   Water ouzel

Bridge's cliff break

Red-osier dogwood

Sugar pine

Lewis's woodpecker   Ponderosa pine

Grizzly bear

Western Mixed Forest: Dominant Plants and Animals.

PLANTS

Trees: ponderosa and sugar pine; giant sequoia; incense cedar; white fir; bigleaf maple; dogwood.

Flowers: monkeyflower; snowplant; tiger lily; false Solomon's seal; cinquefoil; penstemon; scarlet gilia; dusty maiden; oxalis; golden-aster; hawksbeard; orange honeysuckle; elk thistle; wild iris.

MAMMALS

Yellow-bellied marmot; red squirrel; bighorn sheep; black bear; red-backed vole; golden-mantled and California ground squirrel; mule deer.

BREEDING BIRDS

Blue grouse; sharp-shinned and Cooper's hawk; goshawk; golden eagle; flammulated, long-eared, saw-whet, and great horned owl; hawk owl; pileated, hairy, and Lewis's woodpecker; common nighthawk; black and white-throated swift; broad-tailed, rufous, and Calliope hummingbird; olive-sided and Hammond's flycatcher; Western wood pewee; Steller's and Canada jay; common raven; common crow; Clark's nutcracker; Western evening grosbeak; Cassin's finch; red crossbill; pine siskin; white-crowned sparrow; Oregon and gray-headed junco; fox sparrow; Western tanager; purple martin; rough-winged and bank swallow; warbling vireo; orange-crowned, olive, and Audubon's warbler; yellow-breasted chat; Wilson's warbler; rock and winter wren; dipper; brown creeper; red-breasted and pygmy nuthatch; mountain chickadee; Western golden-crowned and ruby-crowned kinglet; Townsend's solitaire; varied thrush; Western bluebird; mountain bluebird; goldfinch; yellow warbler.

Western Coniferous Forest: Dominant Plants and Animals.

PLANTS

Trees: ponderosa pine; Douglas fir; Rocky Mountain juniper. In moist places, quaking aspen; narrowleaf cottonwood; peach willow.

Flowers: false Solomon's seal; mountain death-camass; American bistort; monkshood; baneberry; larkspur; wallflower; stonecrop; bitterbush; locoweed; sticky geranium; blazingstar; biscuitroot; pinedrops; showy daisy; goldenweed.

MAMMALS

Grizzly bear; black bear; red squirrel; coyote; elk; moose; mule deer; golden-mantled ground squirrel; red-backed mouse; deer mouse; beaver; bighorn; yellow-bellied marmot.

BREEDING BIRDS

Ruffed grouse; sharp-shinned and Cooper's hawk, goshawk; red-tailed and Swainson's hawk; golden and bald eagle; osprey; pigeon hawk; screech, great gray, great horned, pygmy, barred, and saw-whet owl; common nighthawk; white-throated swift; black-chinned, broad-tailed, and rufous hummingbird; red-shafted flicker; pileated, Lewis', and hairy woodpecker; yellow-breasted sapsucker; Cassin's kingbird; Traill's, least, and Western flycatcher; violet-green and cliff swallow; gray and Steller's jay; black-billed magpie; common raven; white-breasted, red-breasted, and pygmy nuthatch; dipper; winter and rock wren; hermit thrush; Western bluebird; Townsend's solitaire; golden-crowned and ruby-crowned kinglet; olive, myrtle, Audubon's, and Townsend's warbler; black-headed grosbeak; evening grosbeak; purple finch; red crossbill; green-tailed towhee; white-winged and Oregon junco; fox sparrow.

Western Pine Forest: Dominant Plants and Animals.

PLANTS

Trees: lodgepole pine; in wet places, aspen, narrowleaf cottonwood, peach willow.

Flowers: lodgepole lupine; larkspur; pinedrops; fairyslipper; coralroot; American bistort; bitterroot; serviceberry; thimbleberry;

II. CONIFEROUS FORESTS

8. Western Pine: Lodgepole pine
Trails: Continental Divide,
Lewis and Clark, Oregon

Narrow leaf cottonwood

Osprey

Aspen

Lodgepole pine

Great gray owl

Lemmon's Indian paintbrush

Moose

Golden eagle

Flathead larkspur   Elk   Yampa   Bison   Lodgepole pine

Coyote

locoweed; yampa; Townsendia; little sunflower; false dandelion; twinflower; shootingstar; Clarkia; Lemmon's Indian paintbrush.

MAMMALS: Same as Western Coniferous Forest.

BREEDING BIRDS: Same as Western Coniferous Forest.

Eastern Pine Forest: Dominant Plants and Animals.

PLANTS

Trees: jack, red, and white pine.

Flowers: pinedrops; partridgeberry; crowfoot; Canada mayflower; pine pink; pink and showy lady's slipper.

MAMMALS

Porcupine; red, gray, and fox squirrel; raccoon; striped skunk; big brown bat; black bear; fisher; long-tailed weasel; badger; coyote; Canada lynx; Eastern chipmunk; shrew; flying squirrel; deer mouse, lemming mouse; opossum.

BREEDING BIRDS

Ruffed grouse; mourning dove; turkey vulture; sharp-shinned, Cooper's, red-tailed, broad-winged, and pigeon hawk; screech, great horned, long-eared, and saw-whet owl; yelow-shafted flicker; pile-ated, hairy, downy, Arctic three-toed, and American three-toed woodpecker; crested flycatcher; Eastern phoebe; least and olive-sided flycatcher; blue jay; common raven; common crow; black-capped chickadee; winter wren; blue-gray gnatcatcher; cedar wax-wing; Northern and loggerhead shrike; Parula, magnolia, black-throated blue, myrtle, Blackburnian, blackpoll, and pine warbler; Kirtland's warbler (in Roscommon County, Michigan only); pur-ple finch; pine siskin; clay-colored sparrow.

Southeastern Pine Forest: Dominant Plants and Animals.

PLANTS

Trees: loblolly, slash, and longleaf pine; palmetto.

Flowers: pearly everlasting; goatsbeard; merrybell wood lily; false Solomon's seal; yellow stargrass; showy lady's slipper; rue anemone; columbine; pussytoes; large-leaved aster.

MAMMALS

Virginia deer; black bear; gray fox; opossum; gray and red squirrel; weasel; shrew; striped skunk; bobcat; woodchuck; chipmunk; flying squirrel; deer mouse; cotton rat.

BREEDING BIRDS

Sharp-shinned, Cooper's, red-tailed, broad-winged, and short-tailed hawk; bobwhite; screech owl; chuck-will's-widow; common nighthawk; ruby-throated hummingbird; belted kingfisher; flicker; pileated, red-bellied, red-headed, downy, red-cockaded woodpecker; ivory-billed woodpecker (possibly extinct); Eastern and gray kingbird; crested and Acadian flycatcher; tree swallow; purple martin; blue jay; common crow; fish crow; Carolina chickadee; tufted titmouse; brown-headed nuthatch; loggerhead shrike; white-eyed and blue-headed vireo; Nashville, Parula, and pine warbler, yellow-breasted chat, scarlet and summer tanager; cardinal; blue grosbeak; towhee; Bachman's or pinewoods sparrow; song sparrow.

Northeastern Hardwood Forest: Dominant Plants and Animals.

PLANTS

Trees: yellow, cherry, and gray birch; American beech; sugar maple; Eastern hemlock; tulip-tree; black walnut; butternut; shagbark hickory; canoe birch; Eastern hornbeam; white and Northern red oak; American and slippery elm; hackberry; red mulberry; sassafras; witch-hazel; American sycamore; black cherry; Eastern redbud; red and silver maple; American basswood; flowering dogwood; white and green ash.

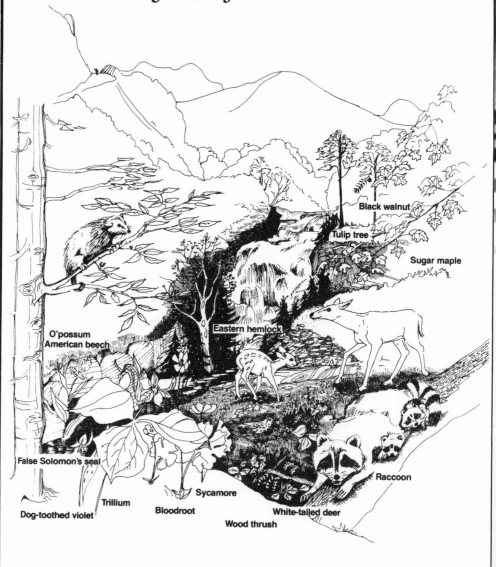

III. TEMPERATE DECIDUOUS FOREST
11. Northeastern Hardwood: Birch, beech, maple, hemlock
Trails: Appalachian, North Country,
Long Trail, Long Path

Flowers: trillium; spring beauty; Virginia bluebell; arbutus; bloodroot; azalea; bellwort; bluet; buttercup; butterfly weed; columbine; geranium; Dutchman's-breeches; foamflower; garlic-mustard; fringed gentian; ginseng; hellebore; Indian-pipe; Jacob's-ladder; wild lily-of-the-valley; May-apple, meadow-rue; merrybells; rattlesnake-root; St. Johns-wort; saxifrage; skunk cabbage; Solomon's seal; troutlily; verbena; wild ginger; violet; wood betony; wood sorrel.

MAMMALS

Virginia deer; black bear; gray fox; red fox; opossum; cottontail; gray, red, and fox squirrel; flying squirrel; weasel; mink; otter; raccoon; mole; shrew; striped skunk; bobcat; woodchuck; chipmunk; beaver; wood rat; muskrat; deer mouse.

BREEDING BIRDS

Wild turkey; mourning dove; turkey vulture; black vulture; sharp-shinned, Cooper's, red-tailed, red-shouldered, and broad-winged hawk; bald eagle (near water); osprey (near water); upland plover; barn, screech, great horned, barred, long-eared, and saw-whet owl; whippoorwill; common nighthawk; chimney swift; ruby-throated hummingbird; belted kingfisher; yellow-shafted flicker; pileated red-bellied, hairy, and downy woodpecker; yellow-bellied sapsucker; Eastern kingbird; crested flycatcher; Eastern phoebe; least and olive-sided flycatcher; tree, rough-winged, barn, and cliff swallow; purple martin; blue jay; common crow; black-capped and Carolina chickadee; tufted titmouse; white-breasted nuthatch; house wren; mockingbird; catbird; brown thrasher; robin; wood, hermit, and olive-backed thrush; veery; Eastern bluebird; starling; yellow-throated, blue-headed, and red-eyed vireo; worm-eating, black-throated blue, and cerulean warbler; ovenbird; Louisiana waterthrush; Kentucky, hooded, and Canada warbler; redstart; cowbird; scarlet and summer tanager; rose-breasted grosbeak; goldfinch.

Eastern Broadleaf Forest: Dominant Plants and Animals.

PLANTS

Chestnut oak; tulip-tree; Eastern red cedar; black willow; Eastern cottonwood; black walnut; butternut; shagbark and bitternut hickory; hornbeam; American beech; chinquapin; white, red, black, scarlet, and pin oak; American and slippery elm; pawpaw; sassafras; sweetgum; sycamore; crabapple; black cherry; American holly; red maple.

Flowers: Same as Northeastern Hardwood Forest.

MAMMALS: Same as Northeastern Hardwood Forest.

BREEDING FOREST BIRDS: Same as Northeastern Hardwood Forest.

Midland Broadleaf Forest: Dominant Plants and Animals.

PLANTS

Trees: Black oak; buckeye; black willow; Eastern cottonwood; black walnut; butternut; shagbark; shellbark, mockernut, pignut, bitternut, and black hickory; pecan; river birch; hornbeam; chinquapin; white, red, black, pin, and blackjack oak; American and slippery elm; pawpaw; sassafras; dogwood; sycamore; chokecherry; American plum; Eastern redbud; honey locust; hoptree; Eastern wahoo; silver maple; box elder; Ohio buckeye; roughleaf dogwood; tupelo; sourwood; persimmon; white and green ash.

Flowers: Same as Northeastern Hardwood Forest.

MAMMALS: Same as Northeastern Hardwood Forest.

BREEDING BIRDS: Same as Northeastern Hardwood Forest.

Eastern Mixed Forest: Dominant Plants and Animals.

PLANTS

Trees: white and scarlet oak; shortleaf pine; Virginia or yellow pine; Atlantic white cedar; Eastern red cedar; black willow; black walnut; mockernut and pignut hickory; American hornbeam; beech; Allegheny chinquapin; post oak; swamp, white, and chestnut oak; Southern red oak; American elm; red mulberry; umbrella magnolia; pawpaw; sassafras; sweetgum; sycamore; Southern crabapple; black cherry; hoptree; American holly; red maple; box elder; flowering dogwood; devil's-club; persimmon; fringe-tree; white and green ash.

Flowers: Virginia bluebell; thimble anemone; white baneberry; columbine; tall larkspur; Dutchman's breeches; rose-mallow; May-apple; wood geranium; touch-me-not; sundew; birdfoot violet; wood starwort; wild indigo; trailing arbutus; shootingstar; bellflower; wild bergamot.

BREEDING BIRDS

Turkey and black vulture; sharp-shinned, Cooper's, red-tailed, and red-shouldered hawk; bald eagle; pigeon hawk; barn, screech, great horned, and barred owl; whippoorwill; common nighthawk; ruby-throated hummingbird; belted kingfisher; flicker; pileated, red-bellied, red-headed, hairy, downy, and red-cockaded wood-pecker; Acadian flycatcher; wood pewee; tree and bank swallow; blue jay; common crow; fish crow; Carolina chickadee; tufted titmouse; brown-headed nuthatch; house and Carolina wren; mockingbird; catbird; brown thrasher; robin; wood thrush; Eastern bluebird; starling; white-eyed, yellow-throated, red-eyed, and warbling vireo; black and white, prothonotary, Bachman's, Parula, yellow, and yellow-throated warbler; ovenbird; Louisiana waterthrush; scarlet tanager; cardinal; painted bunting; goldfinch; towhee; Bachman's or pinewoods sparrow.

III. TEMPERATE DECIDUOUS FOREST
27. Southeastern Oak-Savannah:
Post-bur oak, tall grass savannah
Trails: Chisholm

Prairie cordgrass

Blue-eyed grass

		Post oak	Bur oak
Sand bluestem		Prairie chicken	Compass plant
Indian grass			Texas blue bonnet
Bobolink		Wild turkey	
Meadow lark	White-tailed deer		
	Side oats grama	Pocket gopher	

Southeastern Oak Savannah: Dominant Plants and Animals.

PLANTS

Trees: post, bur, and blackjack oak; red cedar.

Tall grasses: bluestem; broom sedge; prairie cordgrass; sand bluestem; Indian grass; Johnson grass.

Flowers: coneflowers; anemone; bluet; Nuttall onion; johnny-jump-up; bigleaf pussytoes; compass plant; blue-eyed grass; tumblegrass; wood sorrel; tansy mustard; greenthread; buttercup; shooting-star; daisy; black-eyed Susan; rock cress.

MAMMALS

Hoary and red bat; black bear; bobcat; cattle; chipmunk; cottontail; coyote; white-tailed and mule deer; elk; armadillo; pocket gopher; horse; kangaroo rat; raccoon; deer, field, plains harvest, prairie jumping, and white-footed mouse; opossum; jackrabbit; bushy-tailed wood rat.

BREEDING BIRDS

Turkey vulture; red-tailed, white-tailed, marsh, and sparrow hawk; greater prairie chicken; ring-necked pheasant; turkey; killdeer; mourning dove; screech, ferruginous, and burrowing owl; whippoorwill; belted kingfisher; yellow-shafted flicker; golden-fronted woodpecker; Kiskadee and ash-throated flycatcher; horned lark; rough-winged and cliff swallow; purple martin; scrub jay; mockingbird; robin; loggerhead shrike; black-capped and red-eyed vireo; golden-cheeked warbler; bobolink; Western meadowlark; Bullock's oriole; rusty blackbird; boat-tailed grackle; cowbird; black-headed grosbeak; goldfinch; brown towhee; in wetlands, numerous ducks and other waterbirds.

Cypress–Tupelo–Sweetgum Forest: Dominant Plants and Animals.

PLANTS

Trees: shortleaf, loblolly, and longleaf pine; baldcypress; swamp cottonwood; black hickory; pecan; shagbark hickory; overcup and live oak; planetree; Southern magnolia; cane or bamboo; sweetgum; water locust; red maple; Carolina buckthorn; tupelo; buttonbush; privet; pumpkin ash; possum-haw.

Flowers: yellow orchid; green adder-mouth; neverwet; arrowhead; pitcher-plant; sundew; waterlilies; hatpin; hepatica; bloodroot; golden aster; yellow loosestrife; Indian cucumber; trumpet plant; yellow iris; spatterdock; smooth rock cress; tall white lettuce.

BREEDING BIRDS

Swallow-tailed and Mississippi kite; broad-winged hawk; snowy and cattle egret; Louisiana heron; black-crowned and yellow-crowned night heron; least bittern; king rail; purple gallinule; yellow-billed cuckoo; screech, great horned, barn, and barred owl; chuck-will's-widow; common nighthawk; ruby-throated hummingbird; yellow-shafted flicker; pileated, red-bellied, red-cockaded, red-headed, hairy, and downy woodpecker; Eastern kingbird; gray-crested and Acadian flycatcher; Eastern wood pewee; bank and rough-winged swallow; purple martin; blue jay; common crow; fish crow; Carolina chickadee; tufted titmouse; white-breasted nuthatch; Carolina wren; mockingbird; catbird; brown thrasher; robin; wood thrush; Eastern bluebird; blue-gray gnatcatcher; starling; yellow-throated, red-eyed, and warbling vireo; black and white, prothonotary, Swainson's, Parula, yellow, and yellow-throated warbler; Louisiana waterthrush; yellow-breasted chat; Kentucky warbler; American redstart; red-winged blackbird; common grackle; summer tanager; cardinal; painted bunting.

Pinyon–Juniper Woodland: Dominant Plants and Animals.

PLANTS

Trees: one-leaf pinyon pine; one-seed juniper; California juniper; scrub oak; black bush.

Flowers: yucca; wild hyacinth; sego lily; curlydock; thimbleberry; locoweed; blueflax; Indian paintbrush; scarlet gilia; blue-eyed Mary.

MAMMALS

Coyote: black-tailed jackrabbit; shrew; Yuma bat; black bear; coati; ring-tailed cat; spotted skunk; hog-nosed skunk; mountain lion; bobcat; California and rock ground squirrel; Western chipmunk; pine squirrel; deer mouse; porcupine; mule deer: pinyon mouse.

BREEDING BIRDS

Swainson's hawk; harlequin quail; screech, great-horned, spotted, and pygmy owl; poorwill; common nighthawk; red-shafted flicker; hairy, downy, and ladder-backed woodpecker; ash-throated flycatcher; Western flycatcher; Western wood pewee; Steller's, scrub, and pinyon jay; plain titmouse; common bushtit; black-eared bushtit; Bewick's and rock wren; blue-gray gnatcatcher; gray vireo; Virginia's and black-throated gray warbler; Western tanager; black-headed grosbeak; brown towhee.

VI. SOUTHWEST WOODLAND
17. Chaparral
Trails: Pacific Crest

Piñon

Juniper

Washington palm

Blue oak

Mountain mahogany

Ground dove

White forget-me-not

Mesquite

Whip-tailed lizard

Beaver-tailed grass

Prickly pear

California quail

Chaparral: Dominant Plants and Animals.

PLANTS

Trees: scrub and blue oak; foothill ash; mountain mahogany; holly-leaved cherry.

Flowers: wild lilac; California poppy; sun cups; tidytips; larkspur; yellow violet; wild peony; astragalus; gilia; lemon lily; quininebush; white forget-me-not; manzanita; toyon; sugarbush.

MAMMALS

Mule deer; coyote; gray fox; brush rabbit; bobcat; spotted skunk; dusky-footed wood rat; nimble kangaroo rat; California pocket mouse; California mouse.

BREEDING BIRDS

California and mountain quail; scrub jay; wrentit; poorwill; Bewick's wren; California thrasher; rufous-sided towhee; orange-crowned warbler.

Mesquite: Dominant Plants and Animals.

PLANTS

Screwbean mesquite; honey mesquite; arrowweed.

Flowers: spring aster; common reed; quail bush; desert lily; yucca; agave.

MAMMALS

White-tailed antelope; ground squirrel; round-tailed ground squirrel; black-tailed jackrabbit; white-throated wood rat; Merriam's kangaroo rat; little pocket mouse; muskrat.

BREEDING BIRDS

Roadrunner (Cal.); Gambel's quail; ladder-backed woodpecker; Lucy's warbler; mourning dove; crissal thrasher; Abert's towhee; song sparrow; black-throated sparrow.

VII. DESERT
20. Needlegrass-yucca
Trails: Grand Canyon, Pacific Crest

Mountain lion

Century plant

Aspen

Diamond back rattler

Scorpion

Kangaroo rat

Burro

Desert buttercup

Needlegrass–Yucca: Dominant Plants and Animals.

PLANTS

Century plant; agave; cat's claw; desert willow; Bebbia; wooly brickella; Spanish needle; hole-in-the-sand plants; dune blackwheat; dune evening primrose.

MAMMALS

Mountain lion; kit fox; desert kangaroo rat; burro; mountain sheep (Grand Canyon); black-tailed jackrabbit; kangaroo rat; desert cottontail; white-tailed antelope-ground squirrel; cactus mouse; desert wood rat.

BREEDING BIRDS

Common raven; phainopepla; verdin; black-tailed gnatcatcher.

Desert River Bottom Grand Canyon:
Dominant Plants and Animals.

PLANTS

Cottonwood; black willow; narrowleaf willow; honey mesquite; screwbean; arrowweed; quail bush; common tule; common cattail; cat claw; saltcedar.

MAMMALS

Beaver; muskrat; hispid cotton rat; deer mouse.

BREEDING BIRDS

Lucy's warbler; crissal thrasher; Abert's towhee; song sparrow; canyon wren; raven; violet-green swallow; blue-winged teal; varied bunting; white-throated swift; western tanager; black phoebe.

Tall-Grass Prairie: Dominant Plants and Animals.

PLANTS

Indian grass; bluestem; dropseed; meadow foxtail; sand bluestem; little bluestem; broom sedge; tall oatgrass; sand reedgrass; rhodesgrass; orchardgrass; Canada wildrye; weeping lovegrass; sand lovegrass.

Flowers: strawberry; prairie phlox; whorled milkweed; sunflower; aster; goldenrod; nodding ladies'-tresses; evening primrose; many-flowered scurfpea; hairy vetch; gumweed; Canadian thistle; hawksbeard; coneflower; chicory; ironweed.

MAMMALS

Bison (in sanctuaries); raccoon; white-footed mouse; jackrabbit; pocket gopher; coyote; mule deer; thirteen-lined ground squirrel; Richardson's ground squirrel; harvest mouse; white-footed mouse; deer mouse; Northern grasshopper mouse; bushy-tailed wood rat; meadow vole; badger; striped and little spotted skunk; weasel; mink; shrew; mole; kit fox; cattle; horse; pig; bobcat.

BREEDING BIRDS OF THE TALL GRASS

Horned lark; chestnut-collared and McCown's longspur; Sprague's pipit; American magpie; prairie chicken; greater lark bunting; bobolink; Smith's longspur; chestnut-collared longspur; burrowing owl; meadowlark; cliff swallow; common nighthawk; killdeer; long-billed curlew.

Short-Grass Prairie: Dominant Plants and Animals.

PLANTS

Short grasses: crested wheatgrass; Western wheatgrass; winter bentgrass; grama; buffalo grass; prairie threeawn; arrowfeather threeawn; blue grama; hairy grama; mat sandbur; windmillgrass; orchardgrass; witchgrass; porcupinegrass.

Flowers: few-flowered psoralea; hairy golden-aster; daisy fleabane; plains prickly pear; ball cactus; Western wallflower; curlycup gumweed; scarlet globe mallow; coneflower; tumbleweed.

VIII. GRASSLANDS
21. Short Grass Prairie:
Bluegrama-buffalo grass
Trails: Santa Fe; Oregon, Lewis and Clark

Tumbleweed

Blue grama

Pronghorn antelope

Daisy fleabane

Buffalo grass

Great blue heron
Long-billed curlew
Mallard
Avocet

White-fronted Canada goose
White-tailed deer   Kit fox
Cone flower   Sharp-tailed grouse

Burrowing owls
Black-tailed prairie dog

MAMMALS

Antelope; white-footed mouse; jackrabbit; prairie dog; black-footed ferret; mule deer; white-tailed deer; bison (in sanctuaries); raccoon; long-tailed weasel; striped and spotted skunk; kit fox; coyote; bobcat; thirteen-lined ground squirrel; shrew; cattle; horse; pig.

BREEDING BIRDS

Ferruginous hawk; Swainson's hawk; golden eagle; prairie falcon; sparrow hawk; sharp-tailed grouse; lesser prairie chicken; ring-necked pheasant; sandhill crane (migrant but conspicuous); kill-deer; Franklin's gull; short-eared, barn, and burrowing owl; poor-will; common nighthawk; horned lark; black-billed magpie; common crow; goldfinch; grasshopper sparrow; savannah sparrow; lark bunting; vesper sparrow; McCown's and chestnut-collared long-spur; bobolink; Western meadowlark.

Bunch-Grass Prairie: Dominant Plants and Animals.

PLANTS

Blue bunch: wheat grass.
Flowers: lupine; sunflower; Indian paintbrush.

MAMMALS

Coyote; mountain weasel; skunk; badger; pocket mouse; pocket gopher; ground squirrel; white-tailed jackrabbit.

BREEDING BIRDS OF BUNCHGRASS

Golden eagle; prairie falcon; sparrow hawk; sharp-tailed grouse; killdeer; Franklin's gull; short-eared owl; American magpie; chestnut-collared longspur; Western meadowlark.

Northern Desert: Dominant Plants and Animals.

PLANTS

Big sagebrush; rabbit brush; hop sage; antelope brush; prickly pear.
Flowers: yucca; lupine; Indian paintbrush; scarlet gilia; thistle; sage buttercup; balsamroot.

MAMMALS

Coyote; badger; pocket mouse; kangaroo rat; ground squirrel; black-tailed jackrabbit; deer mouse; desert cottontail.

BREEDING BIRDS

Green-tailed towhee; sage sparrow; Brewer's sparrow; sharp-tailed grouse; golden eagle.

Southern Desert: Dominant Plants and Animals.

PLANTS
Creosote bush; burrowbush; indigo bush; dye bush; brittle bush; ocotillo; cholla.
Flowers: desert lily; lupine; Indian paintbrush; cereus.

MAMMALS
White-tailed antelope ground squirrel; round-tailed ground squirrel; black-tailed jackrabbit; white-throated wood rat; Merriam's kangaroo rat; little pocket mouse.

BREEDING BIRDS
Roadrunner; Costa's hummingbird; common raven; Say's phoebe; cactus wren; LeConte's thrasher; black-throated sparrow.

Salt Desert: Dominant Plants and Animals.

PLANTS
Greasewood; iodine bush; inkweed; saltbush.

MAMMALS
White-tailed antelope ground squirrel; round-tailed ground squirrel; Merriam's kangaroo rat.

BREEDING BIRDS
Common raven; horned lark.

*Pine Flatlands–Tropical Hardwood Hammock–Grasslands:
Dominant Plants and Animals.*

PLANTS
(a) Pine Flatlands
Trees: slash and sand pine; cabbage palm; cocoplum; understory of palmetto.
Flowers: coreopsis; pineland pink.

X. SUBTROPIC
Lower Florida

American alligator

Alligator flag   Bromeliades

Resurrection fern   White-tailed deer

Live oak   Purple gallinule

Arrowhead
Water lettuce

Bald cypress
with Spanish moss

Brown pelican
White ibis   Coconut pine
Snowy egret
Marsh rabbit

Cabbage palm   Slash pine
Loblolly pine

American egret

Great blue heron

Yellow-crowned night heron

(b) Tropical Hardwood Hammock

Trees: Eugenia; poisonwood; strangler fig; Dahoon holly; popash; gumbo-limbo; bustic; royal palm; cabbage palm; liveoak.

Flowers: bromeliads; many orchids and lilies.

(c) Cypress heads

Trees: baldcypress; water oak; buttonbush; Southern willow; red-bay; red maple.

(d) Grasslands

Other plants: sawgrass and other sedges; cabbage palm; palmetto; water lettuce; waterlily; arrowhead; spike rush; spider lily; cattail; water pennywort; marsh fleabane; rubber vine.

MAMMALS

Armadillo; opossum; Eastern mole; long-tailed shrew; black bear; gray fox; bobcat; weasel; deer mouse; cotton mouse; wood rat; groundhog; gray squirrel; Southern flying squirrel; marsh rabbit; Virginia deer.

BREEDING BIRDS

Ground and mourning dove; bald eagle; black vulture; swallow-tailed, Everglades and Mississippi kite; Louisiana heron; purple gallinule; broad-winged hawk; barn, Florida barred, and Florida screech owl; yellow-billed cuckoo; Southern hairy, Southern downy, red-cockaded, pileated, red-headed, and red-bellied woodpecker; chuck-will's-widow; flicker; Florida nighthawk; ruby-throated hummingbird; kingbird; Acadian flycatcher; blue jay; Southern crow; fish crow; tufted titmouse; white-breasted nuthatch; Carolina wren; mockingbird; Eastern bluebird; purple grackle; Bachman's or pine-woods sparrow; chipping sparrow; Alabama towhee; cardinal; blue grosbeak; summer tanager; purple martin; red-eyed, warbling, and yellow-throated vireo; mockingbird; rufous-sided towhee; Florida white-breasted nuthatch; anhinga; cattle and snowy great egret; wood stork; Louisiana heron; white and glossy ibis; osprey; bobwhite; limpkin; sandhill crane; laughing gull.

I N D E X

291